FROM THE LOST LETTERS SENT - BOOK FOUR:

1995 - 2001

FROM THE LOST LETTERS SENT - BOOK FOUR: 1995 - 2001

Memoirs From An Invisible Songwriter

LORD CHESTER L. BALDWIN II

A Lord Baldwin Happening

Contents

I

SOME AUTHOR'S NOTES

In 1989-1990, after saving up money for two or three years, I purchased a, '*TASCAM 424 MKIII 4-track PORTASTUDIO Multitrack Master Cassette Tape Recorder*' and started recording songs that I had written words for, or music I had composed and kept in my head since 1966,... and from 1989 through 2001 I recorded a total of 320 songs,... material spread out over time and documented within 38 albums,... I also recorded 65 instrumental compositions of experimental music,... and documented within 6 other albums,... making a grand total of the, '*Archive Series*,' to 44 albums;...

What we have here is, '*From The Lost Letters Sent – Book FOUR: 1995 – 2001*' that documents the last ten of the thirty six albums afore mentioned, along with the memoirs and poetry (Lyrics) of Lord Baldwin, (Lord Chester L. Baldwin II).

These, categorized as the, '*Archive Series*,' comprised within of the 44 albums that were recorded during the, "*Analog*" Era. The varied recordings were accomplished using the, 'TASCAM *Multitrack (4-track) Cassette Tape Recorder.*

Book FOUR; (this present body of work) documents, *83 songs* and represents the cassette tape recordings to be found within the last ten albums of the, thirty six, '*Archive Series*,' of the '*Analog*' Era recordings from 1995 to 2001,... they are;

* 33 – Rise Again *
* 34 – Beyond Our Reach *
* 35 – The Journal's Breaking News *
* 36 – A Day Too Short *
* 37 – Connected *
* 38 – Too Hard *
* 41 – Keep On Thinking Free *
* 42 – Rites Of Passage *
* 43 – Who I Might Be *
* 44 – The Universe Within *

As mentioned prior, originally, "*Words For Songs*" was going to be the title of this and the other books, but one night I was lying in bed trying to go to sleep and thinking I needed something else; something that could signify the state of affairs that is Lord Baldwin's music and the songs he writings.

When I created the first two albums and shared them with my family and friends, I was told that while I was waiting for fame and fortune, I should sell my cassettes to the music stores,... but I let them know that it was my hope and mission to create this portfolio of material, put music to the words, poems, lyrics, then record the instruments, record my voice, engineer the production of the album, and then it was my mission to share that gift and talent with others,... Yes, there always was that erstwhile element in the mix; the ego wanting their genius to be known and compensated, but as recognition continued to allude me, I felt there would have to be a different motivation and I was compelled to keep chasing the dream.

So, as I continued to give my work away, (since 1990), it was like a thank you to my Heavenly Father for my gifts and talents of music,...

thinking spatially, I thought as how each one of my songs was kind of like a special letter, with its own individual message,... maybe making a statement before it is sent out there into the vastness of space and the universe;... a letter from me to you.

At each unique song's particular inception, each letter (song), was stamped with its own time and date postmark before it would go out into the universe, maybe contemplating its own hopes that the message would be received sometime, maybe not today, maybe not tomorrow, but someday,... and these lost letters sent have been drifting in time and space ever since, waiting, hoping for someone to find and open them, to read (or hear), its message,... and these lost letters are out there right now in the incalculable vastness of the cyber-digital cosmos, waiting to be discovered, calling out, "Come find me."

In case you've decided to skip the previous three books to go directly to, 'From The Lost Letters Sent - BOOK FOUR: 1995 - 2001,' please note that the contents of all the books can be broken down into three parts;

First, the album cover art, which, as noted previously, I'm delighted with, because I had such fun designing and creating them (as an icon if you will), to represent the songs, the music, the lyrics and poetry of that particular album.

Second, the words, the lyrics, the poetry – These "Words For Songs" come to me in my daily doings, when I'm riding my bike, when I'm trying to go to sleep and sometimes they come to me in my dreams. Sometimes playing my guitar invites the words for songs to come out and play. Sometimes I take an interest in a happening that needed documentation, even if it is just lyrics to a song. Sometimes I am driven by the administering of injustice and inequity to the down-home folks that have to deal with prejudice and discrimination just to live a life here in America, and I am driven to write a poem to reflect the way I am feeling at that time. I believe in the potential of each song being important, in part from its individual contribution and to its possibilities as a whole especially if it is a concept album. For that sometime in the future.

Third, the, "Memoirs From An Invisible Songwriter" which in and of itself is broken down into *Two* parts; one; the documentations of past happenings, to give life to, and clarify particular activities and undertakings, shed light on projects, explaining where I was, and what was happening at that time in my life; and then perhaps why it was that I felt the need to write the words I did, explain the challenges, the triumphs and failures, and reasonings, and decisions to the song's creation,... and two; a collection of stories that may, or may not relate to the writings of the words for songs.

As I was originally putting this document together in 2001, (as a project that I was doing at The Evergreen State College), some of the stories and antidotes, fresh at the time, made a lot of sense, so I included them,... and besides being fun diversions to the whole, I believe the stories to be essential to help you gain a more balanced understanding, and it was my hope that some of the stories could shed light on who I was, what I was doing, my motivations and what it was that shaped me to go in the directions I did and why I did not go in other directions when the opportunities presented themselves.

Regrettably, there is always so much more to include, but I needed to keep moving to get this work out and so, what you have here is not complete, nor do I think it ever will be. It is a work in progress though, and I reserve the right to revise, renew, renovate and or bring the "**Memoirs**" and "**Notes**" up to date.

Accepting the fact that the twelve percent accomplishments come at the time spent and expense cost of the eighty-eight percent other works that would eventually become, "just not good enough," inside those twelve percent pieces some masterpieces have manifested themselves.

As Lord Baldwin's music is now streaming worldwide, this book may act as a companion guide for the listener of Lord Baldwin's material, and for those who might be interested in what thought-processes and insights that Lord Baldwin was going through or was influenced by, along with stories that may be related to the creative processes.

PERHAPS SOME BACKGROUND

In the mid-50s, my family was living in Iron Mountain Michigan where I was influenced early on to what music was all about and listening to the birth of Rock and Roll in my older brother John's bedroom.

House on Margaret Street – Iron Mountain Michigan

After my brother David,)John's very best favorite brother), left in 1958, I was delegated to try to fill the gap that David's departure left, and so, while John and I would sit on his bed playing a variety of card games, we would be listening to music on his Westinghouse Tube Radio. From fan magazines of that era, like; "**Teen**" and "**Hep Cats**" and "**Dig**" and "**Rock and Roll Songs**" (a few of the titles that John collected along with his "**MAD**" magazines), John was well read and seemed to know everything about the artists that we were listening to, and he loved to share that information, telling me narratives and stories about his favorites; Elvis Presley, Ricky Nelson, Chuck Berry, Bill Haley and the Comets, the Platters, Fats Domino, Gene Vincent, Little Richard, the Diamonds, Pat Boone, the Everly Brothers, the Coasters, Sam Cooke, Jerry Lee Lewis, Tommy Edwards, Conway Twitty, Connie Francis, Jackie Wilson and Buddy Holley. My love for the music only grew even after John went into the navy in 1960.

When John left, he asked me to watch over his stuff while he was gone and he entrusted me with his radio and his magazine collection. I put his radio on the dresser that I shared with my brother Richie and stored John's magazines in a broken wicker hamper in my closet along with my own prized comic books, and then, for safe keeping, I covered the pile with a tattered WWII parachute.

Sadly, maybe six months later, my mother grabbed us kids and ran away (for the second time) from her abusive husband, (we'll just call him; Senior). There was very little time to prepare for the departure and we would be traveling light by Greyhound bus with no space to take wanted possessions; only a change of clothes. I thought that we would be returning after their reconciliation, so I felt all my prized-good stuff was safe. And even years later, knowing the house on Margaret Street had been sold and others were now living there, I felt that I'd be able to go back to that house in Iron Mountain and go into that closet and retrieve all those treasures. That of course, never happened.

It was eight or nine months later, after saving up enough money, that I bought a **1963 Fender King** acoustic guitar.

And that Fender King was the guitar that I learned how to play guitar with, the guitar that I put all my endless hours of practice in on, and it was that guitar that, along the way, I ended up composing most of the music for my songs and tunes for the following twenty years. During that time, I did all of my early public appearances, open mikes, radio recordings, and all of the many auditions, and all of my live performances with this 1963 Fender King acoustic guitar.

Okay, okay, getting off track here. It is obvious that I don't know what to say here or how to say it. Maybe you're asking yourself, why should I care about this book? What is so special about it, and who is this self-proclaimed Lord Baldwin?

Lord Baldwin has spent his entire life writing poetry and lyrics and in his later teens began to put music to the words. After composing maybe seventy-five plus songs, from 1966 to 1989, he started recording his songs and then created a number of albums. This book can therefore be used as a companion for and in behalf of, or with the last ten albums that were recorded between September of 1995, to December of 2001. (NOTE: As will be explained in more detail later on, the folk song,

"Ever On" is the only song ever recorded in a studio, and was recorded
· in April of 1985).

Many aspire to do great things, especially when they recognize that
they've been entrusted with particular talents and gifts. It takes time
and soul searching to discover the potential of those gifts but even from
the beginning of the process, some begin to sculpture and to feed and
to modify and to nurture their special dreams that they might grow
into that distinct singular vision of that one day, where they will shine
and be able to bask in their own *bright* **starlight**.

I Am on a mission; a mission to find substance in my words and
articulate nuances with my voice and to colour the music embedded in
my chord progressions and reach for handles to pilot my vision of what
I hope others to know Lord Baldwin by,... thus I continue to move
forward,...

In doing so, knowing that things too easily gained are too little
esteemed, **I keep chasing that dream**, no matter how far in front of me
it is,... I know that if we want this thing to work, '*I've Got To Believe.*'

As this book may be read on a computer monitor or through a cell
phone, illuminating your display of the pages, it is good to know that
the book also includes all of the ten album's cover art and in full colour
representations. There are also liner notes about the covers included
on the album art itself, explaining some of the reasoning for Lord
Baldwin's art designs;...,... each an esoteric work of computer art and
worthy of being displayed on good-quality, long-sleeve tee-shirts; you
know, the ones with at least three or four buttons in front like the ones
in head shops in 1968,...

As you can imagine, there are many unsung heroes out there that
I want to thank them for their help in making this new endeavor
possible right now. And here is the shout out to my lovely best friend,
Diane who unconditionally loves me and continues to believe in me,
and inspires me to write the many love songs for her that she so richly
and honorably deserves,... and here is my call out to all my children and
their children. Please know that I dedicate all of this thing I do to all of
you and again, to Diane, with my most sincere love and devotion,...

I hope whomever you are, that you can find enjoyment in these pages of this documentation of these next ten albums along with their corresponding songs.

Yours Indubitably,

LORD CHESTER L. BALDWIN II

2

SPECIAL NOTE TO MY FAMILY

I decided that I'd like to say something special, just to you; my children and to my children's children, (my grandchildren), so here goes,... You all know me and know that I love music,... It fills me up with happiness and can help me get out of bad places like when I'm feeling annoyed or angry about something,... Music has healing powers that can mend your soul and repair your broken heart. I want you to know that music can have the same medicinal powers on you too, if you wish.

You may or may not have pondered about this thought, but I want to address this here and now,... There are things in our being that were passed on from generation to generation through our DNA,... things passed on from our mothers and from our fathers that help define the attributes that comprise our physical and chemical makeup,...

New scientific studies now suggest that some of our memories, fears, and behaviors are passed down genetically through generations from our ancestors,... Recent studies done by epigenetic scientists and researchers even suggest that we receive loads of genetic memories from our parents, grandparents, and further ancestors, in an instinctive effort by their DNA to better prepare ours for difficult experiences that they have faced, such as fear, disease, or trauma,... These epigenetic scientists also study how genes are inherited and the changes to those genetics that we exhibit, even when those changes are not essential to our DNA,... These changes can be affected or recalled by our experiences, age, environment, and health.

It came to me one night a couple of months ago that within this receiving of coded genetic DNA that we were all given, through the transferal of genes from our fathers, mothers, grandmothers, grandfathers, etc., we also received special gifts and talents that we, if we so discover, could use and magnify,... Let me be even more plain on this; our Heavenly Father has instilled within us, many gifts and talents, expecting us to discover them and to magnify those talents to accomplish great things while here on this earth.

I believe that examining our heritage can help us to identify some of those gifts and talents,... I don't have too much documentation to extrapolate data from the past because I only vaguely knew my great grandmother Viola Snook, on my mother's side, who, played harmonica in her teens in a band in 1885 and continued playing her whole life till her passing in 1970, but I can say with a certainty that both my grandparents on my mother's side, my mother, who played piano and early on transposed musical documents for my father, father, who played accordion, organ and piano professionally in the early 50s,... and they all inherited and used their special gift of music that were passed down to them,...

Some of **our** ancestors, like my mother and father, knew that they had this gift of music and they shared it with the world as they went about their lives doing what they did,... some of our other ancestors got busy with life and maybe magnified other talents that they recognized early on,... It doesn't mean they didn't have the gift of music, it just meant that that particular gift might not have been discovered or might not have been as important to them as other pursuits,...

Okay, so where am I going with this,... I came to the realization that not long after discovering that I had these special talents and the gift of music, I began to move quickly forward in my understanding of how chord progressions worked, and it all seemed to happen logically in my head,... There is no substitute for **practice**,... but I found that as I was practicing, the tediousness and redundancies did not bother me at all and I found a kind of joy in my eventual progress,...

I had wanted to be a singer/songwriter for a long time, but there was something in my DNA that told me, 'of course you can do that — you and your ancestorial line were instilled with musical talents from our Heavenly Father *many* generations ago with the gift of music' and therefore, you were born with the gift of music,... and how cool is that?

Long story short, you, my children and grandchildren also inherited my DNA which means that you too have these special talents and the gift of music,...

IF YOU WISH, you only need to search for and discover them within, to magnify your powers,... I say, *if you wish*, because not everyone, even those blessed with these talents will feel the need or want to amplify the music powers within,... There is a price to pay for becoming a musician,... beyond your special gifts, as with everything in life, and for even the most gifted of artists and writers, as mentioned before, there is a basic prerequisite and necessity for you to **practice**, and practice and practice even more to get to a higher level of proficiency,...

Still, it is your choice to go in that direction or not, but please know this; not everyone has the special talents and the gift of music like you do,... and unless you hate music and everything about it, which I'm pretty sure is not happening in your DNA, it costs you nothing but your time and effort to explore this fascinating world of music.

One more thing; your talent, that music gift we're talking about is powerful and very much like magic. It should not be used inappropriately. You should not use your powers to hurt others or to puff yourself up and be full of yourself, or to gain advantage at someone else's expense, or to hurt someone that is less talented than you. It doesn't mean you can't be competitive at times or that after you've reached a level of proficiency that you can't go out and make money with your talents. There are many good people in this world that use their musical powers to pay their rent and to buy food. That is okay. You need to value your musical powers and know that if you want the powers to stay, if you want your musical talents to grow, you will need to do it in the spirit of kindness and love and you need to be good.

Now, look inside your being and find your powers and magnify your talents, whether they be music or writing or art or something else,... Those talents are all there, you just have to find them and use them wisely. Please know that I love you, and wish you well as you delve into the mystical universe of music.

3

- 33 - RISE AGAIN - 1995 -

4

❧

NOTES ABOUT THE COVERS

Notes On The New Cover:

At the time I was creating the new cover I was curious about public domain art and after googling it, found this painting had just previously been released. It was the 1909 painting by Pablo Picasso called, "The Reservoir, Horta de Ebro." To be sure, just in case things went awry, I mirrored the painting and felt like it was an all-new piece.

How ironic though that I ended up trading one Pablo Picasso painting for another. I think it was destiny.

Notes On The Original Covers:

The original front cover was the 1903 painting by Pablo Picasso called, "The Old Guitarist." Definitely still copyrighted, but I sure loved the image.

The back cover was created from a JPG that I had found and gleaned off of the internet. I loved the way the swirling smoke, like a visible slipstream of time rises from the past and is in motion, moving towards an uncertain future

5

RISE AGAIN

Rise Again
Always Loving You
Another Time, Another Day
Step Forward
Taking My Time
Carry You
On My Own

6

Rise Again

You had your chance; you had your day.
The time has come and gone. "It's over now." they say.
The magic moments are now in the past
of fleeting memories are all that will last.

But I'm not ready to be led to that route.
There's still some life in me I've got to get out.
I feel a surge of need shaking to my core,
and draws me back to the arena, once more.

From the ashes and dreams of way-back-when,
comes a hope that fuels a fire deep within.
And I know where my heart of soul have been,
and it calls within, to Rise Again. Rise Again.

Fooling myself; disappoint every friend.
Odds are, I'll probably get hurt there in the end.
Give it up, don't take this illusive stand.
Let it go before things get out of hand.

But I'm not ready to go that way,
to live on past glories from some yesterday.
I'm still in there fighting, that says a lot.
I'm ready and willing to give it all I've got.

From the ashes and dreams of way-back-when,
comes a hope that fuels a fire deep within.
And I know where my heart and soul have been,
and it calls within; to Rise Again, to Rise Again.

I'm not ready to be led away; to live on some yesterday
I want to look tomorrow in the face,
know I'm out there, and that I've got my place.

And From the ashes and dreams of way-back-when,
comes a hope that fuels a fire deep within.
And I know where my heart and soul have been,
and it calls within, to Rise Again. To Rise Again.

7

Always Loving You

Your sweet smile and touch, says and does so much,
as I know of your genuine concern.
Your kindness and belief; with sweet gentle relief,
supports me in any direction or turn.
Virtuous and upright; shines a singular light,
that illuminates a devotion for me.

Always loving you; well, I'm always in love with you.
Throughout my life and beyond our true love goes on.
And I'm always loving you.

Faithful and true a whole lifetime through,
I could never want for a finer friend.
Trustworthy and sincere; so devoted and dear.
Beside me through all the trials to the end.
Together and apart; I know that your heart
is mine for time and all eternity.

Always loving you; endlessly in love with you.
Throughout my life and beyond our love goes on;
I'm always loving you.

Into my being you came long ago,
to share with what life, together we might live.
Into my life and so deep within my heart,
you've shown me the way true love can give.

Always loving you; forever in love with you.
Throughout my life and beyond our true love goes on,
and I'm always loving you.

Throughout my life and beyond our true love goes on,
and I'm always loving you.

8

Another Time, Another Day

Running from, and hoping to miss
the gambit of my bout.\
Trying to decide if the problems
are worth me worrying about.
Seems like there's so much to sort out,
and I'm always being called away,
forced to put things off in hopes of returning
for another time
and another day.

The choices have always been there,
so I've made it my life to pursue,
but caught up in the pressures of work,
I end up with other things to do.
Coming and going, without particulars,
as obstacles continue to weigh,
and urgencies balanced as they are imposed
another time
and another day.

Another time, another day. Another go, another stay.
I seem locked within this fate
with the chains too strong to break.
For this cause and delay, I deal with all the pain
for another time,
another day.

Running from, and hoping to resolve
the stratagem of my course.
Trying to reconcile the stumbling blocks
that barricade a subtle force.
There will always be too much to sort out,
with no time to relax and play,
just plan and reschedule; hoping for a chance,
another time,
and another day.

Oh, another time;
another day.

9

Step Forward

Conflict between the past and present
pulls me back and forth; out of place.
There's no escape; no running away,
only a dissension left to stand and face.

Disoriented with no comfort zone,
I grope in darkness, thrashing about.
Stumbling over what's right before me,
in the alarm of fear and the certainty of doubt.

Step forward, matters to be;
responsible with accountability.
Step forward; mind to hand.
Step forward to take a stand.

A loser in a world of losers;
faced with unsureness to contend.
I have such a fury inside me
that screams out, "Lets make an end."

An end to the absurdity of farces
that I carry out without knowing why.
An end to the dread of the failure
before I even stride forth to try.

Step forward, beyond usual range,
in the mind set to make a change.
Oh, step forward; mind to hand.
Step forward to take a stand.

Taking arms against a sea of troubles,
with dimensions of uncertainty.
Is it madness to seek fulfillment
at the price of lost identity?

Aye, there's the rub!
From perplexed images of inner-self,
out of my weakness, who could tell?
A protagonist, an actor, a hero;
I'm not playing my part very well.

Illusion or truth interpreted
through emotions still out of control.
Comparing myself with others,
who have taken the stage with a role.

Step forward, present a case.
Step up there, for position and place.
Oh, step forward; mind to hand.
Step forward to take a stand.

10

Taking My Time

Taking my time; slowly as I go,
reevaluating everything I know.
Having second thoughts of how things have gone,
from where I have been and what's going on.
I'm living my passions one moment at a time;
if there's no success, that will be just fine.

Everything will keep where I am bound,
I'm taking my time this time around.

Taking my time, reversing ways
to get back part of those lost days.
Looking more within and less without,
taking the time to know what it's all about.
All my past existentialism will wait,
as I avoid the B. F. Skinner game.

Taking my time, with feet off the ground,
I'm taking my time this time around.

Taking my time for a closer look
within myself from all that I mistook.
And I'm finding treasures in little, simple things,
that a while ago were hidden from me.
With my bearings lost, I fell prey to "Them"
and I don't want that to ever happen again.

Taking my time, for the love that I've found,
I'm taking my time this time around.

Taking my time; life on delay,
I'm clearing my agenda for the entire day.
Nothing forced; letting everything flow,
planning loose to see where things go.
My business head ruled me back then,
but I won't make that mistake again.

Taking my time; just let their wheels go round,
I'm taking my time this time around;

I'm taking my time this time around.

11

Carry You

For so many years, we've looked to you from day to day.
You always been there for our needs along our way.
But sometimes things happen, and it's not easy to carry on;
feeling obligated with concerns; sometimes it's hard to be strong.

Let me carry you, carry you for a while.
While you try your best to regain your strength
and bring that smile.

Though it's hard to give up control and step out of your role,
let me carry you; carry you for a while.

For so many years, depending on you to make the stand,
to lead the good cause; a generous heart and helping hand.
You want so much to continue and to do what you can do,
as you've always seen things through; let us now be there for you.

Let me carry you, carry you for a while,
in your remission, rest up in loving style.

Though you want to be involved to get the problems solved,
let me carry you; carry you for a while.

Carry you; carry you for a while.
Carry you, just until you regain that smile.

Though it's hard to give up control and step out of your role,
let me carry you; carry you for a while.

Let me carry you; carry you for a while.

12

On My Own

So many years I relied on someone else,
but now, look at me, thinking for myself.
I was always afraid of what I should or shouldn't do;
the fear hasn't changed, but I know I'll get through.

Looking over my shoulder at the past; I see I've grown,
and learned to trust in myself, now that I'm on my own.

So, write me a letter, call me on the phone.
Give me some wisdom how to handle things alone.
Sometimes hearts get lonely living in the twilight zone,
help me to make it on my own.

Mom and Dad taught me well; raising me from a kid,
and I have gained so much from watching what they did.
Mistakes came and went; we had the good and bad times.
They never did get rich, but they had enough to get by.

Looking back to those times, and all the people I have known,
I have experience to use, now that I'm on my own.

So, write me a letter, call me on the phone.
Give me some counsel how to cope with things alone.
Sometimes hearts get lonely living in this twilight zone,
help me to make it on my own.

So much might be different if I'd known back then,
but I can't be worrying how things should have been.
My folks were always preparing for the time I'd go away.
Here I am and guess what; I think I'll be O.K.

I'm looking for some fun, and I don't want to be alone,
I'm still doing my best; here I am, on my own.

So, write me a letter, call me on the phone.
Give me some advice how to manage things alone.
Sometimes hearts get lonely living in the twilight zone,
help me to make it on my own.

13

MEMOIRS & NOTES - 33 - 'RISE AGAIN'

Rise Again

(1995) – The lyrics to this song are about getting back in the saddle, seeing another chance coming along and taking that chance for all it's worth. More than a year and a half passed by between this album and when the, "City Boy" album came out. By this time, Brian had been born and had celebrated his first birthday. I went through a long, dry spell where I not only didn't write much and didn't record much either.

Whether subconsciously or purposely, a literal **wall of boxes** and stuff had been constructed in front of my little area where I was recording. There were times when I tried to break down part of the wall so that I could get in there and record a song, but the wall always returned. I tried to blast little holes through that wall of boxes and junk, but as soon as I left for work and returned home again, the wall would be back to where it had been, sometimes even wider and higher. Diane had had nine children in the past and carried them all with little hassle and great joy in her heart. When Brian came around things were different. First, this pregnancy caused her to take on water and swell up. Second, she became a borderline diabetic, and had to check her blood twice everyday. She had to change her diet, and could not eat anything with fat or sugar. She ate a regimental diet of fruits and vegetables along with some grains, 6 times a day but in such small portions. Her temperature gauge in her body, which usually always goes weird when she's pregnant, went totally off the map. To top this off, she was always tired, from the time she woke up in the morning to the time she went to sleep at night, she was tired. She did not like me turning the light on to record some music at 10 or 11:00 at night, and she would groan and growl at me if I made any noise it all.

And then one day the wall appeared. A wall of cardboard boxes filled with junk. I have to say, some of those boxes were mine, but they nonetheless appeared overnight and stayed there long past the time Brian was born. It did come to a point, after Brian arrived and things began to settle down, that I was able to gradually rearrange the boxes in such a way so as to be able to breech that wall, and then within restricted and limited times,

I started recording again. And because I had continued writing during my lunch hour every day at work, though the urgency to push the whole song creation machine forward, I had enough new of material to record both albums, "Rise Again" and "Beyond Our Reach." Another thing to notice was that both albums did not use any other material from my cache of earlier material. And the wall? That wall did not completely disappear until I deconstructed it in the beginning of the year 2001. That means it took me five years to conquer.

Side Note:

Of course; I love Diane, and I have great compassion for my wife and her circumstances, and I was willing to let my music, and whatever I was doing, go; for a while. And in the meantime, I concentrated on helping Diane get through this last pregnancy that I felt she was enduring for my sake.

Another Side Note:

The long and short of this whole story is that after so much time had passed, I was unsure of my ability to continue on and write music or even lyrics to songs. So, this song, "Rise Again," was my coming out song, or so to speak; my Phoenix album. There are a couple different meanings that one can place on this particular song, and I like that. It's always interesting to have somebody interpret my song in some way that I hadn't even thought of, but nonetheless, I was going to rise again and created this next album.

Always Loving You

(1995) – This poem was written on or around Valentine's Day of 1995. By this time Brian was exactly four months old. Diane had started to recover but was still tired all the time and always in need of rest. For some reason, I said something or did something wrong and I was in the doghouse when this Valentine's Day came around. And it was days, maybe weeks before I played this song for her. It did not stir up any great excitement nor was it that well received, so I put away and recorded it months later. Of course, after I recorded this album and Diane reviewed it, I won't say that she loved this song but maybe liked it?

When I did record this song, I did it in some strange key (D#) that for whatever other reason, made it hard for me to sing, to or with, just right. I was stuck with either singing too low or way too high. Because I was in such a hurry to rush this to record, I didn't have the time to rerecord the song in a good key for me to sing in. I want to do it sometime later in a different key and see how it sounds.

Side Note:

My inspiration for the title to this song came from a caption that I had read on a balloon that was in the hands of some young man as he was walking out of the Mega Foods store in Tumwater. I thought to myself, "hey, you could write a song with that hook." And so I did.

Another Time, Another Day

(1994) – I made more than a few rationalizations for all of my seemingly meaningful objectives, and I saw my projects, developments and undertakings being shelved for some other time and day. Although I mentioned the wall previously, I would like to reiterate some of the facts. From Diane's perspective I was spending too much time in front of that *Tascam Four-Track Cassette Recorder* and the *Yamaha PSR-500 keyboard.*

When Diane was carrying Brian in 1993-94, this pregnancy thing became a sensitive issue. She wanted all of my attention or she at least wanted equal time, and she wanted to sleep at night, not have that guy playing guitar and singing and playing harmonica at two in the morning. At the time I was rather put out, thinking this was stifling my creativity and making me musically impotent. Looking back now I see it was a good thing and helped me to get closer to Diane and her many difficulties with this pregnancy.

This song documents my frustration dealing with the wall

and my own ambition or lack of ambition to overcome that wall and begin to record my music again. There were justifications for all of my best intentions and failings, but I just kept seeing my music, my songs, my expressions to life being put off for "Another Time and Another Day."

Step Forward

(1995) – The lyrics to this song are about recognizing and stepping forward to your position, station and personal understanding in your time, of and in this life. It cannot be easy to find yourself in this day and age with so many distractions and seemingly easy alternatives.

At the time this song was written, Meridith was going through a crisis in her life. She felt unaccepted by her peers and wanted so much to be loved by her friends, but she would only feel rejected and lost. She began to have other problems where she started selectively discontinuing certain foods until all she was eating was Diane's bread; that until Meridith found out there was oil in the making of the bread. And after she had lost a lot of weight to a point where she looked unhealthy, Diane and I took Meridith to a psychologist for counseling. This counseling lasted for a very long time before Meridith started feeling good about herself.

I tried to identify what she might be thinking and how she might receive herself if she was looking at herself from the inside out, and I wrote this song, for her, possibly about her and the conflict and struggles that she was going through at the time.

Side Note:

Taking My Time

(1995) – Young life is so finite. Babies quickly become toddlers and then morph into little people and then teens and then,... All through my time of fatherhood I was inundated with work and the pursuit of the money needed to keep the Baldwin family system successfully working in a positive direction. But after losing Christopher and now being blessed with Brian, this was my one new chance; a time where I could stop and watch the miracle thing, the phenomenon of wonder, happen in front of me. When Brian came around, I was elated with the prospect of being a father to another child. This time, more than any time in the past, I was going to really enjoy being that father. I was given ample opportunity, with Diane being tired all the time, to take care of Brian whenever I was home. We had a rocking chair in our bedroom next to the crib and I enjoyed rocking and singing to Brian almost every night. (Which may be, perhaps, why he has such a strong sense of music and harmony in his soul).

In the past, being the father, it was my duty and expected standard, to work hard, bring home money and devote as much time as I could to my family when the opportunity arose. It was during one of those evenings, as I rocked Brian to sleep that I decided that this time, this singular particular time, I was going to exercise, "Taking My Time" and really get as much out of these first days, weeks, months, years as I possibly could. And like John Lennon, I kind of took some time off to be that father for Brian, for Allison, for Spenser, for Stephen, for Benjamin, for Meridith, for Elizabeth, for Chet III, for Lori, for Diane, and for me.

Carry You

(1995) – Sometimes, if we're fortunate, we may get the chance to step up and carry that parent or significant other person that has carried us for such a long time. It was in this year, 1995 that we found out about my mother's cancer. Mother played the whole thing down, reassuring us that everything was find and that she would be okay. And so, I wrote this song, which in effect is saying, you've done so much for us your whole life, now please, let us do something for you. So stubborn, my mother, not only did she not divulge her true danger, but she stoically carried the fears and anxieties within herself, even unto the end. This picture here of my

mother was taken about a year before her passing in the fall of 1996. (Please note that when I was growing up I hardly ever called her mom; it was always mother, so as I document these things, please don't fault me that I call my father dad but I call my mother, mother. It is out of the utmost respect and unlimited love that I do).

Seven months later, after extensive chemotherapy, mother was in remission and was hopeful for the future. Unfortunately, her resistance was down and her immune system was weak. My brother David thought that Ron, her husband at the time, had grown tired of the whole cancer process my mother was experiencing and that he had actually poisoned mother with raw eggs or something else. For whatever the reason was, mother got an internal infection, which eventually put her into the hospital; a place she would never leave. From a hopeful perspective, I sat on her hospital bed and sang this song to her. I still remember tears in her eyes as she smiled in acquiescence and appreciation.

On My Own

(1992) – Someday, parents have to let their children go. They have to let them journey from their home and go out there; into the cold, uncertain world in hopes of taking that next step and to find out who they are and what they'll do. And finding themselves out there, we as parents hope that they understand that there will always be a base of warmth and love waiting for them whenever they return. Someday, children have to let their parents go too; they'll leave their homes and search for themselves out there in that big world, hoping that there will always be a place of friendliness, warm-heartedness and love that they can return to whenever they want or need. A home base.

Most of us had to go through the rite of passage and leave our home base to try to succeed on our own and be all that we can be. It is scarry out there. There are a lot of obstacles and negative influences, bad people that selfishly was to get ahead by victimization, or exploitation, or by manipulating, cheating and using someone else only to benefit from your loss to compensate for their own shortcomings incompetence and inadequacies, but there are also kind, good people that want to help you on your journey to help you get back on your feet after failures, to help you to succeed with your accomplishments, triumphs, and learning in the steps of progressions in your life.

Side Note:

The poetry to this song was inspired after my first born, Lori, graduated from Tumwater high school and moved on, to Western Washington University. Lori was so determined when she left that I almost felt she didn't love us anymore, but after she made a few visits back home from school I saw a change, and it was from that change that I wrote this poem and composed this song.

Obviously, I was writing this poem from her perspective, but perhaps, it's from everyone's perspective that leaves home to find the world out there and, in the process, find themselves. And hopefully, they have the warm knowledge and assurance that there will always be a home-base to come back to with good people; family waiting to take them in and always welcome them home again.

Side Note:

I know most parents say that they can't wait for the kids to all leave home and I would say, with having ten children, there is something to be said for management with smaller numbers, but the fact is, a piece of my heart went out with Lori when she went to college at Western Washington University.

And arguably it was my fault. My mother always felt that her kids should have had a college education to get ahead in the world. And there I was, working at a community college, totally convinced that education was the key to success. But two years later when it happened again and Chet left for Western too, I was starting to feel a sense of emptiness that I knew was only going to get stronger as time went by. And like clockwork every two years or so, I could expect that it would be Liz next, and then it would be Meridith, and then it would be Ben, and then it would be Stephen, and then it would be Spencer, and then it would be Allison, and then it would be Brian.

I also know that they have to go out into the world and find themselves, and I have to know that they love us enough that they will eventually come home now and then, but I miss those singular, distinct personalities meshing or clashing with one another. Each one of them brings to the table a certain difference and individuality that fills a different part of my heart.

Another Side Note:

I know it was through my insistence that some of my children felt they needed to go to college. I believed then that from all information I was led to believe that it would be the best thing for them. But I have since reversed my stand on this philosophy.

Certainly, by the 1990s, when Lori started college, student loan debt began to skyrocket. In 1993, the average debt of a bachelor's degree graduate was approximately $9,000; five years later, it was about $15,000. There was no single reason why student loan debt had gotten so out of hand, but increased tuition costs, reduced state spending, borrower behaviors, and even choice of major all played a role. And, since federal loans would not cover all of the increased costs, and there could be several numerous even hidden costs, many students turned to private loans.

If I knew then what I know now, I would have encouraged them to approach education differently. I would have had them make sure they knew what they wanted to do before they went to college and have a degree path declared before they went and, I would also encourage them to not go if they were looking to pursue a degree in liberal arts because, as I have found with some of my children, they would be working their whole lives and maybe never be able to pay the loans off.

I was able to purchase a house by the time I was 25. Yes, it took me 25 years to pay it off, but it is mine now. Only two of my children are living in their own house; all the rest are renting. None of the rest can afford to do anything else but rent an apartment or house. And with their student loans, none of the rest can even get a bank to finance them to get into their own homes.

My promise to all of them is that, if I ever make enough money in the music world to be profitable, (and it's not looking so good as of lately), the first thing I will do is to get all of my children out of their college loan debts and to pay off their loans so that they can be free to pursue a better lifestyle.

14

❧

- 34 - BEYOND OUR REACH - 1995 -

15

NOTES ABOUT THE COVERS

Notes On The New Cover:

At the time I was creating the new cover, NASA had just made their entire media library publicly accessible and copyright free; I mean come on! So, what you see behind the lettering is actually three different pictures laid on top of a picture of just stars.

I love the center piece with its detailed Image of the Crab Nebula, followed with the upper-left corner image of the Orion Nebula star-formation region, (rotated 45 degrees) and in the bottom right, hovering in the far-off distance, we see a pair of interacting galaxies called Arp 273. And this also gave me an excuse to put in my flying saucer as it investigates the awesome happenings in the far reaches of space. Clearly for us these astounding scenes are; "Beyond Our Reach."

"Notes On The Original Covers:

Nothing wrong with the original front cover, it's just that it was a "borrowed" NASA image from the internet at the time, so being uncertain as to its availability, it was out.

The back cover was again, created from a JPG that I had discovered and garnered from the internet. It is a unit cell, but I'm not sure anymore what element it is.

16

BEYOND OUR REACH

Beyond Our Reach
A Higher Purpose
When She Said, What She Meant
Finding Myself In Search
Of Finding Myself
Just A Little Tiny Step
I Got The Last Laugh, This Time

17

Beyond Our Reach

In hopeless desperation we cling to the glistening dream,
with all great expectations
of how things soon might be.
From dawn to dusk each day, we labor hard to own our time,
still things pass on to someone else
as we move up in the line.

In hopeless desperation we cling to the glistening dream,
as it sparkles and shines
there; just beyond our reach.

Apprehensions and contemplations of expectations to be,
cause disillusions and frustrations
for the life we'll never see.
Working hard to get nowhere as the time flies quickly on,
while the trophies and the favors
progress by and are gone.

Apprehensions and contemplations of expectations to be,
only taunt us as we find;
it's all beyond our reach.

It's not fair; it's not right that we should ever fight
for the prize to finally rise.
Still we step through the dance, hoping for a special chance
to arrive; oh, to come alive.

We claw in depravation, at the door we'll never breach,
to fill the void of a lifetime
and have all we'd ever need.
A just reward so long deserved, to finally be realized,
still things pass on to someone else
as we move down in the line.

We claw in depravation, at the door we'll never breach
as possibilities and probabilities;
grow more beyond our reach.

18

A Higher Purpose

Two in the Morning, and I'm still not through,
but I have to let it go and get some sleep.
Work comes early and there's so much to do
to circumvent me sinking too deep.
Concerned about the future, and the path I tread,
and for the life that I provide for them all.
Somehow and some way I know we'll move ahead
and these trials will be hard to recall.

With a higher purpose; an understanding with a special sense.
A higher purpose; this family and all that it represents.

Resources fall away, hitting us where we live,
as improvisions gets us by most of our needs.
I wonder if I justify, excuse or forgive
myself for all the inadequacies.
Defending my actions to warrant this plight;
these conditions of doing with less.
Still, deep in my heart I know it's right,
so, I won't regret what I don't possess.

A higher purpose' a reason and resolve for each new day.
A higher purpose; that carries our convictions on our way.

Two in the Morning, and I'm still not through,
but I feel good for all that I've done.
Time spent with children; time spent with you,
helps me forget how much we're on the run.
Somehow, some way I know we'll rise above
these adversities trying to tear us apart.
Spending a lifetime in service and love,
with these people so dear to my heart.

Reaching for a higher purpose;
beyond this temporal plane we're now on.
A higher purpose; that transcends us above and beyond.

19

When She Said, What She Meant

When she said, "I need to find myself"
and, "Our love seems a little bit tired."
What she meant was, "I've found someone else"
and, "What we had once has now expired."
When she said, "We need to try something new;"
what she meant was, "I need to run."
When she said, "I'm no good for you;"
what she meant was, "you're no longer the one."

I knew from the words; what I finally heard
was her saying her ambivalent goodbyes.
Still I wish and believe she could have been honest with me
instead of those cryptic lies.

When she said, "Everything will be the same"
and, "It's not you, it's not you, it's me;"
what she meant was, "It's you that I blame,"
and, "It's time to set me free."

When she said, "Don't worry, I'll be just fine;"
what she meant was, "I'm on my own, now."
When she said, "We aught to give it some time;"
what she meant was, "I'm through trying to work things out."

With my broken heart, I'm back here at the start
knowing in truth; we're finally through.
Now, from all the signs; reading between the lines
I'm not really sure what I should do.

When she said, "This isn't really the end;"
what she meant was, "I won't be opening that door."
And when she said, "We can still be friends;"
what she meant was, "I won't see you anymore."

20

Finding Myself In Search Of Finding Myself

Kindergarten to high school; then college;
many years of learning, to educate.
Never-ending books and studies to be done,
as my childhood was put on wait.
Yet here and there, dreaming of somewhere,
always far away and somewhere else,

I'd keep finding myself in search of finding myself.

Toys and games, matinees, Scouting and sports,
filled my youth in an early dawn.
But dogs and bikes, my old friends back then,
soon disappeared as I moved on.
Friends left innocent play to go on their way
and evolve into someone else,

while I keep finding myself in search of finding myself.

From the anthropology of the earth to the mysteries of the sea;
I'm sure on this great big planet, something's out there for me.
I quest for the love and knowledge, to understand why I'm here,
and fulfill the measure of my creation on all planes; far or near.

Flipping burgers, a busboy, a waiter, a suit,
a carpenter, or driver on the road.
From construction to design, from inside or out
I'd still end up carrying my load.
An ends to a means, continuing the scenes
for me and everyone else,

still, I keep finding myself in search of finding myself.

21

Just A Little Tiny Step

It's just a little tiny step, from that argument last night.
From the attitudes implied,
or things not done quite right.
It's just a little tiny thing that eats like rust; day by day,
till everything is gone
as we step by step by step; away.

It's just a little tiny step, just a tiny move apart.
Not seen by the watchful eye
but felt by a hurting heart.
It's just a small departure; a move in a defensive way,
but felt like an earthquake,
as we step by step by step, away.

And step by step; we move quietly away,
and comes the fateful day; we have nothing left to say.

It's just a little tiny step, from some little innuendos,
the off-balance postures sent
and the way it goes.

It's just a little tiny word, that eats away, day by day,
till everything is gone,
as we step by step by step, away.

And brick by brick, we just build onto this wall.
Then comes the day we know; we have nothing left at all.

It's just a little tiny step; just a moment quickly passed,
but it's not taken lightly,
and the die is sorely cast.
It's just a little tiny thing, that eats like rust, day by day,
till all our love is gone
and we step by step by step;
step by step by step, away.

I Got The Last Laugh,
This Time

Maybe she's thinking her game was a success,
leaving so quick with our affairs in such a mess.
Maybe she's hoping I'll come crawling back tonight,
because I can't live without her by my side.

She's so clever; making me break my heart.
She's so together; while I always fall apart.
She always came up first and was always right,
but I got the last laugh this time.

Maybe she thinks I'm the same person way back when,
but she's got another thought coming to her again.

She knows me too well and thinks that I don't know,
but this time I'm packing it in and hitting the road.

She's so trick; no wonder I'd always fall.
She's so slick; I couldn't get a word in at all.

Well maybe I'm not so clever with all my lines,
    but I got the last laugh this time.

I see her dressed to kill; dining alone.
She never did care too much for being close.

And I know she's waiting for me to give in and try,
    because I fall for the same trap every time.

She's no one's fool; she never does slip up.
She's so cool; like she can take or leave love.

She thinks I need her back here in my life,
    hey, but I got the last laugh this time.

23

MEMOIRS & NOTES - 34 - 'BEYOND OUR REACH'

Beyond Our Reach

(1993) – I believe that there is a special energy of determination or drive; an internal necessity that is present in everyone, especially artists that feels the need to create something; a sock monkey, a painting, a poem, the perfect loaf of bread, a dance piece, that new novel; there's just something inherent in those people that not only can create, but *must* create. Motivated by this dream of a single-minded purpose that they carry inside. It is not a hard thing to keep believing in that illusive dream; that dream that I chase, especially when in the process, it just keeps on manifesting itself and emerging from inside my head, and from inside my heart; where I'm driven (and blessed), to imagine where I'm going with whatever project I'm into at that time, and then maybe an ingenuous idea, considering the possibilities of some simple notion of words, to go on to become the poetry (lyrics) of the song; that will hopefully coincide or correspond with the experimentations of the possible chord progressions, not to mention what key to do the song in, (and for me, it's usually a key that can be accompanied with a harmonica), and then there is the follow through; the timing of the piece, the blending of instruments, the voice or voices, the lead guitar, or prominent saxophone voice or clarinet or 12-string guitar voice; then the mixing down; the engineering of the end product, and then the reviews; the second listening, to be sure that this one is as good as you think it is, and if not, doing what needs to happen to bring it up to the quality end-product that I seek. Now in another world, I would have my entourage of groupies and friendly critics to exaggerate what it is I'm doing, to boost my ego and help me feel like I'm really a big deal; but in my case, beyond the obligatory comments I get from my family, (usually from my eager beseeching), I am my own fan club, supporter, evaluator and critic. Still, in my self-actualization, that is to say, the fulfillment I hope to get out of repeatedly completing the varied creations that spring from my talents and potentialities, there is a part of the dream fulfilled. And there is an exhilarating excitement in the process of creating something from nothing or something from something else. And I do it for myself and as an outward consideration, I do it for my close family and friends. And though most of the time, I have to almost beg someone to have a listen, most times each work of art ends up being created, then put away in some box in my closet, ultimately to be there for myself as I push forward to the next set of poems, musical creations and or albums. And the dream? Well, I could easily get discouraged as I am forever being denied the experience of the larger picture, but the dream is a light of hope; telling me to get ready because that next adventure into the future, that holds such promise, is waiting to be discovered.

Side Note:

This song followed one of my last-ditch attempts to do something commercially with my musical talents. I bought this current *Songwriter's Guide and Listing* book from Barnes & Noble and proceeded to send out solicitations to all of the major recording companies, (and there was a lot of them), to find out if there was an interest in listening to my material. This is standard protocol even when the listing in the book declares that they would be interested, you still need to make sure because the book pads addresses and company information with a lot of bogus listings. I sent out over 150 request cards with self-addressed-stamped check-the-box-if-you're-interested postcards to be mailed back to me. I got about 56 back, with only about 23 that indicated they might be interested in possibly listening and evaluating my material. I created a slew of demo cassette tapes with, what I felt was, some of my best songs, and then sent them out, again with a self-addressed-stamped mailing bag and another card with a check-the-box-if-you're-interested, and then mailed them out. To find out if the cassette tapes were indeed listened to, I put this small piece of tape at the beginning of the leader tape in a corner of the cassette cartridge, that would effortlessly pull off the plastic housing and onto the leader tape when the cassette was put into a player and turned on. After six months I got one of the many tapes back, followed by another three months later and the last almost a year after it was sent out. None of them had the seal broken. They probably just sat on someone's shelf for months until someone else felt guilty and decided to send back the un-listened-to material. All the others were probably thrown into a trash can after they steamed the dollar and twenty-eight cents worth of stamps off the packing envelopes.

Another Side Note:

So, there I was, negated, distraught and disappointed with the fact that I couldn't even get one person to review my material. Denied! I thought about how many other people are out there; people that may have as much or maybe even more talent than me, that, like me, could not be heard because no one cared to do their job and just listen. And in my anguish, I wrote this song, which is one of my favorites on this album, not because I languish in self pity, but rather because it reminds me that if I want to be a songwriter, than I can be a song-writer even if it doesn't come packaged with a positive endorsement declaring that what I'm doing is any good. If for no other reason, I have to do this songwriting for me.

Another Side Note:

And so it has been for so many years. I will just keep going; another song here, another album there, and sometimes reflect or pause and wonder, is anybody out there listening? Meanwhile I'll keep looking to create the masterpiece that will turn everything around. Doesn't matter that I'm always a day late and dollar short, and that my quest for validation seems to always be, "Beyond My Reach."

A Higher Purpose

(1992) – This song was written during another time when I was unemployed, and it reflects the insecure and uncertain madness of the worried family man. The poem portrays a person struggling with some confusion about career choices, worries about family constraints and self-doubting, anxiety, me lacking in confidence, and having to deal with the insanity of complexed bureaucracies and state government organizations, with their systems and procedures designed to maintain excessive control over their hiring practices. This, along with my on-going time conflicts to get things done in different places and my unresolved financial inadequacies and my work limitations. I was working over at the Gages' house, doing yard work and odd stuff on my own time, in between looking for another job. It was so depressing having a degree in Computer Sciences and the knowledge and know how, but with nowhere to apply it. Meanwhile Diane and I went into that, let's-see-just-how-far-we-can-stretch-things, mode. And, I got involved with the state welfare department for possible medical cover-age, and, we were humbly on what was known at the time as, church assistance, (a term to mean church welfare) for our needed food. The night I wrote this poem, I was up after two in the morning, filling out detailed job applications and other paperwork for possible state jobs that never materialized. I felt, and rightfully so, that like Sisyphus, I was in an endless cycle of uselessly rolling a rock up a hill only to watch it fall and roll back down again.

Side Note:

Perhaps this song was a cry of justification for and in-behalf of all my guilt for my shortcomings, but I believe that at that time, more than any other time in my life, I needed to believe that in spite of my failings, faults, problems and inadequacies, there was this higher purpose and reason for me to continue on. I know now that I was right, but at the time I was not so sure.

Another Side Note:

On the other hand, from the comment that I made earlier for the song, "Beyond Our Reach," It can be personally rewarding for a mom or dad to see the rewards return for the many years of sacrifices they genuinely suffered for their children through the years. Yet sometimes the tasks seem to go unnoticed and reap few returns, leaving the reward or prize to be in the very task itself, or seemingly nonexistent. One of the challenges that I faced was the scarcity of time itself; it seemed to quickly drain away. I would find myself looking back on my parenting skills or lack thereof, and what I did or did not provide for my kids, but meanwhile their lives continued to race past me, as I was struggling to keep the train on the track. I do know that we, Diane and I put a lot of our own needs on hold so we could keep going down that good path. Sometimes the reward is the knowledge of the importance of the task that we did accomplish. Still,...

When She Said, What She Meant

(1995) – When a woman says something it may mean what you think it means, but then again, it may not. I was reading in the newspaper one morning about women going through the first stages of separations that would usually always follow with divorces. In this article they recognized many scenarios and documented the differences between what she was verbally saying, and what the true meanings of her words really were. It sounded like a good idea for a song and I went to work immediately.

Side Note:

My brother Charlie was intrigued by the concept of this song when I explained it to him, but after hearing it, he said that he thought it was my best song ever. He was visiting at Ray's house for a family reunion at the time and during that three-day-weekend I must have played this tune for him at least five times. Struggling to remember the name but never getting it, he'd say, "Hey, play that new song again, you know, the one about what she said and meant." I knew what he meant and played it again and again.

Finding Myself In Search Of Finding Myself

(1995) – I have been forever on this quest to find, know and perfect myself, while here on this mortal plane of existence. This seems to be a recurring theme in many of my albums and my life—I have learned to embrace it; I hope you will too. There are many people out there that are certain who they are and where they're going, but like me, there are some that question the direction and the purpose and the cause and effect of the changes of life and philosophies that happen along the way to finding themselves. Although I did graduate from a community college with a Degree in Computer Sciences, and by the time this song was written I did have a good job working for that same college, but there I was, once again, doing some life evaluating and soul searching. No other time prior in my life was I more successful in my career and perhaps family life, but I couldn't help questioning just what it was I was doing as I found myself in search of finding myself.

Side Note:

I think like many people I've been finding myself in search of finding myself. Looking at where I am or where I'm not, and where I'm supposedly going or where (for whatever reason) I'm not going; but there I am, psychoanalyzing myself yet again. And I think we all do, sometimes it's healthy, sometimes, not so healthy. Still, my judgement of myself could be, and is likely to be, subject to being biased. One type of bias that I feel I'm mainly disposed to is, that of a kind of, self-serving bias. It is somewhat of a defense mechanism, and I do tend to judge myself in a favorable way. And I'm like, seeing where I am and convincing myself that it's okay if I'm less than something or someone, or I tell myself it's alright if I'm taking way too much time to get that thing done; when in fact I'm holding myself back with excuses and justifications.

Another Side Note:

In this poem I highlighted a lot of my own previous involvements in certain events, circumstances and work experiences, starting with school. I am not a military brat, but because of my mother being physically abused so often, (from 1955 to 1967 and maybe, more on this subject later), I ended up going to, went to six different grade schools, three different middle schools and four different high schools.

And as my childhood was put on wait, always running away, dreaming of that perfect far away and somewhere else; I'd keep finding myself in search of finding myself.

And then I touch on a few of my work experiences, like, flipping burgers at Burger Chef, (incidentally, where I met Diane), a busboy, a waiter working the borsh belt in the Catskills at many resort hotels, a suit, as a Funeral Director at Forest Funeral Home, a carpenter, working construction in Oregon building bridges and other construction, a driver on the road, driving delivery for JW Electronics, design, as a draftsman for Burns and Roe in Jacksonville Florida; still, I would keep finding myself wherever and whatever I was doing, always in search of that better job with that better pay, always in search of finding myself.

Just A Little Tiny Step

(1992) – If I was a marriage counselor and could offer just one thing that has worked for me over the my many years of marriage, one small piece of advice that might I might offer to someone in hopes of saving their relationship and maybe even bringing it back to life; that advice would be this: listen to that other person when he or she is speaking, and then, really listen. And realize that by listening and communicating with each other, you both get closer to fixing that thing that is broken. Without listening, both continue to get farther away from each other. And even the littlest inconsiderate things will, like bricks to a small barricade, slowly build up to an unfathomable wall that, after a while, cannot be penetrated or scaled.

When I was in junior high, I had this friend named Rory Lewis who never lost an argument or verbal fight. Even if he was obviously wrong, he would never admit it and he was the king of holding out until someone else broke or gave in. His secret was that he could distance himself from his friends by not caring. He knew his opponent's weakness was a need to be loved and he knew that because he didn't need me the way I needed him; he could hold out indefinitely. So, while I was going through the anxiety of love-friendship withdrawals, he would go into his well-equipped solitary world and just wait. And because he didn't care about you as much as you did for him, he could wait forever. And so, I was always the one that caved in and would always say that I was sorry and that it was my fault, even when it clearly was not. I hated him for that strength he used against my weakness of needing to be accepted and loved. And eventually one day after a stupid argument, something about flying saucers, we broke up and I never interacted with him again.

There are times when mistakes and broken hearts can be so misunderstood. Diane and I had a simple quarrel. I don't remember what our argument was about, only that it lingered for days. And because our feelings were so fragile, and our egos needed to be constantly fed with the reassurance that love and consideration was being administered, when I harbored that anger for too long, needing to be right, I started slipping away from that closeness we had. Like Rory, I told myself that I would win, no matter what. We needed to know there is a trust-bond continually happening, and we both wanted to believe that we were not being taken advantage of by the other, but when our communication broke down, we grew more distant. And when that mutual, and or, symbiotic relationship got damaged, even by some small thing that we could not even remember anymore, the purpose for our being together seemed to lose it's strength and purpose.

One night I was laying there in the dark on my side facing the wall, my back to Diane's back who was apparently asleep, I laid there just thinking about how it all came to fall apart. I was amazed that something so seemingly insignificant or even irrelevant could actually shake our relationship. I knew that both of us were waiting for the other to apologize, but who would make the first move? Diane must have been thinking on the same wavelength because we both rolled over to face each other at the exact same time, and we had a big discussion; not about the infraction or the argument; those reasons had long since been forgotten, instead, we talked about our communication problems. And we talked about how terribly lonely and frustrating it was to stubbornly hold on to the pride, and the resentment and anger, and how it served no good purpose. We vowed that we would try to understand the other's point of view if and when this might happen again. And then, we kissed and made up.

Side Note:

Sometimes it's just a little thing that breaks up a relationship. But sometimes that little tiny interaction that says, "I'm sorry" or "het, it was my fault," is the biggest thing you can ever do, to say, "I love you" and doing so can put you on the fast track to recovery, otherwise you might face a long and arduous process of healing.

Leslie

(1960s) – (Instrumental), It was late in the afternoon on a weekday, probably a Friday because my mother had come home early from work; she owned and operated a food vending truck, called "The Chuck Wagon" and a lot of the factories that she serviced and delivered lunches to would close their doors early on Fridays so she did too. Also, it must have been sometime in the afternoon because at Grandma Scarbrough's house, 'Make Room For Daddy' was on. Charlie and Mary were playing, 'Sorry' and Richie was reading an Uncle Scrooge comic that I'm sure he had read many times before, I was in grandma's living room dinking around on the piano.

After about ten minutes Grandma yelled from the kitchen for me to stop playing the piano and said that it was just adding to the already noisy house, and not even waiting for me to respond, she flew out of the kitchen, stood next to me, and with a stern look on her face, she shut the doors to the piano keys as my fingers barely escaped. She went into her room, came back out with a small key and locked the lid.

After about ten minutes Grandma yelled from the kitchen for me to stop playing the piano and said that it was just adding to the already noisy house, and not even waiting for me to respond, she flew out of the kitchen, stood next to me, and with a stern look on her face, she shut the doors to the piano keys as my fingers barely escaped. She went into her room, came back out with a small key and locked the lid.

"Mother?" I heard my mother call. "Were you listening to what he was playing?"

"No." Grandma Scarbrough replied. "Just sounded like noise."

Mother stood up from the kitchen table and came into the living room. She smiled at me before turning to grandma. "You never reacted to John when he was taking lessons here a couple years ago."

"That was different." Grandma replied. "John was learning how to play the piano; not pound on it like Skipper; trying to see how much noise he can make."

Mother laughed and replied, "Skipper wasn't pounding on it, and he was trying to play a song. I think it was 'Oh Suzanna.' And plunking out notes on a piano is another way to learn how to play it."

"It's not the same." Grandma retorted. "He can't read music."

"You know as well as me that a lot of great musicians never learned how to read music." Mother said as she nudged me to move over on the piano bench so she could sit next to me. Grandma, seeing she was losing this battle, unlocked the lid and over animatedly opened the piano back up. With a look of curiosity, mother turned to me and said, "So you want to learn how to play the piano?" Embarrassed by everyone looking at me, I froze.

With grandma still standing behind us, mother pointed to the name on the inside of the lid that read, Farrand Piano Co. Holland Michigan and said, "You see this name here? Where the first letter of the name is,..." she gently grabbed my right hand and pulled to towards her, placing my thumb down. "On every piano in the world, right below the first letter of the name of the manufacturer is always the middle C."

I played the note with my thumb, even though I wanted to use my pointer finger. "Yes." Mother replied satisfied. "Now if you look at the keys, you'll notice there's white keys and black keys. And the black keys are in sets of two and then three and then two and so on, repeating up and down." She then pointed to my right thumb and said, "Just before the set of two black keys, like where your thumb is, that's C. And just before the next set of two black keys is also a C note, just higher or lower C if it's below the middle C.

I felt special to be sitting there on that bench next to my mother, who was always too involved with keeping her family together to concentrate on me. And there she was; sitting there next to me, giving me her undivided attention. And a light went on in my head as I started tapping on the different C notes, up and down the piano. I marveled that I understood what my mother was teaching me; and it excited me inside; I wanted more.

Although there had been a promise of more piano lessons that I hungrily looked forward to, regretfully, they never happened again. After the assassination of President Kennedy, mother, a devout Catholic, was devastated and so, reached out to Senior. After reconciling with Senior, we moved out of grandma's house and back to

Glendora California in the same; Belle Acres Trailer Park, but into a different, larger trailer.

But that one, singular piano lesson from my mother never left me and whenever or wherever I was, if there was a chance to be reintroduced to a piano, I never missed the opportunity to sit down and practice some of what my mother had taught me. Before her passing in 1996, mother was always the first one to receive my musical works and albums. And this album, "Beyond Our Reach," was the last album that she would ever receive.

Side Note

Until we did move in December of 1963, my grandma would still lock the piano at times to avoid any extemporaneous piano noises in her house. Little did she know that Richie knew how to unlock the piano with a hairpin. Problem was, he couldn't lock it back up without a few minutes and when we'd see her driving down her driveway, I would just shut the lid. Seeing it closed, she rarely tested the lid to see if it was unlocked.

After her passing in 1973, I became the owner of that piano, of which I still have today. One of the first things I did was to remove the lock assembly from the lid. I wanted any and all kids to be able to play with it, (I'm pretty stringent about them pounding on the keys to make noise), but they caught on fast and were able to use it when ever they wanted, (as long as someone was not watching TV at the time).

Side Note:

After my one piano lesson from my mother, I began to experiment with ¾ timing, rolling the fingers of my left hand to the 1-5-8 or, 1-4-8 to create the notes of a chord played in succession, either ascending or descending, kind of like an arpeggio but without moving beyond the assigned three notes, and I would play something that resembled a tune with my right hand. The Leslie tune came about with me rolling the base with the fingers of my left hand, which was a neat sound and then I created a little tune that, over the years, evolved to what you hear now. The tune got its name from a friend of mine that, in 1963, lived across the street from Grandma Scarbrough. Leslie had an annoying gift of being able to listen to me play my tune and then parrot the tune, only sounding more like what it should sound like. He had the same parroting ability with a harmonica, and with his talent of sharp recall, he advanced quickly through the ranks in the Boy Scouts of America. (You can read more about Leslie in the book, "Stepping Between The Ants").

I Got The Last Laugh, This Time

(1993) – Sometimes we find ourselves in the most precarious situations, don't we? If a person is in love, truly in love, it can be so difficult for them to ever triumph when it comes to dealing with a selfish, manipulating significant other.

So it was, (and still is), for my friend Ralph who I went to school with in 1990-91. He married an Asian woman, had two kids and was having, what he thought was, a good relationship. That was until she went to work, working for the state, and then started making better money than Ralph and she started hoarding money away, telling Ralph he needed to continue paying the bills with what money he earned. Then she moved her sister and her sister's family in to their home. And there was Ralph, paying for both families with his part-time work while going to college.

One day after he realized he wasn't going to be able to pay the bills, he asked her for help. She refused and threatened to call the police and scream that he had abused her. Wanting to reconcile circumstances and be able to interact with his children, he came back and took on the burden once again and quit going to school full time. Even though things continued to fall apart on their marriage, Ralph kept trying to bandage the problems. He lost his job, but went out and got another part-time position, hoping to keep things going, especially because now, he has two kids in college, that, because his wife felt that her money was hers and to be spent for other things, Ralph supports them on his own. The truly sad thing is, Ralph just wanted to have a happy home and continues to work towards that end.

Side Note:

Things appeared to be fine for a classmate of mine named Jim, who had plans of getting ahead. He saved a lot of money and his wife did a great job of making their ends meet, taking care of all the finances. That was, until Jim got a much better paying job. Over the course of a couple months, she not only was spending more than he was making, but never let Jim know what was going on with their finances. That was until things started falling apart. Jim tried to pull the expenses back into some semblance of control, but his wife, who was now accustomed to her inflated lifestyle, got angry. Somehow, she got control over everything they owned; the bank account, the house, both cars; everything of monetary value. And one day Jim just decided that he had had enough. He determined that he would let her think she had the upper hand, but all the while he made preparations to leave her and be legally free of all the financial burdens and binding circumstances. On one fateful winter day, Jim left her suddenly, and then went underground and incognito, so to speak, and now lives somewhere on one of the ferried islands on Puget Sound.

Another Side Note:

As reported earlier, less than a year after this album came out, my mother took a turn for the worse, her immune system was already compromised by the chemotherapy she was going through and ended up in a hospital in Miami Florida. All of her children showed up; John and David, lived in Miami, Ray flew in from Oregon, as did Richie and his wife, Mary came down from New Jersey with her son Dennis, and I flew in from Washington State.

While we were going through the process of dealing with all the finalizing arrangements, Ray found out from one of his daughters that his wife Shawna had broken into the back of Ray's construction truck and was selling all of his expensive tools and equipment in a lawn garage sale to get money for her and her boyfriend to buy drugs. Ray was decidedly upset about Shawna's actions and though he wanted to stay for his mother's funeral, he had no recourse but to find and take an early plane back to Oregon in hopes of salvaging what he could of his marriage.

By the time Ray got back to his house, Shawna had locked all the doors and windows to the house, claiming that she now had full possession of it. But after Ray got the police involved, she was not only informed that the house belonged to Ray and was not in her name, but was told that what she was doing was illegal and that she had to let Ray in his house. She eventually got evicted.

And as you can imagine, there is a lot more to this story here but I don't think that I am the one that needs to tell it.

And Another Side Note:

I wrote this poem for all of them, and their problematic circumstances, and for the hope that there might be a time in their lives that they might recognize their shortcomings and maybe even try to reconcile the sad but true circumstances. Otherwise they might feel that in the very end, they got the last laugh.

And Yet Another Side Note:

I played with this cliché for a few minutes before I came up with the basis for this poem and then wrote the first set of words in about a half an hour. A little later I didn't like the comedic way the words fell and started over. Also, there is the sound in the background where if you listen, you might hear the sounds of people talking. I wanted to have it feel like you were in a restaurant and there was a slight din of people enjoying their dinner out. This did not turn out well though because the engineer was not able to pull it off successfully.

And Yet One More Side Note:

And then there was Larry, one of the instructors at the college that became a good friend to me. He told me one day how his wife had not only maxed-out his credit cards, she cleaned out his bank account and then left the country, leaving him in unbelievable debt, to raise their kids, to pay off the bills and to deal with his sudden, horrible debt. Somehow, Larry managed to rise above all the adversity and although he was still in minor debt the last time I saw him, his positive attitude helped him manage to unbury himself. I do wish him well.

24

-35 - THE JOURNAL'S BREAKING NEWS - 1998 -

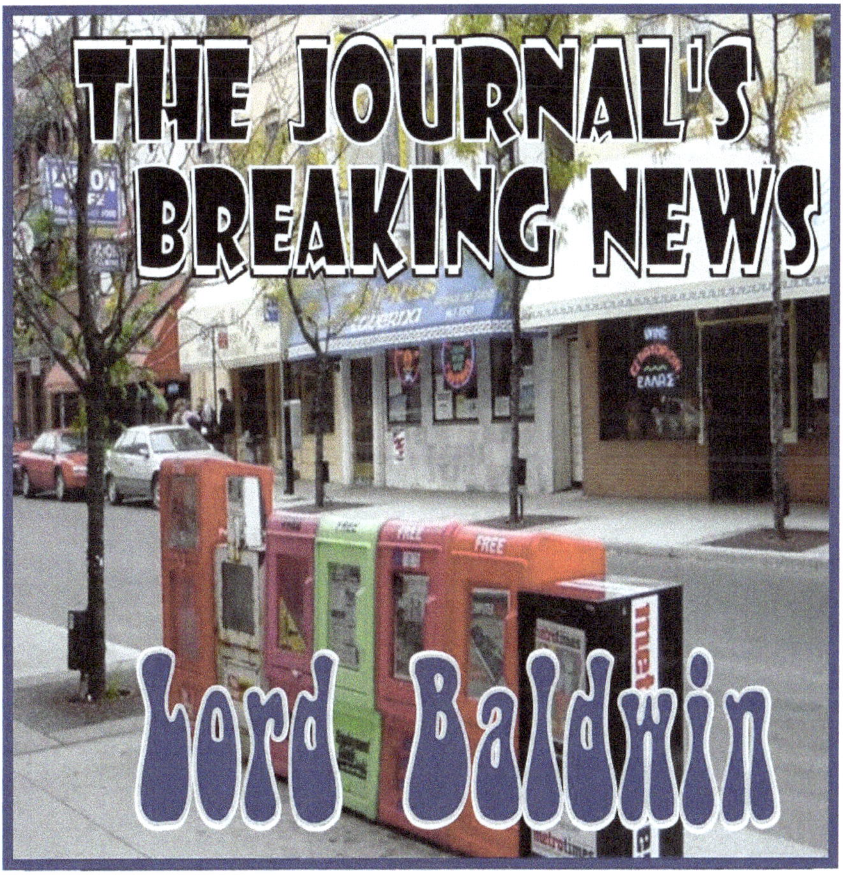

25

NOTES ABOUT THE COVERS

Notes On The New Cover:

Nothing spectacular here – I was tempted to use a collage of tabloid clippings of OJ Simpson and Princess Diana and Michael Jackson and maybe borrow bat boy from the American supermarket tabloid, Weekly World News, but I wasn't sure how copyrighted the images might have been. Maybe I should have done it anyway. But, maybe then the paparazzi would hunt me down, chase after me, get way too close behind the vehicle I was driving and then cause me to crash into a wall. And then say it wasn't their fault. But anyway, as you can see, no copyright here – I just changed the lettering and shortened my pseudonym to Lord Baldwin

Notes On The Original Covers:

The original front cover showed seven newspaper boxes, many saying, 'free' and the town on the other side of the street looked a lot like downtown Olympia.

The back cover kind of looked like this unfortunate man was posing in front of a firing squad, but I do believe that at the time this photo was taken, it was of a politician in a South American country getting ready for a photo shot for his campaign. .

Notice the use of the colorings in the lettering; 'yellow' and, 'black' kind of like, 'Yellow Journalism' and black printing press ink.

26

THE JOURNAL'S
BREAKING NEWS

The Journal's Breaking News
That You'll Be Back Again
Is This What You Wanted?
She Remembers
Come To Me
I'm Older Now

27

The Journal's Breaking News

Truth and lies are twin brothers that know each other's heart.
The problems that won't go away are the ones that become part
of the fabric of the business of the intractable wrecking crews
that roll twenty-four hours long
for the journal's breaking news.

Deals and sellouts; the good air time exploit the helpless and weak.
sell fabrications to the gullible that keep coming back each week
A product for the money, a bribery or just paying dues,
it's all in a hypocritical day's work
for the journal's breaking new.

Scientific testing of demographics, to see what markets bare,
continues as people scream out "foul" to the factions hiding there.
Ambiguity that leads to profane
manipulated by the public's views
only fuels newspaper and TV stories
for the journal's breaking news.

Anyone can be a player in the ratings and tabloid cast,
payoffs to the whistle blower as the deepest pockets, bid last.
No one backs out or walks away when they get their final ques
there's no innocent or guilty party
in the journal's breaking news.

The cash cow keeps producing and the monster must be fed.
Still, it's a world of entertainment, with a price on every head,
anxiety runs amuck with speculation to despairing blues,
as they wonder whos' the next target
for the journal's breaking news

It may be manipulative and unethical, misleading and a lie,
by morning it's front-page news back-hoed into everyone's lives
As character assassinations, with no evidence of truth,
but who cares about particulars
in the journal's breaking news?

the innocent retaliates to the courts and its proper guards,
but the journal's legal jargon, mumble jumble lawyers
hold all the cards
And they shuffle and deal and litigate
toe-tapping in wing-tipped shoes
settling for a highly disclosed amount
in the journal's breaking news.

There's no wall between fact and fiction; nobody knows for sure;
victims bought and sold each week on the seventy-five cent tour.
Pedaling ribald to the masses,
prognostications to inform and amuse,
with the sad voice of indiscreetness
by the journal's breaking news.

28

That You'll Be Back Again

They say I'm a fool to wait here for you,
they say you lied when you had to leave.
And with each passing day, the longer you're away,
the harder it gets to believe.

I knew that you'd changed success finally came,
and I was a part of all you'd end,
but when you said goodbye, I felt something inside
say you'd be back again.

Still as each day comes and goes
with all the news; nobody knows.
Though my heart says it's been too long,
I'm hoping all along that my feelings weren't all wrong.

It's easy to go when you finally know
the good or bad of how things are.
But if you never know, you live your life in hope
things will work out from afar.

As I turn out the light, my prayer every night
is you'll return from where you've been.
Things are not what they seem, so I can only dream
that you'll be back again.

And the madness returns as that feeling just burns
all the questions; the uncertainty and the doubt.
Am I wrong in this case to go on with my blind faith
for someone or something I should do without?

Tomorrow will near and I'll still be here,
waiting like I've done before.
Although you're not around, my faith is fairly sound
I will never want for more.

You said you would be someday back for me
so I'll wait for that there and then.
And while we are apart, I'll promise to my heart
that you'll be back again.

Things are not what they seem, so I can only dream
that you'll be back again.

29

Is This What You Wanted?

I'm broken and falling apart
don't know what to do with this lost, broken heart.

I'm shattered; so hard to go on,
without you here with me my life's purpose is gone.

I'm so sorry things aren't like they were before.
I'm still trying to get myself together once more.

Is this what you wanted, to see me fallen this way,
with nothing but emptiness left to my day?
Is this what you wanted, to have me suffer this joke?
Are you happy now that I've finally broke?

Uncertain, and this is more than enough
to keep me worried if there's a future for us.

And the madness; the one thought in my mind,
is I'll live with regret for the rest of my life.

And yes; I made mistakes I wish I could change,
but are you going to make me relive things over and over again?

Is this what you wanted, to see me fallen this way,
with nothing but emptiness left to my day?
Is this what you wanted, to see me sink in the rough?
Are you happy now? Have I suffered enough?

My heart when I think of what we had back then
but I don't know what to do to put us together again.

Is this what you wanted, to see me fallen this way,
with nothing but emptiness left to my day?
Is this what you wanted, to have me struggle and fall?
Are you happy now that I've finally lost it all?

30

She Remembers

Her heart could belong to me
we could chase each other's dreams for romance.
There's a special kind of love
that I could easily be part of, given the chance.

It would be nice to start again where we left off back then;
the way things were before I finally fell,

but she remembers; too well.

From a distorted point of view
thought it was alright to say and do for my sad gain.
I took advantage from the start,
exploited her kind heart and caused her pain.

Is it any wonder then as I come back here again
that she hesitates to believe the tales I tell?

but she remembers; too well.

She remembers the times she was alone
and the nights I never did come home
she remembers all the chances that she gave
in hopes that this time; I'd finally change.

Her heart could belong to me
we could chase each other's dreams into the dance.
There's a special, kind of love
That I could easily be part of; given the chance.

I 'd love to be there to see us back where we used to be
but right now, she's closed up inside her shell.

She remembers; too well.

Yes, she remembers; too well.

31

Come to Me

Come to me all who are weary and I will give you rest.
Learn from me for I am gentle,
humble in heart and here for your quest.
Remember always I love you; I'll be your comfort to ease your pain,
I'm here to share the trials you go through,
so don't give up; have hope and faith.

I am your friend, I am your guardian.
I am your power — a beacon in the night.
I am the way, the truth and the life,
so you may walk as children of light.

With the love your heart's endowed,
love one another, as I have loved you,
and when a brother reaches out,
if you know me, you'll know what to do.

I am your friend, I am your guardian.
I am your power — a beacon in the night.

I am the way, the truth and the life,
teaching charity to children of light.

When it seems like no one cares, you're alone and in despair
impelling you beyond what you can bare.
When a twisted truth gets crossed and it feels like all is lost,
reach for me, I will be there.

From a contrite spirit and broken heart,
to make amends in humility,
mercy and grace I will impart,
and with resolve you will find peace.
Remember always of my love.
My yoke is easy and my burden is light.
My peace I give unto you to be of:
let not your heart be troubled this night.

For I am your friend, I am your guardian.
I am your power, a beacon in the night.
I am the way, the truth and the life,
so you may love with the pure love of Christ,
come to me my children of light.

32

I'm Older Now

I'm older now, I know things aren't like they were.
I've gone through some alterations and I know more will occur.
Accepting what's real as well as hypocrisy run wild,
I may look ancient, but I feel like a child.
I'm older now, and I've come to realize
my place in this world has changed and not just from my eyes.
Perception can cloud the truth but the truth can set you free,
I'm older now but I'm still me.

I'm losing my teeth and I've got this gray, receding hair.
I wear glasses sometimes to see what is really there.
my memory fails at times so I learn all over again,
what it is and is not, and who I really am.
In the mirror I see the face of a man that isn't me.
As others discern my countenance, I wonder what they see.
Is it the face, the shell, the body,
or the mind and heart they perceive?
I'm older now but I'm still me.

Beyond the denial, there's a fear of me missing pace,
as each day goes by so quickly and another takes it's place.
Running to keep racing with the brightest and the best,
more tired than ever before, and always needing a rest.
I still take on injustice and I'm ready for the fight.
I hold to the resistance to stand for what is right.
At times I'm tempted to pass, but I can never just let it be,
I'm older now but I'm still me.

I'm older now, yet I still choose the hit or miss,
between the horror of the nothing and the everlasting bliss.
It doesn't get any easier just because the years pass by.
Existence can be what you believe but also what you deny.
I'm older now so I must stand by what I am,
the search for the great unanswered questions,
I leave to wiser men.
And for all it's worth, I've found that life
is what you make it to be,
I'm older now—but I'm still me.

33

✥

MEMOIRS & NOTES - 35 - 'THE JOURNAL'S BREAKING NEWS'

The Journal's Breaking News

(1997) – There is a special process that the news and the media follow, and there are ethical and unethical methods or procedures that they, the media, deem justifiable. Primarily brought on by the OJ Simpson fiasco, but fueled by the Princess Diana tragedy, by the Michael Jackson circus and the Whitewater and sex scandals of Bill Clinton.

"The Journal's Breaking News" was an observation of the grinding, manipulative nature of the news media, but it's important to note that the craving for sensationalism by certain audiences as well as the desire for unscrupulous muck runners to prompt their own form of expressive input or to voice their one-sided opinions and spin the

facts have gone on for centuries. Whenever there are people that are prominent and are in the public's eye, there will always be men and women whose jobs are to comment on, reveal facts, point out the oddities, give praise to the praiseworthy, and to tell the story that the public is hungry for. If though, those stories and accounts are not selling newspapers or magazines, or when the advertisers are not happy with the news reported on the broadcastings of the radio or television,

there will always be men and women whose business it is, to dig into someone's personal life and, through different forms of shock tactics, maybe a slight overstatement of the circumstances, can and will, reveal secrets, true or false, allude to wrongdoing even when they know none has been committed, or even create and declare lies and spread gossip; whatever sells the product. And the bigger the personality is, the bigger the target is on their back and the more the public has an appetite for.

A huckster is anyone who sells something or serves biased interests, using pushy or showy tactics. Hucksters can be a positive or negative force for and in the media. Historically, the term meant any type of vendor, but over time it has assumed pejorative connotations, and although the media can be used for power and influence in a good, positive way, to bring about social change where change is needed, that self-fueled mechanism that is relied on for honest information and reports of important intelligence, has, especially since the early-nineties, drifted off course from their trusted perceptions to informative journalism, to a reduced state of carnivalistic atmosphere and in the process not to be left behind by other outlets, began to substitute plain truths with flagrant gossip, self-created rumors, planted hearsay lies and tittle-tattle facts, to create or fuel scandals with little to no consideration for the individuals or the families of the individuals they are exploiting.

What is the news? Some say the news mirrors the times and facts of our society, and from what I can differentiate through evidence shown from the past, I believe to be partially true, but news has a new normal that can include hearsay, rumors, gossip, idle talk, unfounded information and unconfirmed reports.

And when there is no privacy or rights left to the VIPs or celebrities or the somebodies; the dignitaries and public figures, the common man or woman have no way of fighting this machine. When it comes to the truth; there is no truth, only shades of gray that redefines our sad culture.

That You'll Be Back Again

(1998) – Originally this creation was an instrumental and after being recorded as such and can be heard on the, "When That Second Chance Comes Again," album that came out four years later. At the time of creation, I couldn't quite decipher the feelings of the music, combined with the thoughts of poetic words, or where those thoughts and feelings were taking me to. But one night around eleven I was playing the tune and this poem materialized. I stayed up till past two, working on and finalizing the piece. To me, when the marriage of the poem, (lyrics) and the music come together to form a song, there is a special magic that fills my heart. There is an elevated bliss that cannot be compared to anything else. And when it comes together so seamlessly like this one did, it is doubly magnified.

Side Note:

As maybe mentioned before, when I construct the concept of any distinct album, there are certain elements that thread through all of them; a kind of formula or science if you will that helps to guarantee that particular album's success. The first element is to put your best, fast song, first, so as to ensure the attention of the listener, and hopefully, he or she will want to hear more. The second element is to always follow the first song with an excellent second song. In the listening of that second song, in any album, is usually where most listeners stay or leave, but to me, it also sets the stage for the rest of the album. If the first and second song are good, then the chances are, the listener will tolerate the rest of the material. To me, this second song is most important and is more versatile than the first, because that second song can be fast or slow, up or down tempo, anything, but it has to be good. Sometimes what I believe to be the best song of my album is too slow in tempo to put as the kicker, (first song), so it positions itself as the second song. Because of this philosophy, when I listen to my own material, I always look forward to the second song because I know it will be as good or better than the one that I had just listened to.

Another Side Note:

This philosophy of song positioning and type of song and concept album viewpoints is draw upon by my generation's experiences and maybe a few generations before mine.

On June 21, 1948: Columbia's Microgroove LP made Albums Sound better than the 78 rpm records prior. That same year, Columbia Records put the needle down on history's first successful microgroove plastic, 12-inch, 33-1/3 LPs in New York, sparking a music-industry standard, so strong that the digital age has yet to kill it.

In my generation, the listener would put on a 12-inch, 33-1/3 LP vinyl record album that usually had multiple tracks with short, two or three second pause spaces in between each track for the listening audience's consideration. Long before the Beatles,' "Sgt. Pepper's Lonely Hearts Club Band" was Released on May 26, 1967, (June 1, 1967 in the United States), there were artists putting out concept albums that invited their audience to listen to the tracks in the order they were put on the album. It should be no surprise to the true listener that I was influenced by *the Beatles*, but also from the 50s, *Elvis Presley, Chuck Berry, Miles Davis, Frank Sinatra, Ray Charles, John Lee Hooker, James Brown*, and early 60s, *the Beach Boys, Booker T and the MGs, Simon and Garfunkel, Sam Cook, Bob Dylan, the Rolling Stones, the Animals, Paul Revere and the Raiders, the Loving Spoonful, the Young Rascals,...* I could really go on and on, but my point was, before Sgt. Peppers came out other people and groups had already embraced how they wanted their audience to hear their material as it came out.

We could all argue about the true meaning surrounding the controversy of the original cover image of the Beatles' "Yesterday and Today" album, known as the "butcher cover," where, the band members, or representatives for the band declared that it was a statement against the Vietnam War. but I tend to believe what was said early on but then retracted 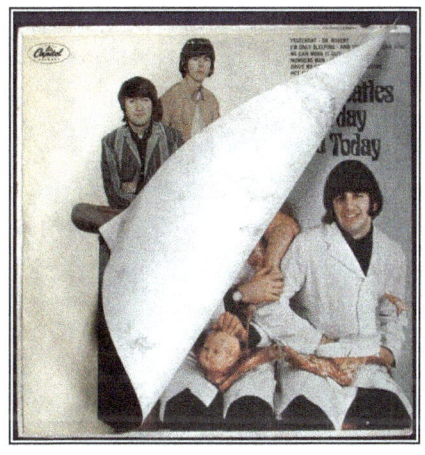 to save face as other sources close to the Beatles reported, that it was the Beatles protesting the Capitol Record Company's policy of "butchering" their UK albums by excluding tracks and rearranging the remaining tracks for a chance of profiting in on the Beatles in the North American market.

I digress. In the later 60s and certainly in the 70s people began to use cassettes to make their own mix of artists and cuts where you just take what you want and leave the rest, losing the ideas and the ride intended by the engineers and artist's intentions for album concepts.

We now live in an era of the Get-It-And-Go, where everything is digital and available with playing units that can play an album or a track or a mix and randomize and exclude or include whatever the listener desires. And I'm not saying it's bad, I do a random listening thing with my albums all the time, but what I am saying is, for you out there that might want to get a feel of what Frank Sinatra was trying to convey with his 1965 studio album, "September of My Years," they might try listening to the vinyl record recording from the first song on side one to the last song on side two. I really took a big detour from where I started from, didn't I. Sorry, I just wanted to say that track positioning used to be a big deal. And even in the digital age now, it still is to me.

Is This What You Wanted?

(1998) – Who knows what truly lurks in the minds of madmen? When I worked at the Forest Funeral Home, I learned that we were unique in our community because unlike any other facility in the county, we maintained our own crematorium and we were responsible for offering special, rock-bottom cremation deals to the public. Because we were small, there were only two of us funeral directors working at the facility. This meant we wore many hats.

One day, not too long after I started working there, I placed the remains of this huge, un-embalmed, well over 300-pound woman, who had been dead for three to five days prior to my removal, into the crematorium and fired it up. I then went down into the office to finish up some of the final paperwork. About 20 minutes later I got a call from one of the neighbors named Andy that lived on a property adjacent to the cemetery. Andy was an older man in his 60s that would sharpen all of our shovels and other tools once or twice a year.

Andy told me that there was thick black smoke coming out of the crematorium stack and there was a very bad smell in the air. I looked out my office side window and sure enough, Andy was right.

Crematoriums have after burners, and like catalytic converters, at a temperature of 2000 degrees, those after burners incinerate all the superfluous smoke and soot, leaving a clear and clean environment.

I ran up to the crematorium and, this was my first mistake, I panicked and turned the machine off. The residual thick, black smoke and soot from the burning fat continued to fill the chamber where her half-burnt remains lay smoldering.

About 15 minutes later, I tried to restart the cremation, but the jets as the two spark plugs were now all clogged with soot. It had a failsafe switch that would not allow it to start up unless everything was functional.

I called up Gary, the other funeral director, who was in Columbus Ohio at the time visiting his parents, and I asked him what I should do.

He told me how to retrieve the spark plugs by climbing up on top of the workings of the cremation machine and how to replace the old spark plugs with new ones. He also told me that there were replacement spark plugs in a separate cabinet in the prep room. I followed all the instructions but I still couldn't get the machine started. I then checked all the fuses and switches but they were all apparently operational.

By this time the smell of the partially cremated remains of that lady filled the room and it was horrible. After calling Gary back again, he then told me that one of the afterburners was probably clogged and the only thing left to do was to clean the soot off from the causeways and the natural gas jets. I asked him where the jets were and how I was supposed to do this cleaning. He said they're inside the crematorium, sticking down just a bit, located in three areas of the ceiling brick walls.

"So," I replied, "You want me to climb into the hot crematorium with that stinking, decrepit, half-baked corpse and clean the jets that are all clogged with fatty soot and smoke from some dead body?"

"No." Gary said in a matter-of-fact and are-you-kidding questionable tone. "You'll need to wait until the bricks cool down a bit before you go in."

"I'm not climbing into that box." I retorted. "What if Rick shuts the door after I go in?"

Rick was the groundskeeper for the cemetery. From the time I arrived at the funeral home, I never got on good terms with Rick. Arguably I could tell right away that Rick had some mental issues. When I was first hired Gary let me know that Rick had difficulties processing instructions and needed to have them repeatedly given. He was methodically slow and rather incompetent in the follow through, sometimes even with the lawnmowing which he had been doing for three years before I got there. Gary said that Rick had problems, except when it came time to digging graves. Then he was in his zone. He could excellently dig squared off, with perfect depth rectangular holes, in all seasons and weather and in record time; every time.

What I did not know when I first got there was that the person I replaced at the funeral home, let's say his name was Bruce, was good friends with Rick and had told Rick that he would be the replacement guy for Bruce when Bruce left. And then I arrived, Rick took it badly and hated me from day one.

Now, to be sure, I was his immediate supervisor and if and when Gary was gone, which, because he had ailing parents in Ohio, was the case all the time, I was to give Rick his instructions, which he followed to whatever wide semantics' perspective interpretation he could come up with,... and Rick was quietly but forever vindictive.

Anyway, I told Gary that I was not climbing into the crematorium for fear that I would be at the mercy of Rick who could very easily shut the door after I went in.

"We'll he couldn't start it up." Gary joked and then said. "Hey, all kidding aside, there's no other way to get that thing started again unless you fix it."

"Are you sure?" I asked. "Can't we just call someone?"

"No." Gary fired back. "This is a small facility, just you and me; and because I am in Ohio and you are there, you are the someone. Besides I'd be surprised if Rick is even there, he..."

I turned around and looked out the window to see if I could spy Rick's truck.

Rick had a sweet 1961 Car-ibbean-Turquoise Step-side Ford pickup, which he used on the job, every day,... throwing tons of dirt in the back bed every time he dug a grave,... if that truck was mine I wouldn't a wanted to tax it there,...  but that's another story too,... and to be fair, Gary took on all the mechanical work on Rick's truck and Rick got to use the gas card every week, even when business was dead,... so, couldn't see Rick's truck,... I went outside and looked all up and down the cemetery and then looked up at the garage and the prep room, no Rick,... I went back inside and picked up the phone, "You're right," I said with a note of relief, "he's gone."

"Make sure you go easy with the bricks," Gary cautioned, "they're fragile and,.."

"Okay," I interrupted. "But you owe me, really, really big time."

After a long wait, the bricks cooled down enough and I threw a piece of plywood over the top of the remains and with a bucket, a scrub brush and a dimly-lit flashlight, I climbed inside.

The platform teetered from side to side as I was on he remains rib cage, but then as I balanced in the center, the platform sank a bit and I settled in. I thought of how bad the stench was when I was outside the crematorium, but now inside, the stench made my nostrils shut and many times I kept from almost puking when my stomach would involuntarily convulse, in between my scrubbing down parts of the black bricks. My flashlight, which was balanced close to my head so I could see the jets above me, rolled off the platform and with a thud landed somewhere with the remains. The light upon the impact of hitting the bricks brightened it up.

"Why didn't I think of that?" I said out loud to nobody in particular. "Well at least I have more light." The smell was atrocious,... as, all the while, I was scrubbing the bricks around the jets and applying pressure to clean the dirty areas, the plywood platform kept sinking a little bit and then a little bit more. I soon realized that the remains were squishing below me and seeping out from the sides of the crematorium and onto the edges of the plywood platform I was on. The steady slow goo creeping up on me, reminded me of the 1958 movie called, "The Blob" and I was gonna have to get this job done before I was consumed.

All of a sudden, there was the sound of the flashlight as something popped and I was in semi-darkness. By this time, I could feel the areas that needed to be cleaned and working faster. With the goo rising, I cleared whatever soot I could see or feel from the jets, then raced out of the oven and, leaving the plywood platform where it was, I closed the doors. Nervously I turned the knobs, pushed the buttons and fired it up. As flames shot brilliantly out of the jets and the loud hum of the burners roared, the crematorium oven took off, looking and sounding better than it had ever heard or seen before. It looked like the afterburners were functioning but I still had to go outside to check the smokestack. There was no smoke; just the trail of intense heat rising from the flue conduit. My arduous task was over.

I called Gary back and without a word, I lifted the phone receiver up to the edge of the crematorium so he could hear the engines and the sounds of the gas jets creating the two-thousand-degree fire blasting and burning within.

"Is this what you wanted?" I yelled triumphantly over the phone.

"This is Gary's father," a voice returned in the distance, "I think you may want to talk to my son."

She Remembers

(1997) – There are times that I think that don't really know the mind of the woman, and there are other times that I know I will never really understand the thought processes of the woman. I worked with this guy named Martin, who liked to get drunk after work, drinking dozens of bottles of beer and then he would go out with his other coworkers, cruising through bars looking for action. Unfortunately, he forgot or didn't care that he was married, and he let things escalate till they went too far. He might have even loved his wife Daisy and his kids, but the fact that he became a repeat offender over the course of a few months only made things for him harder. Eventually his wife packed up things, grabbed the kids and left for New York. For a while, he was indeed a broken man, and he seemed even repentant and regretful of his actions. For a while he wanted to put his marriage and family back together again. Daisy even came to visit once and I talked with her, over at a mutual friend's house. She told me that the thing that hurts the most is that she remembered how things were and knew that it was a life she could not return to. And unfortunately, Martin's regret was short lived, and after Daisy left to go back to New York, I never saw her again.

One day I was driving home from work and I got this song in my head, but it was the idea for the musical harmony for the chorus that seemed to motivate me the most to complete this song, and because the whole song was pivoted from that idea. I had visions of a little bit different sound then what I ended up with, but this came pretty close and I was by no means unhappy with the results.

The premise of the words reflects a truism that women, no matter what they say, never forget. I don't mean that they are an unforgiving lot because, quite the contrary, most women seem to possess the capacity, like Daisy, for compassion and forgiveness, and I don't think in general that most women want to or need to maintain some type of database on the faults of their men, to be used as evidence against us at some other critical date later on, but in fact, I do believe that most women's means and abilities of storing memories of facts and trivialities are different than that of most men. And I mean that in a good way, otherwise how would I find out where anything is in my home; or in my life?

Come To Me

(1997) – Around Christmas of 1995, I got a phone call from my friend Darryl Wade, who at time, was working in Las Vegas as a limousine driver. Even though it was during the holiday season, I knew that he was not calling to wish me a Merry Christmas or a happy new year. After all, I hadn't heard from him for years. And after a few short pleasantries Darryl started telling me a story about one of his recent passengers; a young Arab woman named Victoria, that wanted a song written with Jesus Christ speaking as a second person. Darryl worked with Victoria on this project for couple days, off and on, and then decided that what she wanted was far more complicated than what he could deliver and so, I was called in.

At first, it was implied that what they wanted me to do was to just add the music to their lyrics; and that sounded fine to me,... After I said that I was interested, Darryl gave me her phone number and said she would call me later on,... A couple days later I got on a conference call with Darryl and Victoria, and we discussed what it was that she sought and what was required of me. I quickly realized that what she wanted was far more than what she could deliver herself, and I made some suggestions, giving her some critical ideas,... I then listened to other expectations, both from Darryl and from Victoria, and I told them that I would be glad to work on this piece,... and suggested that I play with the words a little,...

I did not realize what a can of worms this was going to end up being. After two or three phone calls, having her recite certain key scriptures and ideas, I finally figured out what it was that she wanted and I went back to work. I started over from the scriptural references, 'Matthew 11:28 and came up with another idea, where Christ was looking at us and saying, "Come to Me."

At the time, I had this neat little tune that I was playing with on the guitar that had no name, or destination for that matter, and I put that tune with some of the words that eventually became the song, and the mood or feel of that tune fueled the rest of the creation along the way. It probably took three months working with this piece, off and on, before I came up with this finished product. Meanwhile, all the time, I had Victoria calling me, pushing me to get this song finished. Victoria wanted to record and publish this song, hopefully, before Easter so that she could promote it in the Christian genre market.

After I finished, at my expense, I made special copies of this song, and along with the words, I sent both Darryl and Victoria copies through the mail. I also sent a copy to myself through the mail and threw it up in my closet so that it would be copyrighted from that moment that I received it. Not more than a week after they were sent out, I got a call from Victoria who suggested that we needed to copyright this. At first, she asked, "did you copyright this?" And before I answered, she said that she

Christus Consolator by Carl Heinrich Bloch

was going to have a musician come in to document the musical part and then she was going to have it copyrighted for both of us. There was something new in her overly-assertive demeanor that bothered me;

I could tell that there was definitely something off in the tone of her voice with that foreign accent, and the way she said things made me feel uneasy. At that awkward moment, I also felt like I was about to be betrayed or cheated by somebody thousands of miles away. My guard went up, but I tried to convey otherwise with a calm pleasant demeanor.

A week later there was talk about money that might come in if this song took off. Our verbal contract called for a percentage, I think it was 10 percent for the music and five percent for the words that I had supposedly added. In fact, the end product had a few sayings that she suggested but that were taken word for word from the New Testament. Still, after finishing the words to this song and adding the music, I put all three of our names as credit to this song.

About a month later, around Easter, Victoria called me up and talked about the finalization process. She said that she had gone to a musical lawyer and had had special papers drawn up, a contract to legally put claims on the song, and she said that she was sending that contract to both Darryl and I for our approval and signature. She then asked me if we could change some of the credits on this song itself. She wasn't worried about Darryl's name nor about her name playing second fiddle to mine, but she objected to the term "Lord" in front of my name. She asked me if that was my Christian name, and I told her no. She asked if I had changed my name to include it, and again, I told her no. She went into an intractable mood where she let me know that she felt that I was being blasphemous by wrongly taking upon myself the name of the Lord. I told her that my particular pseudonym stemmed from a happening long before she was even born, in the summer of 1967, and that I meant no disrespect. I also told her that I was a Christian myself. I didn't like the insinuation but I dealt with it. She asked about changing the tempo, and although I wasn't too keen on that idea, I said it was okay. She asked about some other changes, like a few words here and there, which I was willing to work with.

But then she got me angry. She asked me, if I got paid a little more, would I mind taking the Lord part out. I told her at first, I would think about it, but then instantly replied "No!" I told her that this was part of my creative name and it was what I wanted to be documented and to be represented for my contribution of this song.

Perhaps I made the mistake of not giving in to her requests, because I told her that there was no way that I was going to change the name on that song and that it was not negotiable. After talking with her for over an hour, (it was her call and her money), she finally agreed to leave my name alone, and she reiterated that she would send the written contract so that I could review it and hopefully sign it as soon as possible.

I never heard from her again. A couple of years later I did hear from Darryl, and when the subject came up, he said that he had never received a contract or heard from her either. It would seem that this experience would be another one of those things that you chalked up to a learning experience and let it go at that. But I loved this song, especially the music and after revising the song and the words back, so as to be my own words, (the scriptural references stayed), I recorded and included this song into this album.

I'm Older Now

(1997) – I dread the fact that I am older, but there is some reward to learning from mistakes and growing from all the things I've learned, so that I may know with some assurance, what to do when I face those problems again. And there's also all the things that we did and the things we learned from experiences and mistakes,...

Those of you that have ever heard me sing this song live, you know that there is a story that goes with this song, and you could probably forgo the retelling of it, but for the sake of those reading this memoir, and who know nothing about it; here goes.

I had this dream. I was at work at South Puget Sound Community College, and I know, even in my dream, that it was a Thursday, because, while Dr. Minnaert was President of the college, he would designate every lunchtime on Thursdays at SPSCC to be used for the arts like musical concerts or comedy groups that would come in to entertain the students, and this being a Thursday in my dream, there was an outdoor concert staring Neil Young and Art Garfunkel. This did seem to me to be an odd couple to be touring the local circuits, but I went to it anyway. They were doing songs from Buffalo Springfield and Crosby, Stills and Nash as well as some Simon and Garfunkel material. After they had finished doing a song, Neil Young came down from the stage and walked right up to me as I was standing behind the corded off area and asked, "Didn't I see you at one of my concerts in 1971?"

Okay, I know this was a dream, but you know how dreams go. And yes, I did go to a Neil Young concert in Portland in 1971. So, after some brief pleasantries, Neil Young asked me if I had my guitar, and of course, somehow, I did, so then, I got invited to get up on the stage with them. And we did a few more songs from that same itinerary before Neil Young turns to me and says, "I know you write your own stuff, so hows' about we do a couple of your songs?"

Okay. Now keep in mind that this is a dream, because I turned to him and said that I not only had a new song, but it was folded right here my front pocket and then I pulled it out. We quickly went over some of the chords and then started doing this song. We all sang the first verse, Art Garfunkel sang the second verse, Neil Young sang the third verse and I sang the first half of the last verse and they all joined in to complete the song.

It was wonderful and well received, and after a large ovation, and after the crowd noise subsided, Neil Young turns to me and says, "You know, that's some good material that the world should be hearing." He reached into his tattered wallet and pulled out a frayed business card and handed it to me. "This is the name of a guy that will bring you fame and fortune, Chester. Tomorrow I want you to call this number and this guy will hook you up." I stashed the card into my front shirt pocket and we started playing another song.

It was about this time, maybe three or four o'clock in the morning that I woke up and immediately sat up and reached for that magic card in my shirt pocket. It wasn't there; no pocket; no shirt. And I sank back down on my pillow for a moment, thinking about the dream. Then I jumped up out of bed, went over to my tape recorder and recorded the melody of this song. Then I wrote out all the words to the song as best as I could remember and then went back to sleep.

By the time I woke up suddenly the next morning, everything was gone; I had forgotten everything, but I did have the notes and after reviewing the recording and the words, it all came back to me and that evening I put the finishing touched to the song.

Side Note:

If you've been following my Memoirs & Notes, you know how strange this side note will be, if not, well, I'll try to get you caught up. It was October 10th 1998. The Baldwin family had been invited to go to Jack and Frances's house to celebrate Jack's fiftieth birthday. At this point, we were down to five kids still at home; Ben, 17, Stephen, three weeks out from turning 15, Spencer, 12, Allison, three days away from turning eight and Brian, four day from turning four. A lively group, none the less.

There was a lot of people there from both sides of Jack and Frances's families and because the day was dry and reasonably warm, there was a lot of activities going on outside.

I did bring my guitar to help everybody sing happy birthday, but before that happened, I pulled out the guitar and told everybody I had a special song just for Jack and the occasion. Jack looked like he thought I was going to prank him or embarrass him with some sensitive memories, but I pulled out this here song, "I'm Older Now."

The Scarbrough Family Reunion Summer of 1997

As I began singing, the mood and timber changed. I could tell that Jack was leaning into each word and phrase that I was singing, and I could tell that he was touched. I was in the middle of the last verse when tears filled his eyes as well as his wife Frances, who had her hand over her mouth as if that would hide the tears in her eyes. When I finished Jack came over and gave me an uncomfortable hug. Apparently, he though I wrote the song about him. I did not tell him different. He asked for a copy of the words and I gave him the copy that I had brought with me. Jack and Frances trailed off looking at the lyrics and talking to each other about the song.

This was a man that had probably plotted and planned, and waited for his father, the owner of the JW Electronics company to go on vacation to Hawaii in the spring of 1982 so that he could covertly fire me from my job. This was a man that had wanted me out for years; arguably at the time, to him and probably to much of the other upper echelon working there, (and maybe even some of my coworkers), for whatever reasons, personal or professional, I was not a liked person and this was a good move and he was even applauded by some. But I have grown from that past happening and become a better person from it.

Diane, who had heard and witnessed everything that had just gone on at that Saturday afternoon birthday party, looked over at me; her watered eyes beaming with approval, maybe for what I had done and how I let her brother believe that I wrote the song especially for him.

34

- 36 - A DAY TOO SHORT
- 1998 -

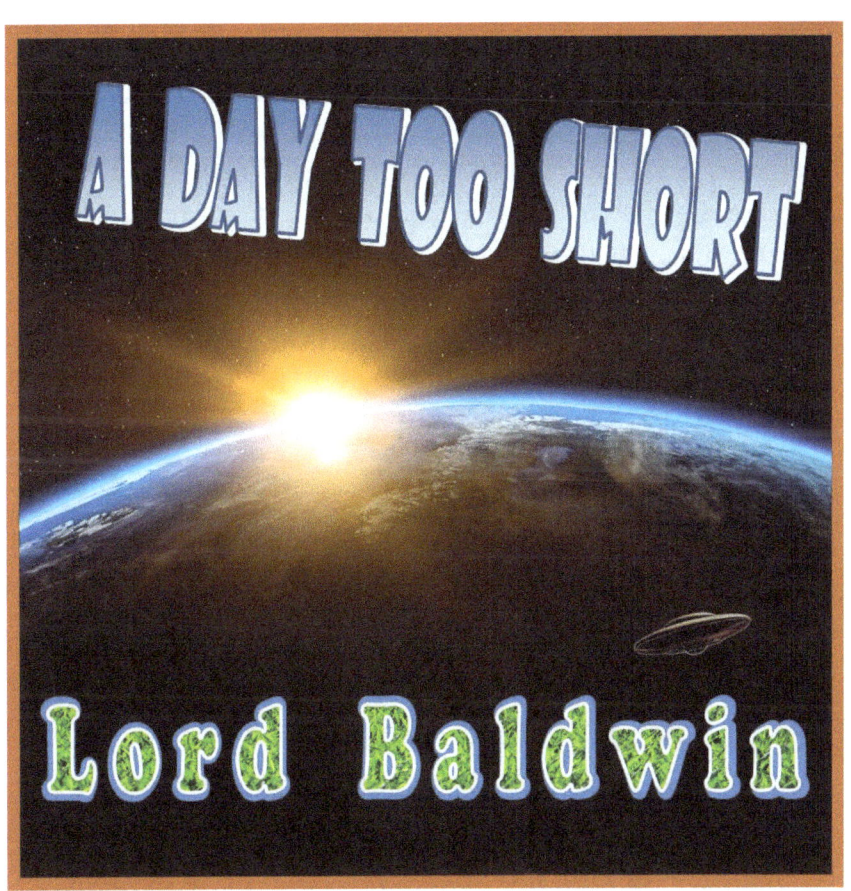

35

NOTES ABOUT THE COVERS

Notes On The New Cover:

It's sunrise over the earth, and we all know that that daylight lasts for twelve hours, but from space, it might seem longer. Still it's all a day too short, except for maybe the flying saucer that, depending on its orbital directions and speed, could end up changing that equation.

Notes On The Original Covers:

Sisyphus is a figure from Greek mythology who, as king of Corinth, became infamous for twice cheating death. Ultimately, Zeus dealt him the eternal punishment of forever rolling a boulder up a hill in the depths of Hades.

I created the back cover by taking another drawing of Sisyphus and turning it into a pencil sketch watermark, making it look like Sisyphus was rolling his rock up the letters of the titles of the songs.

36

A DAY TOO SHORT

A Day Too Short
So I Lie
Here I Wait
Further Apart
No Words Tonight
I Have No Control
Henry Hit Your Hammer
You Know What You Want

37

A Day Too Short

A day too short for what should be,
and time divided is incomplete.
A price to pay, demands to meet
will all be met before he sleeps.

Sometimes it seems that it must be wrong
for a man to believe in his dream too long.
Still chasing words that rhyme for song,
for a distant chance that might never come along.

So many hours are lost away
for a purpose only he can relate.
The cause is right though the path is vague,
yet he would push forward anyway.

Through wind cold rain, in dead of night,
he walks the streets to ponder life.
In moments brief, he knows the right
is the gray between the black and white.

He seems to have that specialness t
hat sets him apart from all the rest.
The style, the sight, the constant test;
to pursue and achieve his very best.

And yet because his age shines through,
he doubts himself and what is true.
He sees himself as one who can't choose
and who's lost in the age of the new.

Still, his warm empathy always shines
for the lonesome soul or some long lost times.
His quest and purpose, his cause and designs
all fall into place within the few lines.

Sometimes it seems it must be wrong
for a man to believe in his dream too long.
But he'll write the words and sing his song,
for a distant chance that might just come along.

38

So I Lie

One more lie to cover my back and a past that follows my track
and the lies that came before to validate what my life is for.

There's so many reasons a person lies,
for protection; fear or a truth he denies.
At times it seems so natural, yet a quirk;
the easy way to make it all work.

So I lie. I just lie. To shield my lies, I tell more lies.
And I lie; I just tell lies; I tell more lies to cover my lies

Lying to myself for so long, started feeling like nothing was wrong.
But lie after lie left alone,
builds up momentum, with a life of its own.

Worst of all, I lie the most to myself,
while a part of me was hidden from myself.
Maybe I just was afraid of what I'd see
and have no one to blame but me.

So I lie with colourful lies. And I tell more lies to live in my lie.
So I lie. I just lie; then I shield my lies by telling more lies.

And on and on and on it goes, and what it all means, only I know.
Held captive by the words I speak
and I'm doomed to carry it all in me.

One more lie to impress a friend;
one more lie and that will be the end.
One last lie and I'll let it all go then; come clean, start over again.

But that time never does take place,
because it's easier to dodge truth than to face.
In the end when things get tough on the lines,
a moment of weakness overcomes my designs.

So I lie. I just lie. To shield my lies, I tell more lies.
And I lie. I tell lies. I tell more lies to carry my lies.

Yes, I lie; I tell more lies just to cover my lies.
So I lie with colourful lies that lead to more lies;

So I lie.

39

Here I Wait

Here I wait like a knight without a lance.
Too late to join in your dance. I'd hate to lose my only chance.
Is it me, is it really me?
Have I been blind so long, my eyes and heart can't see?
I am drawn to the something that could be.
The moment, the rapture and passion, so hard to express.
And I know; I know I need to make my press.
Yet, I know you're special.
Here I wait with my fears and my lies.
Too late to hide from your eyes.
I'd hate to have to come back another time.
I was in a dream for so long,
but that dream for me, it seems, must have been wrong.
I Saw the gleam in your eyes and my song was on it's way.
And I knew, I'd changed from that day.
But the longing; the burning always stayed.
Still I know you're special.
Here I wait to see this thing through.
Too late, still I don't know what to do.
Here I wait; for you.

40

Further Apart

It so easy to play the "your fault" game
and shift all the blame over with lies.
But beyond what's played and transgressions made
what we finally saved is of no account to what dies.

The disdain we perceive, all that vengeance we need
for the bad we believe treads on our path,
only justifies how we get lost in our doubt
and then finally toll out our spiteful wrath.

But if you don't care and if I don't care
we won't get anywhere and we'll forsake the heart.
And if you don't try and if I don't try
then we just get by and grow further apart.

It's so easy to fall and surrender to it all,
throw up your arms and call it a day.
And if things get tough, turn your back on well enough
cut your losses; don't look for love, just walk away.

The sad truth no doubt is we could work things out
if we'd only reach around like we did back when.
Another second chance might revive our romance
we could step out to the dance together again.

But if you don't care and if I don't care
we won't get anywhere and we'll forsake the heart.
And if you don't try and if I don't try
then we'll just get by and grow further apart.

41

No Words Tonight

No words tonight, no exaggerated lies.
I hear you speak through the magic in your eyes.
There's been too much said
from the mind and the head
that the heart expressions all fall away.
No words tonight,
let the passion voice what the words can never say.
No words tonight, no questions asked of how.
We know the course we're heading to right now.
It's time to let go and just let it flow,
slip away from demands of the day.
No words tonight,
let the passion voice what words will never say.
No words tonight, in our own time and space.
All that we seek is within our warm embrace.
There's been too much talk
as we're chasing the clock
that true heart expressions fall away.
No words tonight,
let the passion voice what the love will always say.

42

I Have No Control

It feels like I'm on this one-long ride
with no say in what or where or why.
Subject to fickle gods with little sense
amusing themselves at my expense,
that cast my fates like wind-blown sand
to see where or when I might land
and how adversity shapes my role;
I have no control; I have no control.

They come and go with tiny forks and knives
carrying off fragments of my life.
I come up empty for no reasons because
there's nothing left to show for what I was.
I grasp at anything to get back where I'd been
but slip and fall down further again,
and look up and out from within my hole,
I have no control;
no, I have no control.

This power or authority I think I own
is challenged daily as new boundaries are grown.
Like a battle waged, I step out into the loop
I lose ground, fall back, retreat and regroup.
The strength I gather with each new hour
is just an illusion, I have no power.
I live my life, I own my soul,
but I have no control.
I have no control.

I yell and scream to invoke their fear a
nd let them know I'm standing here
but their willful actions only grow
in answer so that I might know.

And round and round and round it goes;
where it stops nobody knows.
Governed by the laws and rules at large,
I find out who's really in charge.
They give me respect, consider what I say
but in the end do what they want anyway.
As the fate of youth extracts its toll,
I have no control.
No, I have no control.
I have no control.
I have no control.

43

Henry Hit Your Hammer

I say, Henry hit your hammer on the steel rail,
Henry hit the spike fore we land in jail.
I got no money to pay no bail,
Henry hit your hammer on the steel rail,
Henry hit your hammer on the nail.

Well now, who complains from the sack to the table
saying, "How come I get no mail"?
"If the suns' gonna shine like this all day,
well, I ain't getting no work done anyway."
And it's a shame a man works on a morning like this,

Henry hit your hammer on the steel rail,
Henry hit your hammer on the nail.

I say, Henry hit your brains on the new morn,
Henry tell us why we done got born.
To slave away a lifetime don't seem right;
a working all day and a sleeping all night.

Henry hit your hammer on the steel rail,
Henry hit the spike fore we land in jail.
I'm right behind you so we just can't fail,
Henry hit your hammer on the steel rail,
Henry hit your hammer on the nail.

My friend Henry, oh Lord, Henry,
my, my, my, my, my Lord, Henry,

I said, Henry hit your hammer on the steel rail;
Henry hit the spike fore we land in jail.
I got no money to pay no bail,
uh, Henry hit your hammer on the steel rail,
Henry hit your hammer on the nail.
I said, Henry hit your hammer on the steel rail,
Henry hit your hammer on the nail.

44

You Know What You Want

Shadows follow; a single silhouette on their own.
Regress, sadness, someone knocks but no one's at home.
You lied; you said you tried, so everyone would leave you alone.

You know what you want; you know what you need,
but love for you is just too hard.
You know what you want; you know what you need,
but you don't really know who you are.

Hope weighs; you say, "I'm alright; nothing is amiss."
But truth please; you're lonely, and you don't want to live like this.
As stars gleam; you dream every night of that passionate kiss.

You know what you want; you know what you need,
but love for you is still too far.
You know what you want; you know what you need,
but you don't really know who you are.

Baffled; Puzzled; confused that there might be something wrong.
Coping; yet hoping for that distinctive one to come along.

Burning; yearning to finally sing love's special song.

You know what you want; you know what you need,
but love for you is just too hard.
You know what you want; you know what you need,
but you don't really know who you are.

Maybe someday; you think you'll step out forward and away.
But right now; right now, it's enough to dream of that day.
And careful, yet hopeful; in secret you plan out your day.

You know what you want; you know what you need,
but love for you is still too far.
You know what you want; you know what you need,
but you don't really know who you are.

45

MEMOIRS & NOTES - 36 - 'A DAY TOO SHORT'

A Day Too Short

(1984) – There is a strength in commitment to purpose and duty and all that, but sometimes we do what we do because we just love doing it. It was 1984 and following a good shot of self-confidence in the arm and with creative juices finally flowing again and an appreciative audience of friends and family pushing me on, this song followed my third big attempt to do something commercially with my musical talents. Now armed  with a programmable typewriter (at Forest Funeral Home) to type up my written work, a $25.00 microphone and a fairly good cassette deck to record my music, I set out to introduce myself once again to the world.

I sent out about 85 request cards that had self-addressed-stamped post-cards to all these major and minor record company addresses that I gleaned off the back of album covers in a Warehouse Record Store. I sent them attention to whoever the producer of that album was and figured with 85 cards I'd get some good percentage of a response to work with.

Nobody responded; apparently, not even one contact was remotely interested in possibly evaluating or just listening to my demo cassette tape. And as I've mentioned in the past, I can only guess that the letters and postcards hit the trash can right after they arrived or went home with some copyboy to be used to help start a fire on some cold winter morning. For maybe five months I was optimistic that I'd get some re-sponse, but after that, I became rather despondent, then cynical to con-temptuous with the whole process. For a while, feeling sorry for myself, I stopped playing music and just concentrated on my family and doing the funeral home work that kept on coming in. I think I might have written two songs up to that point in the 1984 year, and for a while, it looked like that might just be it; my songwriting days were over.

But that, for a while ended when Darryl Wade came along to take over Rick's job of grave digging. Rick, as maybe mentioned prior, did not like me, rather he was resentful of me coming in off the street to take the job where he felt he should have been picked, never mind the fact that prior to my arrival, Gary Rook had no intention or desire to have Rick represent the funeral home in any other manor than as the gravedigger, but Rick was envious of the fact that I was able to rise to the occasion and do the work needed to be done and he felt he was being treated as a subordinate, (which, in Gary's case may have had some foundation), and so, Rick decided to leave.

After Darryl was hired to be the part-time caretaker and part-time gravedigger, he was touring the facilities with me and came across my beater guitar that was sitting by the Cherry Casket in the corner of the casket room, and he asked me who's it was. I think I might have come across taciturnly or emotionlessly reticent as I dismissed the fact that the guitar was mine and that it was there for me so I could accompany the occasional song that I might write in my spare time when things were dead at the funeral home. I moved on into another part of the facilities and the subject was, I thought, forgotten. The next day we got a call to go pick up a body at a rest home and Darryl went with me for the removal. By the end of the call he had become comfortable enough with me where he felt he could bring the subject up again; and he did.

"Okay," He quarried, "Can you play me one of your songs?"

I played, **Lonely Too Long**. He was mildly impressed and asked if I had another. I told him I had more and then played, **Ever On**, to which, with astonishment on his face, silently but excitedly motioned with his hands for another song. This time I played, **Something Must Be Wrong**, and seeing his enthusiasm and eagerness for more, followed with, **Crazy Cars**.

That day Darryl became one of my biggest fans and critics. And it was that optimistic, confident encouragement, and that whole-hearted, enthusiastic shot in the arm that woke me up and caused me to rise to the occasion of what this unknown stranger's expectations were. And suddenly, after taking stock of my past works, I started moving forward; and suddenly I had renewed value and purpose to go forth and write new songs. And although I haven't heard from Darryl in years, he remains devoted to my eclectic material and distinct style of music.

Side Note:

Unlike **Beyond Our Reach**, this song was intended to be a more positive philosophical perspective of someone with a perception of their mission and the open mindset of the songwriter, that, in spite of obstacles and apathy by the fickle audience, recognizes the peculiar perspectives to the offbeat problems, offset by the individual's inspiration, quirky sensitivities, challenged by the more than certain innumerable disappointments of either facing sure failures or the indifferences to his or her audience,... and yet, you do. Yet you must continue because you believe in what you're doing and ultimately, you're holding onto the slim hope that somebody will be listening,... and all those pie-in-the-sky hopes of the songwriter may end up being appreciated by only one person; you, but that's okay,... You get it. And then, how do you know if that someone out there might not only have found you, but is connecting to your words, to your ideas, to your inner feelings,... you just don't know,... and how can you know that that someone out there isn't getting that concealed understanding or special communication that was created by you, for and in behalf of that audience that was looking for the hidden messages? You can't know,... and how will you know if that other someone is making the connection that you were hoping to convey? Again, you won't,... How can you keep throwing your life's work wrapped up and around your heart; out there and up into the vast void of uncertain space to a seemingly ungrateful universe? As a true believer,... you know you must.

Side Note:

I think I brought this story up before, but here's to another rendition of it,... There was this friend of mine, well, kind of,... He had a really nice Martin guitar that he kept in a hard shell case and brought it out once in a while to polish it,... but one day I asked him why he didn't play his guitar and he told me that he got a capo, but after using it for a while came to the conclusion that he was cheating by using the capo because he couldn't make the proper fingering for bar chords,... so he threw up his hands in defeat and eventually stopped playing his guitar altogether. I let him know that there was a learning curve using a capo on different frets but it opened up possibilities that my limited guitar playing would not be able to come to be without it. He carefully put his guitar back into its hard shell case and looked at me with sad but defiant eyes, and maybe with a sense of reluctance because he'd decided to just give up and he was not open to any other discussion.

Another Side Note:

Sometimes I feel like I just need to stop feeling sorry for myself and just get on with my life as a poet and songwriter, you know what I mean? It's debilitating to just be waiting for my moment to arrive,... and I realized long ago that if I stopped producing the poetry and music to wait for that something to happen, the creativity I'm experiencing would go to seed or worse, disappear,... and so I push on, with hopes of a brighter future, but all the while, the ideas and stuff are still populating my mind and crying to get out.

So I Lie

(1998) – Unless we lie about it, we all do this. I strive to be an honest man but I must admit I do fall short. So, what is a lie and is there ever justification for that lie? When I exaggerate the truth, is that a lie? When I embellish a story, is that a lie? When I am trying to save some-one from getting hurt feelings, is that a lie? When I am in a threatened position for life and death situations, is that a lie?

Of course, whenever the truth is compromised, no matter what the reason or motivation or desired good or bad outcome, the resulting thing you end up with is a lie. And although I like to think of myself as an honest person, I know with that honest introspection that in the end I exaggerate the truth, I embellish stories, I am try to save someone from getting their feelings hurt; I am by association to living, a liar.

After pondering the reality of lies and then reflecting on our predis-position to deny we even use them, I spent a week working on the poem here, then it was not an effort to get the music to gel with the words, and then I found myself revising certain parts over and over until I got this special ambiance that I ended up with and that you now hear.

This is a "*second song*" and because of such, it is valued greatly to me. I just love the way the story unfolds about this guy that, like someone addicted to a drug, admits that there is a problem, but then says that he hopes, he wants, he's sure that this will be the last time. He recognizes the problem, even evaluates his own spin on it, but in the end, like an alcoholic going to an *Alcoholics Unanimous* meeting, him standing in front of a group saying, "Hi, my name is Bob, I'm an alcoholic," he says, "Hi, my name is Bob, well, that's not true, but this is the way things are, and so I lie."

And the music rolls on as he confesses his one untamable sin. But then again, my impression or thought that follows after his confession is, isn't he really the honest one in the circle there, because he can admit that he's a liar?

Like most of human behavior, lying exists on a spectrum, from sometimes harmless "white lies" to egregious and highly consequential fabrications told to gain or maintain money or power. Research suggests that while most people may rarely lie in ways that are intentionally hurtful, pretty much everyone is untruthful, at least in small ways, and for many, quite often. Experts do agree that lying is part of our human nature and that it is sanctioned and even encouraged by many parts of different societies.

Side Note:

When I first played this song to Diane, she responded disapprovingly and commented that the song seemed to accentuate, justify and maybe even glorify the negative traits of deception through lying. I agreed, but then told her that she might be missing the point of the song. I told her that everybody has a tendency to lie. Lies occur between those we love and trust as much as they do with those we dislike, and lies can even happen among complete strangers. We don't like to sound stupid. If we don't know the answer to a question, we fill in the blanks and sometimes make the answer up. And it is just to what extent that each individual justifies his or her stand that determines the severity of the crime. She didn't agree and never came back to review this song and I respect her perspective. She is the most honest person I have ever been associated with.

Still, the creation of this song accomplished a small part of what I had hoped for, and when I put on this album, I continue to look forward to hearing this one song more than any other.

Another Side Note:

As I may have mentioned earlier, I was forced to move over to the new *Information Technology Building*, (building 34), in 1997. I was to work in the *Computer Resource Center* and in *the computer labs*, assisting the students with their computer program homework and other usages like word processing. It was not too far from what I had been doing the past five years, so I adjusted.

Right after I arrived, I met a woman who was having trouble with not being able to view certain computer monitors, saying that they were making her feel ill. I told her that I would find out what we could do and after some research, learned about photosensitivity, which is a condition detected on the electroencephalography (EEG) as a paroxysmal reaction to Intermittent Photic Stimulation (IPS). This EEG response, elicited by IPS, or by other visual stimuli of daily life, is called Photo Paroxysmal Response (PPR). PPRs are well documented in epileptic and non-epileptic subjects. I digress.

After finding the right monitors with acceptable refresh rates and she could get her school work done, I became good friends with her. She told me that she had been a missionary and after talking about music she also told me that she had an operettic voice and that she specialized in singing Italian folk songs. Long story-short, she became interested in Lord Baldwin material and even reviewed many of my albums. *A Day Too Short* was one of the cassettes, (albums) that she received and reviewed. Maybe two or three weeks after I gave her this album, I was walking up the hallway of building 34, and seeing me, she smiled, and with a pleasing melodic voice, she sang, "So I Lie." She then went on to tell me that she enjoyed the album and most especially, this song declaring that it was one of her favorites. Ironically, (but not revealed to her), the last song on this album may have been written about her.

Here I Wait

(1969) – In December of 1968, I moved in with my dad on his farm in Aurora Oregon. I was a senior at North Marion High School, which was a rural school out in the farmland of Donald Oregon. There was this girl named Wendy that was in a couple of my classes and also a member of the LDS Church, which I eventually joined later on. She had long blonde hair, a quiet confidence in her smile and this country wholesome look that shined out of her clean continence, and made me believe that if she loved me,

I would walk to the ends of the earth for her. She flirted with me on a regular basis, wanting to know about New York and the east-coast and the hippie movement, but I could tell from her smile and her general body language that all she really liked me for was the oddity of that guy who came from the East Coast.

After I started going to the LDS church, I got to know her family a little better and found that, from the beginning, her father did not like me at all. He was a farmer that owned and operated a construction company and built houses in the area. At first, he would say things with back-sided complements, confusing me for the most part, but then, after a while, his set-in-his-ways farmer attitude came out and he just told me how he really felt about my peculiar New York customs and how he felt about me.

He told me straight out that he didn't like me. He probably sensed my intentions and then let me know he would have nothing of it. But her dad was just a small obstacle as far as I was concerned. I moved ahead.

One cold morning about a week later I got up at 5:30 and, with a 3-gallon pail of warm water, I navigated my way through three-foot drifts of snow to get to the barn to milk the cows. Richard said he wasn't feeling good and refused to get up so I did his chores first before doing my own. As I was milking the first of two cows, my thoughts drifted away to that Mormon girl and then I just started to sing. That pure, uninhibited expression of lamented love was almost perfect and the music in my mind reinforced the raw words or lyrics. The words hinted of a quiet loneliness; of a forlorn hope for a love, distant and doubtful. After I finished straining the milk on the back porch, I trudged through the snow to the street above and got on the school bus. On the way to the school, I wrote down the words to this poem. Because I had no instrument to play this on, that night, I pulled out my dad's accordion and played around with chords and progressions before I composed the music to this song. I envisioned my triumphant arrival to Wendy's house with this wonderful song in hand and Wendy, in amazement and admiration would be swept off her feet. Even her father would be impressed.

A few weeks later I went over to Wendy's house only to find out that she had a boyfriend. I still wonder why she was so nice to me. Did she have thoughts of letting him go for me? Should I try to hang around and see what happens? I flashed back on another one of Brian Wilson's songs ironically called, "Wendy" where he sings, "Wendy, Wendy left me alone." Then my song suddenly took on a melancholy aura as with the song itself, there I was thinking, "Here I Wait."

Side Note:

After a while I shifted my attentions to another girl, Sarah Meyers, who had a lot of the artistic stuff going on that interested me. We hit it off really well and I thought things were perfect, until the day I found out that Sarah was also seeing my brother Richard.

I'm still not sure what hurt me more, Sarah pretending to like me while two-timing me, or my brother Richard sneaking around behind my back and stealing my girlfriend. Not long after, Richie and Sarah got married.

[Here is a poignant picture taken at their wedding; Richie and Sarah are talking about their honeymoon arrangements and plans for what they'll be doing shortly thereafter. And me; I can be seen behind them, sadly drifting off and away] After Richard and Sarah got married, they left for New York. I went to Reno to rekindle a love lost there and when things turned sour, I went back to Oregon and got into Portland State University, taking night school classes and trying to stay out of the draft and out of the country's involvement in the Vietnam war. Later in the fall of 69 I was driving around with Mike, one of Ray's friends and we ended up going out in the middle of nowhere, over to one of Mike's friend's houses to do a couple of numbers. I was silently looking over at this long-haired, bearded guy that lived there, trying to figure out who he was and why he knew my name and seemed to know me so well.

There were cockroaches crawling around the floor and on the walls in the dimly lit living room and one was heading straight for me till I kicked it away, into the darkness. With no idea where I was or who this long-haired, bearded guy was, I pleasantly nodded to the conversations and tried to keep the roaches at bay. Then, out of the kitchen with a plate of freshly baked cookies came Wendy. She had cut her hair and was now wearing this long cotton see-through-like dress that, even in the dim room, was revealing. She had lost that innocent church-girl appearance, and traded it for a newly reborn hippie air. Although I was all for the hippy movement and profess to maintain some of the ideals of hippiedom even today, at that moment, I sadly thought about some lyrics from one of Brian Wilson's songs; '**Caroline, No,**' from of the, '*Pet Sounds*' album;

> *Where did your long hair go,*
> *where is the girl I used to know*
> *How could you lose that happy glow*
> *Oh, Caroline, No.*
> *Who took that look away;*
> *I remember how you used to say,*
> *you'd never change, but that's not true,*
> *Oh, Caroline, you break my heart;*
> *I want to go and cry*
> *It's so sad to watch a sweet thing die*
> *Oh, Caroline why*
> *Could I ever find in you again*
> *Things that made me love you so much then*
> *Could we ever bring 'em back once they have gone*
> *Oh, Caroline, No.*

It was all there. And although I liked this new look; like Brian

Wilson, I really missed that other girl I used to know. I wondered why she had compromised and forsaken the church; but then, was I in any better position to judge her? I mean, I wasn't obeying the word of wisdom either. When I finally looked into her eyes and she looked back into mine, I was able to see that extraordinary spark; that glow; that spirit and energy, and perhaps there was a hint of a connection,... a small flame of love left over from another time that quietly hinted; "we could have had something."

But then again; that bright but swift glimpse was revealed only momentarily, and then, perhaps for and in behalf of her boyfriend, the vision was instantly and abruptly concealed. She commented on my psychedelic paisley shirt and we both just let the moment pass. I never saw her again, but I do wish her well.

Yet Another Side Note:

This is kind of crazy; a couple of months after that encounter with Wendy, I was out of work and went to work doing construction and roofing for Wendy's father. He was not really very impressed with my quality of work and complained about everything from the time I got there till I left for home, but ours was a symbiotic relationship; I needed money and he kept me on because he couldn't find anyone else to do the hard labor as cheap as me.

And as I carried the asphalt roofing shingle bundles on my shoulder up a ladder to the rooftop of a two-story house, I tolerated his incessant criticism for a long time before I snapped. One day he was saying something derogatory about me after lunch and I flipped him off and started to leave. He actually apologized and said he was just seeing what I was made of.

I said something stupid in return like, "go to hell." and hitch-hiked back to Aurora. Not long after, I had gone to work, shoveling manure at a chicken farm, and Wendy's father came over to my dad's farm, to ask me to go back to work. He even said that he would pay me more money. I told him that I like my new job, (which I didn't), and he drove away. I never saw or heard from him again either.

Further Apart

(1998) – Again, accepting responsibility for poor communications is as important as forgiving the other for the same. It was a week before we were to celebrate our 25th wedding anniversary over at Diane's sister Sue's house. We had a disagreement dealing with how things were going to come about, with Ben graduating and kids coming home, there was a lot of outgoing expenses, money we didn't have, and at some junction, as it was hot and Allison and Brian were outside playing in the water with Spencer supervising, we were disagreeing about activities that should or should not be happening in keeping the sabbath day holy on that particular Sunday, when things went sour,... frankly I'm not sure what the catalyst was to bring about this disagreement, but that particular argument was a familiar one, and there we were, about to celebrate the 25 years that we'd been married and we were not speaking to each other. At one point I remember I was mumbling this phrase to myself walking to my room, "If you don't care, and if I don't care, we won't get anywhere!" while trying to avoid hostility with Diane.

The Family at the 25th Wedding Anniversary

In my need to disown the justification for my position, or to shirk the responsibility of that quarrel, I realized the truth in the phrase. At that point I was confined in our bedroom, so at the same time, I documented my feelings and tried to see her side and understand things from her supposed feelings, and thus, this song was born.

No Words Tonight

(1992) – Love needs no words to say what's in its heart. I love the fall season; football, weather changes and most of all, we fall back in time and it gets dark earlier, which under ideal circumstances, gives me more time in the evening to do my songwriting. When I am in a mood to do music, I love to have everyone asleep, and the TV turned off, and the quiet stillness inspires me to a greater awareness of my music and creativity. It was one of those fall nights when conditions were just right that this song came to be.

Side Note:

Actually, the title to this song came from an instrumental that I composed back in 1992, and I liked the phrase and just sat at the piano and threw it and a few chords together to make the song. It takes on a different meaning to Diane, but that is just fine, I like double meanings in compositions.

I Have No Control

(1997) – We all like to think we have a handle on things, but we know deep inside that there are some things that end up running on a hope that nothing goes wrong. Oh boy,... this song was written at a time when I was dealing with some rather drastic changes in my own life. Why is it that just when things are going well and you think you got it all figured out, your life starts falling apart?

As maybe mentioned before, one of the directors of physical education coveted my little office space and through a private clandestine campaign of deception, convinced the powers that be that my lab facility could be a consolidation project of the gym facilities and the exercising equipment room, which would open up more space for others elsewhere. So the computer lab at South Puget Sound Community College that I had manned and managed for five years was being shut down by the Vice President of Instruction and I was forced to close shop and move over to another section of the college into the new Information Technology Building, (building 34); creating a rather hostile environment for me, to have to work with two other computer guys, two of which had little to no intent to be ingratiating or gain approval or favor with me, and they were reticent to have another tech share their already crowded space and assigned responsibilities.

I was assigned to work in the Computer Resource Center and the computer labs, assisting the students with their computer program homework and other usages like word processing. It was not too far from what I had been doing the past five years, so I adjusted. I worked directly with a man named Pete who was also brought over from the other side of campus and was assisting the running of the three computer labs with Pete, whose other duties included running the affairs of the student workers in the labs, keeping their work schedules and maintaining and calculating the monthly timesheets for the lab techs left me to work there in the labs for the most part, by myself.

At first, Pete and I were supervised by Dorna, the assistant to the vice president along with a guy that always wore new jeans, (we'll just call him Jeans), and his compadre who was always snooping around to find fault in what Pete and I were doing, (we'll call Ferret), both of which came over from the other side of campus.

I knew Jeans from when we were taking classes together in 1990. Jeans was an overconfident, self-important tech that had come over from building One where he was supervising the computers used for the students taking computer programming related classes. Ferret was a tech working somewhere over there too, but I don't know where he came from and I had never seen him before.

Soon after I arrived, Ferret was given the job to be our immediate supervisor by V.P. 'Mike, who would be, 'Lee Marvin." Jeans, who had been used to being in charge, was resentful that Ferret was chosen over him, but Jeans was not open about it. Jeans, who had a huge ego, did not like taking a second seat to someone he felt he was a superior to, and Jeans felt he was superior to everyone on campus that had anything to do with computers, including most of the instructors. (More on that maybe later).

When I first came to the college, I was hired to be a *Lab Assistant II* (Two) and was not even classified as a computer tech. Pete was classified as a *Computer Tech I* (One), where Ferret and Jeans were both classified as *Computer Tech II* (twos).

It quickly became an inside joke to Jeans and Ferret that Pete and I, (but more specifically me), were underling subordinates. It was annoying that I was always the butt of inside joke between Jeans and Ferret, who would imply and draw attention to my lack of knowledge and seeming stupidity, while they would spend most of their day sitting in an office drinking coffee and shooting the bull, or wandering around the campus, schmoozing any and every birthday or retirement gathering or party they caught wind of,... meanwhile, telling Pete and I that we needed to hold down the fort at building 34. Feeling very uncomfortable, I found myself once again looking around for work in other places.

After a frustrating and unhappy set of experiences, I realized that I was not prepared for such a move and so, I reevaluated my circumstances and concluded that I was like a locomotive engine to this long train of railroad boxcars, (kids—wife), depending on me and my support. And I came to know that I would have to do what I could to make the best of things with the way things were. I fine-tuned my way of thinking and decided that I should try to re-train myself to do something else. This would not fully happen for another two years, but it was at this time that the seed was sown.

Side Note:

I have many children. And they are all so distinctly different that there is little to no way that I can predict anyone's behavior and functioning operations, even from drawing from their past or present actions.

And they all have a mind of their own; always moving alternately in different directions from and back to one another, and it's all the time. It is a full-time job just to keep up with all the happenings in just one of the kid's lives, but with children ranging from six to twenty-eight, I would be foolish to believe I have any chance to really be in command of the whole situation.

Control to me implies that I have this power to offer some type of influence on and oversee and govern the happenings of my kids while managing my own life. Perhaps to help them to organize their own thoughts and actions to help them to move forward in a positive direction, (maybe more on that subject, some other time).

But there is a difference between suggested ideas and manipulation where choice is taken away and am to I rule or to run their lives, while I have some strong hold over them; you know, power? But taking away free agency has never been my way of doing things, especially to the free-thinking philosophy that I roll with, and that is the essence of the problem. I encourage free thought and then I expect to be able to turn that free thought on and off when the occasion dictates? I don't think it works that way.

On or around this time, (as maybe mentioned before), Meridith was having problems, and after losing a considerable amount of weight and becoming anorexic, ended up in counseling with Diane and I in tow; to me, Diane and I were in a kind of freefall where there was little to no influence we could propose on what was happening. Here was another instance where we had very little control of the circumstances, and for almost two years, as the three of us went bi-monthly to Meridith's therapy meetings, I realized just how much control I did not have.

This same time, Ben, who was a sophomore in high school, went through a period in his life where he felt dejected by his peers and became despondent to authority and school in general. He came home with an "F" on one of his report cards (math) and we felt we had to make some major changes in his lifestyle. Ben argued that the real reason that he had gotten the bad grade was because the math teacher was also the Tumwater High School wrestling coach and Ben had turned the teacher down when Ben was asked to join the wrestling team.

Although I talked with Ben on a daily basis and did manage to get him to stop hanging with the "Goths," it wasn't until he changed schools, moving from Tumwater High School to the newly built Black Hill High School, and then his art teacher helped Ben discover his potential, and then Ben began to do a thing called, "Running Start," which is the taking of college courses during high school time, from all of that, Ben started valuing himself and his circumstances. Again, I'd like to think that, over the course of events from my interacting and concern, that I influenced him to some degree, but at the time, I felt like I didn't have any control over him or the circumstances.

When it comes to being a parent, I think about good management; being in command of my home Boy Scout Troop, not as a dictator, but more as their Scoutmaster and friend, that suggests direction, demonstrates how to do things, guides them as they go about doing that whatever, help them to keep the big problems in check, and allow the Troops the opportunity to grow through their trials, adversities and eventually, successes.

Still, after I got myself involved, and expended all of my energy going in so many different directions trying to make it all work, trying to keep everyone happy and maybe staying on top of things; as they go their own way to do their own thing, in spite of the valuable council that I might offer, I must realize that parenthood is still rather an illusion, and that ultimately, I have no control.

Henry Hit Your Hammer

(1971) – One very hot summer afternoon I was digging some post holes with a pulaski and shovel in the front yard of my dad's farm. While I was hard at it, Henry, my dad's black and white cocker spaniel, walked off the front porch, came over to where I was working and sat on the grass next to me, keeping me company and watching everything I was doing. As I swung and hit the hard, rock infested deadpan ground with the pick end of the pulaski, I kind of felt like I was working on the railroad line, pounding down the steel nails on the iron rails. I turned to the dog, and in syncopation with my overhead swing of the pick, sang this song to the dog. Henry perked up, seemingly interested as I called out his name and maybe a little interested in what I was singing about, so I continued.

It was really hot and at one time I stopped singing and just pounded away hard at the ground. Then I turned to Henry and said, "When I get through here, we'll go down to the river and cool off. What do you think?" Henry looked up at me with that same face you see in the picture as if to say, "You bet!"

Then, pounding the hard ground again, I started singing the song. The direction of the song took a funny turn as I realized that Henry didn't have to work, he just sat there watching me. I reflected this attitude in my words and after about the third time through, I was getting to know the lyrics to the song really well. But Henry, who seemed rather reserved, exhausted from the heat and bored with the song, wandered off and disappeared. I kept working and about a half hour later Henry reappeared, friendly, revitalized and dripping wet from his swim without me in the Pudding River.

Side Note:

My dad had an infatuation with boxer dogs, and early on, in the late 50s and early 60s he had a boxer named, Rocky.

My sister Wendy believed that Rocky was her dog. After Rocky died, my dad wanted to get another boxer but purebred boxers, even then, cost a lot of money.

And so, my dad waited until all the kids left home before he finally brought one home. Inez might have seemed disinterested in this boxer pup as it arrived, but she was secretly excited to have this new boxer dog; Rocky II, come into their home and like my dad, she grew to love the dog. I was told that Rocky II held a very strong bond to Inez; sleeping at her feet when they'd watch TV at night, following her around waiting to see what she'd do next, and Rocky II seemed to mind Inez more than my dad when he was being disciplined.

Rocky could be a lot like a mischievous little kid; always doing things that he shouldn't while they were off to church or away visiting. But both Inez and my dad were in seventh heaven with this new addition to the family.

When Rocky passed away many years later, my dad got two more boxers and then another and then two others. At the time of his passing, my dad had four boxers, two of which were rather unmanageable, but they were my dad's best friends, loyal watchdogs and everloving constant companions.

Another Side Note:

After my dad's passing in 2007, because I was the computer guy in the family, the responsibility of scanning all the family photos fell to me. I bought two scanner/printers at Fry's Electronics in Wilsonville to do the job, and, because I had a job and I was a family man, it took me over three months to accomplish the task. When I took on this task, I had no idea how many pictures there were to scan and found that there were bags and boxes of over twenty-five hundred pictures of his boxers in various sizes, types and in varied conditions that made it hard to go through quickly.

The reason I'm relating this side note to you is that perhaps five hundred of those pictures were of his varied boxer dogs; some with my dad in the picture, most without, and without documentation on the back of the photos, my dad would be the only one to distinguish which was which. And when I finished and presented the digital copies to every one in the family, no one but my brother Jack thanked me, and when he did, he said, "Oh, you didn't need to do the dogs. No one knows which one is which anyway."

You Know What You Want

(1998) – Sometimes it's hard to know what you want in life when you still don't know the specialness of who and what you yourself are. This is a commentary of a very nice person that I am friends with. This person has a charming disposition, a friendly, demure way that makes people at ease when they are around this person; but this person is alone. This person doesn't choose to be alone, but that is the end that this person is resigned to. This person believes they know what it is they want in life and can freely express such to others, but there is a problem and it is within. The justification or settlement to this end is what prompted me to write this song. For although this person professes to want and need love, this person has been hurt in the past and doesn't want to experience that pain again. Perhaps the worse part of this scenario is that although this person knows what they want and need, this person doesn't realize who they really are and what they mean to others and to the rest of the world. This person doesn't realize there is a wall that they have constructed to keep others, even close friends, away or at a very safe distance. If this person understood that true love exists out there; that the companionship that they want and need so badly is theirs for the taking, and that when they open up their heart, that special love can come streaming in; and from all directions. If this person could stop being afraid to get hurt again than there's a chance that they don't have to be alone; that facing the world with someone else could not only bring a sense of safety, but a protection against time that is edging ever so closely in their peripheral vision. Is there a chance that they might get hurt yet again? Of course, there is. There are no guarantees when it comes to love. But the adage, "nothing ventured, nothing gained" is such a sad alternative, isn't it? The gift of someone else's love, to have someone to care for and who would care for them; someone to bring their own brand of happiness to life, wouldn't that tradeoff be worth the chance of another heartache? The upside to this could be that that person, might find that that love that they so deeply want and need, might just turn out to be all they ever dreamed of.

I hope that they can give love another chance.

46

- 37 - CONNECTED - 1998 -

47

NOTES ABOUT THE COVERS

Notes On The New Cover:

Arguably the dominoes cover could have remained, but I was up for a change in scenery. and I thought about new technology, and computers, and so many things are connected to each other on a motherboard for it to work properly; it just felt right. Plus,... I love the colour green.

Notes On The Original Covers:

The dominoes cover was kind of cool and I did like the font to the original lettering,

The back cover was a connection to nature and to the universe; a scene, that with the Boy Scouts, I had had a lot of experiences while camping with my boys. (But also, with my whole family, because Diane and some of my girls actually liked going camping too).

48

CONNECTED

Connected
She Loves Me Anyway
From The Lost Letters Sent
Dreams Where I Have Been
When Love Comes Calling To Me
She's Floating In The Air
The Boy Scout Code

49

Connected

As a man staring into the face of God,
the child gazes back at me,
waiting for the assurance or approval
of what I wish or please.
And as this child is, I once was,
in search of what to be.
Yet I grew to be a part of all selected
and joined the family
to forever be connected.

Silent, like their shadows they walk
out the dire streets alone.
Many unwanted, un-comprehended,
lost or unknown.
Yet most in search of a happiness
or a place they might call home,
where lonely hopes and fears are redirected
in a warmth of acceptance
to find they might be connected.

From those that came before
to the newborn's chance to be
there's a sense of awe to feel the power
of their posterity
that flows from the dawn of time
to somewhere into eternity;
resting within the knowledge and love collected
and continuing on,
called together to be connected.

Trying to comprehend
the solemn wonders of the night,
while aligning myself with the planets
nd the stars in the sky.
As burning beams bolt across
a void of speckled light,
I'm moved by the architecture reflected
and I feel somehow, in a way,
I too must be connected.

Yeah, I'm connected.

50

She Loves Me Anyway

I know that I've heard it said
there's nothing better than a friend,
who'll stand beside you to the end
with a love that never wanes.

Somehow in my desperate call
she joined me for the long, hard haul.
She sees my faults and in spite of them all,
she loves me anyway.

Ravaged by times of high and low,
from the daily battles and things let go,
I stand before her, off the mark I know,
from what I'd hope to portray.

The outward image of what I was;
she sees through with her special love.
She knows the changes of what time does,
and She loves me anyway.

I come to her in my fallen state,
completely guilty, and somewhat late
anticipating a deserved fate
for my lost; wayward day.

It doesn't matter that I'm falling apart;
she has this ever-growing heart
and a perfect love to always impart
for she loves me anyway.

And over time you'd think I'd learn
the right or wrong when it's my turn,
but with my stubborn streak and lack of concern
there's always a price to pay.

And yet for all that I'll never be,
and all of my insensitivity
she seems to know the heart of me:
she loves me anyway.

I know that I have heard it said
there's nothing better than a friend
who'll stand beside you to the very end.
Oh, she loves me anyway.
Anyway; anyway.

51

From The Lost Letters Sent

And it would seem that life has a peculiar flow.
In a mystery we come, as into a mystery we go.
There is so much in life I do not understand,
I can but hope in time I would improve my hand.

Yet too many times I'd grope only to realize
all the verity was right before my eyes.
And from my garden would grow all of the fruits I sow
all the thoughts, the deeds and the good I know.

There is a difference, that seems to hide,
from all we perceive and what is inside.
He would walk his path with souls lost to the night,
to help them to get in touch with their inner light.

And so like him I try to be a better man
and not get lost on the path or lose sight of that plan.
Though judgmental and guilty of insensitive deeds,
I hope to see beyond my own needs.

In my heart of hearts, I know what to do.
Leave my past behind, to carry it through.
From the lost letters sent for an arguable atone
to coincide with misdeeds I own

thoughts scale the skies for meaning and design
or for reassurance that there's something besides
that ambiguous; simple, peculiar flow,
of the mystery we are, and the mystery we go.

The mystery we go.

5²

Dreams Where I Have Been

Yet the tragedy or madness that I face
is that when the morning finally breaks,
everything's returned—returned back in its place.
I return again to the dreams where I have been.
And you stand waiting there for our walk through your domain.
Digressive; terse, I speak to converse all in vain.

I want to hear you as I draw up near you
but your voice seems illusive like the breeze.
The cry of my heart burns but there's nothing in return,
Oh, I'd give anything to hear you call to me.

Then as we walk, I do know it's just a dream,
yet deep in my heart I want this moment to be real.
I want to touch and hold you so much
but I know that this can never be.
You're so close at play but yet, so far away,
I'd give anything to have you come with me.
Come with me. Come with me.
Dreams where I have been...

53

When Love Comes Calling To Me

This must be serious to move me this way;
I question my reasons and ties.
I want to be sure my directions are just
as I search beyond illusions and lies.
Looking for that someone real and alive,
with sincere compassion and grace.
Where am I going to find someone like that,
who might understand my needs and place?

Well I know that I'll know when it happens,
where and how and who it will be.
I know that I'll know when it happens,
when love comes calling to me.

There's something happening, unusual
something I can't think with any clear design.
Wonder and anxiety follow me around
and those girls are always on my mind.

Looking for that someone compassionate and sincere,
for all that it might possibly be.
I know that my time of romance will come
and that she's out there looking for me.

And I know that I'll know when it happens,
where and how and who it will be.
I know that I'll know when it happens,
when love comes calling to me.

I've thought about it a lot, who hasn't?
People spend their lives engrossed in love.
But it all comes down to a personal belief
of who might be that true, special one.

Well I know that I'll know when it happens,
where and how and who it will be.
Yes, I know that I'll know when it happens,
when love comes calling to me....

When love comes calling to me.

54

She's Floating in the Air

Here I am on the ground, trying to keep safe and sound
from all the dangers all around.
Keeping close to the soil to avoid turmoil.
Here I am on this earth trying hard to keep at work
marching on for all it's worth
just to keep things afloat, but there's a hole in my boat.

She's floating in the air; I can't seem to reach her there.
She wants to bring me along; up and away from all the wrong,
still, I can hardly leave the ground
with all this weight holding me down.

Here I am in this place, holding on, keeping pace
with the other rats in the race
thinking, "Someday I'll be there." but I'm not going anywhere.
Here I am on the wall, wondering how she never falls.
She says there's nothing to it all.
But when the smoke and mirrors clear,
she's up there and I'm down here.

Oh, she's floating in the air and I believe I could be up there
if I could only let things go; step away from all I know.
But I can hardly leave the ground
with all this weight holding me down.

She's floating in the air; I can't seem to reach her there.
She wants to bring me along; up and away from all the wrong,
still I can hardly leave the ground
with all this weight holding me down.
All this weights' holding me down.

55

The Boy Scout Code

When I was young, I believed
in the *Scout Oath* and *Law* and, *the American Creed*.
To be *Trustworthy, Loyal, Helpful* and a *Friend*
to the helpless and weak—to the very end.
Many years have passed since my last roll call,
yet still even now I'm reminded of it all;

To, 'Do My Best' to, '*Do what's right*'
'*Help Other People*' with all my might.
'Strive for good' with all my heart and soul.
Believe and Live
the *Boy Scout Code.*

I tried real hard to be *Courteous* and *Kind*,
Obedient to my elders and *Cheerful* in mind.
Thrifty with my earnings, *Brave* at heart,
Clean thoughts and *Reverence* from all I'd impart.
I fell off the path from those standards I learned
but I never denied them and in time I returned,

To, *'Do My Best'* to, *'Do what's right'*
to, *'Help Other People'* with all my might.
'Strive for good' with all my heart and soul.
'Stand On My Honor'
for the *Boy Scout Code.*

And so it was beyond my own want or need,
I could not waver from what I truly believed.
From a boy to a man to a father at large,
to the teacher of children in my own special charge.

When I was young, I believed
in the Scout Oath and Law and the American Creed.
And through years passed I still search to find
compassion in my heart and a just purpose in mind.
From all my shortcomings to all I'll never be,
this way feels right as it comes back to me

To, *'Do My Best'* to, *'Do what's right'*
to, *'Help Other People'* with all my might.
'Strive for good' with all my heart and soul.
'Live the Golden Rule'
'Stand On My Honor'
Believe and Live
the *Boy Scout Code.*

The Boy Scout Code.

56

MEMOIRS & NOTES - 37 - 'CONNECTED'

Connected

(1998) – As the windows fall away and we find ourselves alone, if we might look to find that connection we have with our environment, our nature, and how about our relatives; past, present and future? If we open our eyes and our heart, we might find that we are all part of something bigger; more profound, and that we can never be alone when we are connected.

This wasn't a spiritual thing... well maybe it was and I'm just minimizing things, but this poem was written from so many different standpoints of comprehension that I became overwhelmed with the possibilities.

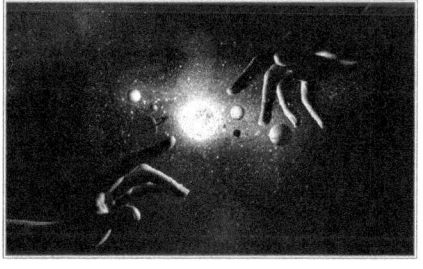

Allison came to me with a problem and asked for me to solve it. It was a simple question, simple for an adult to answer, and I treated the answer as something trivial until I looked back at her and her sincere concern and belief in every word that came from my mouth, and I remembered asking my mother about the clouds in the skies and waiting for the answer with the same confidence and assurance that what I was about to hear, the words of wisdom from my mother could be nothing but the truth. From this new comprehension, I realized that the power and responsibility I had could not be treated lightly and it was my responsibility to pass that important information on, in the best and most all-inclusive way that I could.

I was just standing outside one evening, staring at the stars and feeling like my whole world was just one of the dots in the puzzle waiting to be connected. I thought about the idea that the light I was seeing from most of the stars began from that place around the time of Christ. At first, I wondered if the light they saw back then was different than the light I see now, after all, two thousand years had passed since then, but then I realized that it doesn't really matter, what makes a difference is that the positions of those stars have remained relatively the same. It was as though I could be looking up at the stars from any given point in mankind's time and, except for a few changes, I would be seeing the same thing that they were seeing. And I felt a sense of togetherness or, that we are all, in some way or another, connected, and not just in time and space, but in another sense, at that moment in time, connected to each other.

I was led to a group of photographs of our family taken many years ago and I saw faces and resemblances from parents, grandparents, children; and I found that, in this way of course, I was connected; not only to my own family and the generations of genealogy that went with that, but I was now connected to my wife's family, and all of her genealogy, and I realized in a large sense, that my circle of connectivity grows larger with each generation. And that connection; that ever-growing connection, would have to include the people out of my immediate circle; the destitute, the liars and thieves; the lost, the ones seemingly unconnected.

Just like the bards of old, that passed on from generation to generation, that sense of purposeful belonging through oral stories, myths and folklores, I could feel the magnitude of how important it must be for us to maintain that sense of connectivity, especially in this day and age of impersonal information explosions via television, computers and the Internet.

Allison, an inquisitive ten-year-old girl, asked me what kept the world, our earth, from falling down from the sky? Is it because we're spinning so fast that we're like flying in space or is there some invisible power that keeps us where we are, circling in place? Kind of a heavy question for a ten-year-old. And as I pondered the answer, I remembered my own question to my mother about the clouds in the sky; and I asked, did the clouds stand still and just look like they were moving because the earth was in its rotations, or were we standing still and the clouds were moving on their own because of the wind? My mother thought about the question for a moment before she finally answered. And I believe my answer to be the same as my mother's; "I think you could say, maybe both."

Side Note:

As with the title of the song, I wanted this to be a concept album where all the songs would have some connection to each other and the theme; "Connected," so in between each song, and there are seven songs, there is a brief interlude of music called, "Connections," each leading into the next song. There are six "connections," each composition with its own special inflection, timbre, intonation and feel. I'm sure that I was not able to make everything connect quite the way I envisioned, but when the album was finished and I had engineered all the songs into their perspective places, I felt a sense of fulfillment, and listening to the album, my heart was full. I felt good about their allotted positions and I felt good about what they had to say individually as well as collectively for and in behalf of the perception of the concept of being connected.

Connections (02)

(1998) – So initially I thought of creating this little melody to make a connection to weave through all the other songs and after a lot of experimentations, I came up with something I was happy with. Then the thought came to me that maybe I should use the tune with an altered treatment or motif to kind of change it around adding different tempos and using different instruments (voices), to give variety to the concept album. As noted above, this is Connections (02) meaning it was the second treatment to the tune. I used a #13 organ and a side of bells to get the sound you hear.

Side Note:

I began with Connections (02) because I liked how it felt between "Connections" and "She Loves Me Anyway." And moreover, I felt like Connections (01) was a better fit to follow "She Loves Me Anyway." See what you think.

She Loves Me Anyway

(1998) – One evening while I was getting ready to go to bed, I rushed into the bathroom, grabbed my toothbrush and started brushing my teeth while I casually walked into the bedroom. Diane was sitting on the bed reading her scriptures while I mumbled two or three inaudible sentences with my mouth full of toothbrush and toothpaste, and she stopped reading and looked up at me, and with an endearing smile she kissed me and said, "I didn't understand a word you said."

I laughed and walked back into the bathroom, spit, rinsed out my mouth, and then took a good look at myself in the mirror. Staring back at me was a man in need of a shave with uncombed hair; with a face that time had not been kind to; moles prominently protruding from all over my face, and I couldn't help but wonder; how she could possibly tolerate dealing with all of these imperfections, let alone love this peculiar, imperfect individual. And then a warm feeling came over my heart and confirmed that the answer was that, "She Loves Me Anyway."

In the weeks that it has taken for me to write the words to this poem, there were other occasions that reaffirmed that asymmetrical confirmation of her unconditional love for me, in spite of my imperfections, my shortcomings and failures, and my inadequacies. I hope that she might know that the sentiments, compassion, heart-felt feelings and the devoted love are all mutual, and I think... no, I know for sure, that she understands that I will always love her more.

Side Note:

My brother John was my earliest and biggest fan for my music. He is the only one that had a complete collection of all my cassettes. And he listened to them,... all the time.

John loved this particular song so much that, after hearing me do it live during my visit to Miami in 2016, John wanted me to send him the lyrics so he could dedicate the poem to his girlfriend, Debbie.

This inspired me to rerecord the song when I returned to Olympia, and a year and a half later, in 2018, included the song on the "*Nevertheless,...*" album.

Another Side Note:

(Dateline: November 26th 2020) Today is Thanksgiving. This morning I got the news that my brother John had passed away. I sulked around the house all day, and after we finished our Thanksgiving Zoom meeting with the kids and family, I went back to work this evening,... Ironic as it turns out, I am reediting and working on this very album, "*Connected*" and I have come upon this poem, "*She Loves Me Anyway*" and I think to myself, this was one of John's favorite songs of mine,... that really means something special to me.

I don't know who the others are but John is the big guy on the right

The hospital did not deny or confirm whether John had died from COVID, and he had been going through some issues of him incessantly coughing and his lungs had been deteriorating for a while. John wasn't a smoker but he was in Viet Nam in places that had chemicals roaming through the air. He was a teletype operator for the Air Force and was stationed on many different Air Force bases, some of them on the front line.

John was a gentleman's gambler and like his favorite brother David, played the cards on off season and frequented the rooms where they could gamble,... and win,... sometimes bigtime.

All of the varied card rooms were always filled with the cigarette smoke of the desperate and the lucky. That insidious Second-hand smoke can do a lot of harm too.

I have been sharing music with John since we lived in Iron Mountain Michigan. It was John that turned me on to music and Rock and Roll. After David was chased out of the house in 1958 by Senior,... and I fell in place or was the next in line to be John's apprentice. We had a musical connection that was really exceptional and extraordinary.

He took me to my first, (and only) Zydeco concert when I was visiting in 2016. There was a moment there, at the concert where John just sort of lost his balance and just fell over. He had a hard time getting to his feet. That resulted in another challenge John bravely faced later, finding out that he had a case of hydrocephalus, with excess fluid putting pressure on his brain.

My heart goes out to my brother David. Unbeknownst to most people who would have thought the opposite, David has been taking care of John since they were baseball kids. David was always quietly in charge and John loved it. Almost like twins, they had some serious chemistry between them. Those Concord Hotel waiter brothers always took care of each other. And everyone in the family knew that besides my mother, John loved David the most.

I'm gonna miss him too. I'm gonna miss bugging him about the Seahawks. And college football games that we disagreed with and then for my team to get destroyed, just like he predicted.

The thing I think I'm gonna miss most of all is to call him on the phone and talk about the good days and good times.

And then there's Jeff; John and David's brother from another mother, and in the end, because Debbie, John's girlfriend, was miles away taking care of her mother, and because Kristen, John's daughter chose not to come, (not sure why), and because I was not able to travel there, (I have been sick and two days ago I got tested for COVID and have not found out what the results are yet), and because David has no transportation to get back and forth to the hospital, Jeff was destined to take charge and negotiate between a bizarre hierarchy of a hospital in lockdown, the doctors taking care of John and communicating to the rest of the family and extended family what was happening and eventually the harbinger of sad news to everyone. Thank you Jeff, I know from experience that that was not an easy row to hoe.

And then there is John's daughter Kristen,... John knew he was in his last days and was desperately hoping to see his only daughter Kristen before he passed,... it was COVID times and hospitals were not letting anyone in to see John, including David and Jeff,... but there was talk that they would let her in for that one-last visit,... still, for reasons of her own, and after a lot of excuses, Kristen ultimately decided not to take the opportunity to say goodbye to her father,... and I think those last few days John was holding on for that last look at his daughter,... and it would be easy for me to judge her actions,... but I won't,... it is on her to reflect on a father that loved her so much,... a father that had been supporting her financial needs for well over a decade,... support that continued till the day John died.

I'm hoping that one day Kristen will come down,... and maybe reassess how she conducts herself,... maybe, but maybe not,... maybe if she can stop long enough to reflect on John's deep love for her,... she will miss that illuminating smile that John saved just for her,...

I think in memory to John, I'm gonna go get the, *"Connected"* album and listen to *"She Loves Me Anyway."*

Connections (01)

(1998) – As noted, this motif is Connections (01), meaning it was the original treatment to the melody that the other Connections were based off of. And I used a #16 Accordion, along with a #77 Fantasy, chorus voice as a lead and the bass to #17 Accordion for the rich bottom. As noted previously, I liked how Connections (01) sounded after the song, "She Loves Me Anyway." It had a real nice home-feel of happiness to it and preceded, "From The Lost Letters Sent" nicely.

From The Lost Letters Sent

(1998) – How many prayers go out into the darkness of night with a hope of some instant returning insight or enlightenment? To some, the trite or rudimentary airs of a person speaking to a deity, trying to find out who they are, why they're here, what is their life all about, and where are they going after they've passed on, are all pointless articulations, but not to me; with curious and lofty thoughts, I want to know where I'm coming from, or going to.

Just as we are connected to each other in some strange, maybe mystifying ways, I feel that we are connected in some other astonishing, perhaps to some, enigmatic and unfathomable ways, to a God that chooses to administer bits and pieces of his knowledge and existence, to us; through an almost incomprehensible but simple conduit or that is to say, a still, small voice.

I can't say exactly how this whole thing fits together, I have my own bits and pieces of intelligences that I operate from, and besides the Prophet and the twelve apostles, I'm not aware of anybody else on earth that really can. But from the truths that I have come to know over the years, I have come up with my own set of truths and beliefs that comfort me and reassure me at times that I am indeed not alone.

Side Note:

Like my lovely Diane, I not only feel a responsibility to teach my children right and wrong, I need to let them know of the standards and possible parameters to operate under, like the, 'Word of Wisdom' that they might give consideration,... that they might find joy in their lives and to pass on from my own testimony how I feel concerning spiritual things.

And I could easily feel a certain sadness come over my heart when I see my children choosing the wrong, or even worse, seeing what's right and knowing what is right but having to make that wrong choice over and over again,... because that's me; I'm the one that walked down those wrong paths myself and I would like them to gain the benefit of my experiences, but mistakes will be made by them and rightfully so, learning from those mistakes should follow.

Another Side Note:

Prayer, like, "*From The Lost Letters Sent*," are not always answered in the way we want or need, and many times it would seem that no one is listening. And there is so much in life I do not understand, but I try to be a good person, the best friend to Diane,... to be a good father to my children and grandchildren,... to be an accepting neighbor,... a caring community-minded fellow,... to be an individual armed with kindnesses and charity in my heart.

From the lost letters sent to my many experiences with and without heeded suggestions, while working on gaining a better insight from my spiritual encounters; I'm enhancing and refining my understandings, my inner feelings, all from a desire to strive to be more like *Jesus Christ*.

On my journey, as you find me humbly endeavoring to do what is right, practicing and preaching to love one another, I strive to live by love and mercy, and of course, I continue in my own way to keep communicating to God through prayer.

Connections (04)

(1998) – I knew that I needed to have something special and subtle here because of the delicate nature of, "Dreams Where I Have Been." Connections (04) was not, like some of the other pieces that were recorded one after another, then picked out of a lineup; rather, I created this motif specifically for this particular connection between the, "From The Lost Letters Sent" song and the, "Dreams Where I Have Been."

Here I used a light clockwork-sounding set of bells, #80 Bell Strings to carry this arrangement, overlapping the voices to get the effect you hear here.

Side Note:

It may sound simple and easy listening to you, the listener, but I worked for hours to get this 32 second arrangement to sound this good, and, I was still thinking it needed a little more work but I settled.

Dreams Where I Have Been

(1998) – Sometimes our lucid dreams and our incoherent nightmares have little distinction from each other. This poem was born out of a need to get these feelings and ideas out into the open. A couple of years after my son Christopher passed away, and for some time, I would have these recurring dreams; well at times I might interpret them as nightmares, but these nightly visions would come to me, sometimes two or three times a week, and these provisional imaginings continued for quite some time.

One night after I awoke in the dark I laid there staring up into the darkness and decided to try to document what was happening in this recurring pseudo dream-mare.

In the dream I was walking down a dirt road with an aura of a sepia, (Sepia is a reddish-brown color, named after the rich brown pigment derived from the ink sac of the common cuttlefish Sepia), black and white movie, kind of like in the beginning of the Wizard of Oz.

I don't remember the first time I had this dream, but I do remember that each time afterwards, when it occurred, it seems to spark my memory like a Déjà vu of a place I'd already been,... or like I was going through the motions I'd already done.

I felt in a way that I had been there before but, in a way, I didn't know why I was there. Up ahead there was a bridge, not a very wide bridge, maybe wide enough for one car and maybe a little bit of pedestrian space. And as I approached this bridge, I was aware that he, (my son Christopher), was there, but I couldn't see him. There was an eerie feeling; I knew that he was there, but looking around, I could tell that he wasn't. And almost to the time that I got to the end of the short bridge; there he was. I called to him; calling out his name, *"Chris-boy!"* He looked inconsequentially over at me with slight interest, like he might look at a fly crawling on a wall. But the expression on his face was without emotion, unchanged and, unmoved. There was a burning inside me that cried out for him to recognize me and acknowledge that I was his father, and for him to say something, anything.

And then, we were walking through this strange dreamscape where the trees and the bushes and ground cover all looked fake; plastic-like, and I was mindful that everything was in a sort of, ill-omened black and white blur to my peripheral vision; hovering just on the outside of my foggy perception.

I was aware that we were in that same recurring dream; and yet, that same feeling of emptiness and regret that I had experienced shortly after Christopher passed away, was now with me; overwhelming me as I walked next to him. And I became conscientious of the fact that I could not touch him, I could not embrace him, I could not love him, I could only walk in solitude by his side; just as much a ghost to him as he was to me.

And then there was a brief moment where we stopped, I looked down into his face and looked back emotionlessly as if to say, this is the way it is; there is no more.... And then I would wake up.

Side Note:

After I wrote the poem, composed the music and recorded this song, this strange reoccurring dream ceased. In a way, I feel that the dreams drove the need for the song to be created because the song needed to get out; but in another sense, in spite of the ominous dreamscape I had to endure those many times, I'm sure you can understand that I miss not seeing my son, Chris-Boy and I miss not being there with him, even at the emotional expense of dealing with the pain and anguish of the menacing dream's poignant circumstances.

Another Side Note:

The music was kind of unnerving, which is what I was going for, made only more poignant with my soft-sung voice. And yes that last high note was hard to reach and took a lot of tries before I was satisfied. But when I did finally get it, I was elated.

Connections (03)

I wanted something different here, especially after the listener has just come from a heavy song like, "Dreams Where I Have Been." I wanted something kind of pleasant and melodic to put the listener into a happier frame of mind and help to lead them into the fun cowboy bop song that would follow, "When Love Comes Calling To Me."

Side Note:

Connections (03) came about with me playing with multiple harmonicas and using the keyboard, #57 Harmonica to act as a bass harmonica. It was a lot of fun and the 37 second piece took less than an hour to complete.

When Love Comes Calling To Me

(1998) – The summer that my Mother was dying in the hospital, (1996), all of her children rallied at her side with a sense of hope and loving support. I may have mentioned that while my brother Ray, who owns his own construction company, was in Florida sharing Mother's last days on earth, his wife Shauna was having a yard sale with all of his expensive and needed tools. She put a restraining order on him so he couldn't see, or had limited access to, his children until after their day in court. She also tried to enforce that restraining order while taking over Ray's house, but she found out that she was indeed trespassing on Ray's property and had to find somewhere else to live. And for the next six months his life was in the process of defensive retaliations, offensive attacks and retreats as his once blissful third marriage eventually fell apart.

On one of my visits there, Ray stated that there was no way he would ever get married again. Although he eventually got custody of all the children, including his step-son and Shauna's first child, Michael, Ray became despondent towards any type of relationship and he was reluctant to even socialize again.

Side Note:

Originally, in the creation of this song, I had this nice tune running through my head, so I followed it up with the poem that is laid down here. But the poem demanded a certain feel that, I found myself changing the music more than a couple of times before I finally settled for this version. After a while the tune seemed too familiar to me and I felt that it was lifted from someone and somewhere else. I put another tune to the lyrics and played with it for a while, even recorded it, but the contrived alteration seemed to take the magic away and I lost interest in the whole thing.

After recording "Dreams Where I Have Been," which is a pensive but melancholy song, I knew that I needed to follow it with something upbeat and positive, so I dusted this song off again, recorded it with a kind of honky-tonk piano and went with the original version. After putting the album together, I was pleased with the results. After months had gone by, I couldn't relate this song to any other, but even if I could, at that point, I just didn't even care anymore.

Another Side Note:

It is a given fact that every songwriter faces the worry (or not), that the song they just came up with might be influenced by another song they had heard in the past.

For songwriters who resonate with the music and or lyrics of another artist that they feel connected to, it can be appealing to work out of the same playbook of that musical artist. I have to know that my listeners can be a lot savvier than I might think.

When I moved to New Jersey, my girlfriend there gave me all of Bob Dylan's early albums that belonged to her brother. He was an avid fan of folk music in its purist forms, but after buying, "Bringing It All Back Home," he felt betrayed and thus the albums fell to me.

And so, I started writing poems set to tunes Dylan had laid out in his early albums. And after I bought my first guitar, Dylan was my first go to artist to from. And I believe it was Oscar Wilde that said, "Imitation is the sincerest form of flattery," but after a while my own early material sounded way too much like him and people told me so.

I'm sure that there were a lot of people that felt they could make their careers out of doing someone else's persona, but I wanted to be recognized for the sound and persona that I created; that would be me, Lord Baldwin. And, I don't think it's a bad idea to be inspired and motivated by influences such as; *Brian Wilson, the Beatles, Jimi Hendrix, Simon and Garfunkel, Donovan, Arlo Guthrie, the Moody Blues, Bob Dylan, Supertramp, James Taylor, Frank Sinatra, Country Joe and the Fish, Billy Joel, Cat Stevens*, oh my goodness, there's just too many to mention, but if you want to be original, I don't think it's a good idea to imitate those influences too closely because you'll become them to whatever degree you embrace them.

I heard a song on the radio where the artist took the fundamental nature and substance of the catchy Dylan song, "I Want You" and shamelessly created a song, arguably in a different key, but used all the same chord structures and though he put different words to the song, there were phrases that were undeniably Dylan's.

My point here is that I worry about taking the essence of someone else's material and then calling it my own. I want my material to embrace my own new ideas and I want to grow from my own visions and draw from my own well of inspirations and creativities. It is well for me to know that a small part of Roy Orbison is in my soul and comes out now and then in an aria or a poetic phrase, and I believe he knows; I believe he's is listening and I like to think that he's saying to himself, "Hmm... I like it."

Connections (05)

(1998) – Frankly, I felt at the time, (and still do), that anything I was to put between, "When Love Comes Calling To Me" and, "She's Floating In The Air" would work. Both had rather positive messages and both carried themselves well. The determining factor was that "When Love Comes Calling To Me" was in the key of F and, "She's Floating In The Air" was in the key of E, (actually played with a capo on the fourth fret and using C fingering), so with Connections (07) also being in the key of E, and Connections (05) being in the key of D#, I went with Connections (05) to break up the chance of possible repetitiousness or monotony.

Another Side Note: With many different voices and sounds, I tried to make this connection to be kind of regal and stately. I wanted to come back to this one and embellish it with trumpets and maybe slight French horns in the background as the music faded, but I ran out of tracks and arguably, time and ambition so you see, that did not happen.

She's Floating In The Air

(1998) – Living with a true saint, my best friend and marvelous love, Diane, can sometimes be a challenging undertaking. If you know anything about Diane, you'd know this song was all about her. She is a woman on a mission to offer care and give charity to all she finds in need. In the church we have this phrase, "Calling and Election Made Sure," which comes from 2nd Peter, Chapter 1, Verse 10, where Peter advises;

"Wherefore...give diligence to make your calling and election sure:
for if ye do these things, ye shall never fall.
To have one's calling and election made sure,"

... which implies that a person can receive a divine witness or confirmation while still alive that he or she will inherit eternal life, or put simply, they have already been cleared for landing into the Celestial Kingdom. I joke with her about the fact that she has obtained this *"Calling and Election Made Sure,"* and that she is just waiting here on earth for me to get my act together.

I wrote this song for Diane; my enchanting extraordinary, partner, whose charitable heart and compassion; with her sincere consideration for others, encompasses a shared joy and sincere empathy; kindheartedness and a genuine thoughtfulness to all others, no matter who they are. For her and her caring gentleness that is sensed by everyone, but most especially by children, who are attracted to her like a magnet; it is for this extraordinary, magnificent individual that I wrote this song.

Side Note:

And here am I, weighted down with all the trappings of the earthly man with my many possessions, my slothful ways and carnal desires, while she resides on a higher sphere, gently suggesting certain behavioral modifications to improve the spirituality of me and our family, while quietly yet fervently praying for my eventual redemption.

Connections (08)

(1998) – Now this here last connection, Connections (08) was the "pièce de resistance," is perhaps the most memorable accomplishment of to the series of connections. Instead of following the connections motif like all the others, Connections (08), done in the key of G, is a collection of themes from all seven of the songs on this album, including the last song, "The Boy Scout Code," of which, I was torn on whether or not to include because the audience had not heard the piece yet. And how could I lead the ending of this five minute and two second piece which ends with the essence of "The Boy Scout Code" into "The Boy Scout Code?" Enter the original connections motif at the beginning and end of Connections (08) so as to leave the listener with a sense of finality. And anyway, if you ever go to a musical, they do something like this all the time. And actually, I liked the way the end of Connections (08) into "The Boy Scout Code" flowed.

Side Note:

Because Connections (08) was so long, (five minute and two seconds) the 13 pieces ended up being 47 minutes and 37 seconds, too long to fit on the standard 45-minute cassette tape so Connections (08) could not be included. Still, I kept the concept of the album in my head, in my notes and in my heart for that someday in the future. And as providence would have it, not long after this album was completed, Electronic Resources Inc. (the phoenix company that rose from the ashes of JW Electronics) brought in a shipment of non-name-brand cassettes; of which I bought a few of their 90-minute cassettes. To my surprise, unlike Sony cassettes which reel off an almost perfect to the minute cassette, this no-name brand actually had about 98 minutes on their reels which meant there was 49 minutes on each side. So, at least for me, I had the whole album on my set. But for everyone that got a cassette with "Connected" on one side, and, "Too Hard" on the other, Connections (08) was not included and so, it was really first introduced to the Lord Baldwin universe on June 24, 2019 when the newly reengineered and restored "Connections" album was distributed world-wide by the folks at DistroKid.

Another Side Note:

You might ask, what happened to Connections (06) and Connections (07)? Sadly, they never came off my masters and I have no way of retrieving them because my TASCAM 4-track Cassette Recorder (which I still have), needs all new belts and wheels to be operative, and even then, I'm not sure where all my master tapes are. I know where most of them are, but I'm afraid that some of them have been lost to time and relocations of my stuff.

The Boy Scout Code

(1998) – Living the ideals and principals of the Boy Scout that I will always be. For as long as I can remember, I have always been a Boy Scout. Even before I was eight, I was involved with Scouting in 1954 through 1955 when my dad was Scoutmaster for my big brothers, John, David, Jack and Ed.

And as a young man, I believed in the program; I worked hard to advance towards my Eagle and, through involvement in the program, was shaped along the way.

When I was 13, my mother had run away from Senior (yet again), after he had gotten drunk on wine

That's Five-Year-Old me going on a camping trip with the Boy Scouts

and physically abused her. We ran away to the same place we always did; to Grandma Scarbrough's house in Portland Oregon. Richie and I got registered in a Troop at the Boy's Pal Club in the Lents District. I was soon on the fast track to earn my Eagle rank and had earned my First-Class advancement badge. I was working on multiple merit badges, going on campouts, and that summer, I went to Camp Meriwether, a Boy Scout summer camp located near Tillamook, along the Oregon Coast. I was also in line to go to the 1964 National Jamboree to be held at Valley Forge, Pennsylvania where I would meet and shake hands with President Kennedy. And things were looking up for me until his assignation. After that, my mother, a devout Catholic, was devastated. She was contacted by and soon after reconciled with Senior.

We had not been in Glendora California for more than a month before Richie and I contacted and got registered with a new Boy Scout Troop. From the beginning, we both felt uncomfortable there; our family was living in a trailer park, living on a limited budget, while the rest of the Scouts in the Troop had come from more affluent families.

Scouting relations for Richie and I got stymied to a degree after one of the other Scouting parents had driven us home following a weekend campout, kidding us about living in the "boondocks," just before they dropped us off at our space in the trailer park. Word quickly got out about our situation and we took a lot of ribbing from the other Scouts about where we lived, but I figured that it would all pass after a while.

Unfortunately, as a few months passed, I could tell that the Senior Patrol Leader was taking a particular disliking to me, and with subtlety, he started finding fault, beginning with my less-than-perfect uniform, and then, fed by the attention he was receiving from the other Scouts, he would go out of his way to humiliate me and to a lesser degree, my brother Richie. To make matters worse, the Senior Patrol Leader's father was the Scoutmaster. Although the magic I had known in Scouting was disappearing, I kept going, hoping things would change after we had settled in with the group. Things did change, but not in a good way.

One afternoon after all the Scouts had collectively recited the Scout Law and Scout Oath we broke up into patrols and began elections. Richie was no sooner nominated for a leadership position of Patrol Leader by his group, (must have been his effervescent smile), when the Scoutmaster objected and personally nominated and effected the election of someone else. I could see that Richie was upset, but he bucked up and didn't say anything.

That evening, just before the Troop broke up to go home, the Scoutmaster turned to me and said in a calm, clear voice, "Skip? You and your brother need to see me after Scouts is over tonight."

Richie and I looked at each other not sure what we'd done, but from what I felt was a positive tone in the Scoutmaster's voice, I was confident it was for something good. I raised my eyebrows and smirked and said in a quiet voice to Richie, "he's probably going to say he's sorry for what he did there to you."

"Why?" Richie asked with a whisper. "He's the Scoutmaster, he can do anything."

"But he's not supposed to do that." I whispered back. "That's not the Scout way."

The meeting adjourned, we sat in folding chairs and watched as some of the other Scouts joined up with their parents and began to leave. The Scoutmaster was discussing something with one of the fathers when he stopped, motioned for the man to wait a moment and then he walked over to us. With a few of the Scouts and their parents standing around us, and the Senior Patrol Leader standing next to his father, the Scoutmaster breathed in heavily before he said, "Both of you have been coming to a lot of our meetings..." He looked over at the Assistant Scoutmaster who looked disturbed and turned away. Turning back to us with a trouble-free grin, the Scoutmaster casually continued, "You two boys have gone on a couple campouts and there's been some activities you've participated in; and..." He paused to say just the right words before continuing, "I'm sure that you both know, it costs money to do Scout stuff; you know? to go places, to go on campouts, for the food on the campouts and all the extra stuff?"

He paused for an answer but seeing our dumbfounded reaction, his face went from laidback and casual to determined and resolute. "There must be over three months of dues that both of you owe us right now..." He paused again, staring firmly at us to be sure that we, and anyone else watching, might get the full effect of his authoritative performance.

"We paid some money before, didn't we?" I asked, looking at Richie, straining my brain to remember when that last time was.

The Senior Patrol Leader stood up straight and looked pretentiously at Richie and I. "I don't think so." He said, mimicking his father's imposing, stance.

"It doesn't matter." The Scoutmaster said, looking at his son and back to us. "You boys need to pay your money, Plain and simple. You need to stop burdening the rest of the other Scout's parents. It's not fair to the other boys here in Troop 86; it's not fair to the other parents you've been burdening, and it's not fair to our Scouting organization here."

"Mike?" the Assistant Scoutmaster called from behind.

"Don't get me started, Greg." The Scoutmaster said without turning around to acknowledge his assistant's objections. His eyes remained, steady and unmercifully rigid; down on us. "Do you think it's fair?" The Scoutmaster asked firmly as his eyebrows lowered.

Upset, I looked to the floor and nodded with my head as I voiced a timid, "No." Horrified that our financial circumstances had been made public, and embarrassed to be brought to this level of humiliation, I could do nothing but continue to stare at the floor; so perfectly sure that, all the eyes of the remaining Scouts and their parents, were all staring at me.

"Well so, here's the deal..." The Scoutmaster said firmly as he looked around the room to be sure that everyone's attention was on him. "Unless you both bring..." The Scoutmaster looked over to a woman sitting across the room and asked, "Regina, what was it?"

The Woman named Regina looked down a ledger sheet before answering, "Thirty-six dollars..." She called back with no emotion in her voice. "And some change."

The Scoutmaster spun back around facing me again and said, "Thirty-six dollars and some change,..." He paused for effect and then continued, "Each." He breathed in heavily again before he said, "You both need to pay up." He breathed out, looking at his son momentarily before he looked straight at me and continued, "So... don't bother to come back next week until you both have the money. Do you understand?"

As the look of astonishment crossed my face, I was sure that I saw a sort of blissful twinkle in his eyes.

The Scoutmaster stared at us as if we were going to object or put up a fight, but when we didn't, he looked around the room again and with callousness he said, "And don't you two think you can just go somewhere else and join some other troop; at least, not around here. I know all the Scoutmasters in the area, and I'm gonna let them know they'll need to look out for you two boys. You won't be able to get in anywhere."

"We'll..." I said softly, "we'll bring the... the money next week."

I rose softly, turned and literally pulled Richie up to his feet by his Scout shirt, and then we both cowered as we slithered out of the room. If I had ever felt worse in my life, I couldn't remember when it was.

We had walked half way home before Richie broke the silence. "We're gonna bring the money next week?" He asked. "Where we gonna get the money. Senior sure ain't gonna give it to us, and Mother..."

With anger I turned and said, "It's over, Richie. I'm never going to Scouts again."

(There's more on this story found in the book; '*Stepping Between The Ants* – Book FOUR; *The Fall Behind*')

Side Note One:

I was not LDS at the time, otherwise this episode in my life might never have happened because the church would have absorbed my debt,... And I wonder at times what would have happened if I would have stayed in Portland. Would I have continued to advance to Eagle? I believe I would have.

Side Note Two:

When I moved to Olympia as an adult, through a church calling, I reconnected with the Scouting program and since 1976, I have remained active with the Boy Scouts of America in one roll or another; sometimes in dual roles simultaneously, and I have served as *Explorer Post Advisor*, a *Den Leader*, an *Assistant Scoutmaster*, the *Webelos Leader*, a *Committee Member, the Cubmaster, Committee Chairperson*, and *Scoutmaster*. Not to mention I have remained a registered *Merit Badge Councilor* all that time and continue to be of service.

Side Note Three:

As of 01/01/2020 the Church of Jesus Christ of Latter-Day Saints has disassociated itself from the Boy Scouts of America, deciding to discontinue its role as a chartered partner.

**"The reality there is
we didn't really leave them; they kind of left us,"**

Said **M. Russell Ballard**,
Acting President of the Quorum of the Twelve Apostles.

**"The direction they were going
was not consistent to what we feel our youth need to have,…
to survive in the world that lies ahead for them."**

And in spite of all of that time spent; arguably most all of the church callings that I have so gallantly and happily carried out since 1976 when I was called to be an Explorer Post Advisor for the Teachers Quorum,… that was a big learning curve,… and what was once, for many in the leaders and hierarchy of the church, a kind of gateway for young boys between eight and eighteen, to certain ideologies, values, philosophies, principles and even doctrines to eternal perspectives, is now a distant memory,… and even before the break off time, after the announcement was made, many of the members of my ward (Tumwater Second Ward), and the stake (Olympia Stake), precipitously disassociated themselves with the BSA program and even some of my older Scouter associates ditched Scouting altogether.

I was left in a precarious position, a kind of man without a country. Even though I was still working with boys to help them work towards their Eagle, I was no longer treated with the respect and honor of being a Scout Leader but instead, I was suddenly an unrelatable outsider.

I also felt a sense of disassociation with my fellow ward members, and I felt unexpectedly but abruptly excluded, and there was (and still is), a sense of being ostracized for my continued connection, involvement or relationship with the Boy Scouts of America.

It is good to note that there have been many Boy Scouts that have gone on to become good citizens of their communities, in their respective States, and in the United States of America. And as mentioned before, my sons, Chet, Ben, Stephen, Spencer and Brian have all honorably earned their rank as Eagle Scouts.

Side Note Four:

I asked the bishop to give me a little time before assigning me another church calling, but before that happened the COVID-19 pandemic came along and with the church and our ward, a kind of diminished operations came in place,... it was amazing to see how quickly the church's Wards and Stakes rewired their connections to address the pandemic and to keep the needed information coming in, and then broadcasting services, messages and instructions over Zoom and moreover General Conferences and other valuable information sent out on the the internet (YouTube),... and our Bishop helped to maintain a sense of calm with his caring leadership styles,...

And can I say, it was (is) not so easy being a Democrat in an ecclesiastical/pseudo-political environment where only 17 percent of American members in the Church of Jesus Christ of Latter Day Saints are Democrat,... and in an age where ideological lines are drawn where the very existence of COVID is questioned, where Republican members refuse to get immunized or to wear a mask,... Good to know that there are more members outside of the United States than inside,...

It can be a challenge when certain prominent respected members of the Ward are propagating and moreover, promoting conspiracy theories and falsehoods all in the name of Trumpism and/or restrictive party lines,... when the church is the one place where I should be free of pro-paganda, political inventions and fabrications,... but it is what it is and I take solace in the words of President Uchtdorf who said, "I suppose the Church would be perfect only if it were run by perfect beings."

Side Note Five & Back To Scouting:

Just recently, I have graciously volunteered to be a *Unit Commissioner* for the Pacific Harbors Council. The Unit Commissioner is kind of the connecting link between the local Boy Scout Troops and Cub Scout Packs and the local Council.

I hope to be able to help the Scouting program in our area flourish at a time where, numbers are down because of the pandemic as well as the boy's moral from non-existent or stifled troop meetings that in many cases have been reduced to in-home, computerized Zoom conferences,

The 12 principles a Boy Scout lives by with the **Scout Law**:

a **Scout** is;

**Trustworthy, Loyal, Helpful,
Friendly, Courteous, Kind,
Obedient, Cheerful, Thrifty,
Brave, Clean,** and **Reverent**."

I am still living by and upholding what the Boy Scouts of America stood for when I was a young man.

Most importantly, the whole foundation of Scouting i.e. building Character and virtuous principals of the Boy Scouts of America's pro-gram is tightly held within the **Boy Scout Oath**:

**On My Honor,
I Will Do My Best, To Do My Duty,
To God And My Country
And To Obey The Scout Law;
To Help Other People At All Times,
To Keep Myself Physically Strong,
Mentally Awake
And Morally Straight.**

And for me, I continue to believe in and aspire to live by the *Scout Law*, and the *Oath and Promise* of the *Boy Scouts of America*.

Side Note Five:

In the final days of my Scouting as a youth, I did not get my *Eagle* to become an *Eagle Scout*. But I have five boys that, through the span of 28 years, from Chet starting in *Cub Scouts* in 1983 and him getting his Eagle in 1989, to Ben starting in *Cub Scouts* in 1989 to him getting his *Eagle* in 1997, to Stephen starting in *Cub Scouts* in 1991 and him getting his *Eagle* in 1999, to Spencer starting in *Cub Scouts* in 1994 to him getting his *Eagle* in 2001, to Brian starting in *Cub Scouts* in 2002 and him finally getting his *Eagle* in 2011, again, through the span of those 28 years, I had the awesome pleasure and honor of being with my boys and working with them on rank advancements, on merit badges, required and otherwise, of taking them to Boy Scout camps like Camp Thunderbird on Summit Lake,...

(which was done with every boy, and for some, who also went to other various camps),... and going on 50 mile hikes, (Ben and Brian) and on a 50 mile canoe trip, (that was with Chet in 1988 at the Ross Dam up by the Canadian border), and walking on five or ten or even 20 mile day hikes, (that was with all the boys, but mostly it was a Spencer thing, and he still prefers walking everywhere), and so many Scout outings over the years, going to so many diverse places and the boys interacting with so many other Scouts that many have kept in touch with. And except for Chet where I was an Assistant Scoutmaster, I was able to be a Scoutmaster, (through three different calls of duty), for and with my boys. It was a long but wonderful journey that will stay with me forever.

Side Note Six:

I believe all of the boys were able to go to *Camp Thunderbird* but not all were able to go in its greatness when it was part of the Tumwater Area Council,... and unfortunately, due to so many regrettable circumstances, the Pacific Harbors Council, after some poor accountability choices,... The financial problems at the Pacific Harbors Council had been building for years, but then the executives at Pacific Harbors Council decided to log 30 acres of Camp *Hahobas* to receive $55,000 for the timber in hopes of offsetting other financial losses,... and I went on an LDS Encampment with Brian at *Hahobas* after they'd clear-cut much of the camp,... Troop 005 was assigned to camp in the stump-town area literally a mile away from the mess hall, and where we were, there was no tree covering and no shade,... and that was the most unorganized camp I'd ever experienced,... and to be fair, a lot of the boys, (like me) lamented the loss of all those trees,... and ultimately, it was too little too late and the council ended up having to repay a $650,000 loan,... and was forced to close down *Camp Hohobas,* in Tahuya, Mason County, on the Hood Canal, *Camp Curran,* south of Parkland, Pierce County; *Camp Delezenne,* near Elma, Grays Harbor County; and *Camp Kilworth,* in Federal Way.

Side Note Seven:

Refusing to give up, the *Baden-Powell Northwoods Experience Board* met with the logging company, which has agreed to lease the camping areas and keep the scout camp running,... however, because the agreement is for a lease and not a sale, some of the donors that had pledged are unable to give their pledged amount. (Some of the pledged donations were from conservation groups, and it would be a conflict of interest to support the lease as the land is owned by a logging company.) However, conversations between the logging company and *Baden-Powell Northwoods Experience* continue to work towards an eventual sale. We will miss them all.

Side Note Eight:

As a Scoutmaster many times over, I was looking for an alternative to the *Pacific Harbors Council* camping facilities and in my search, I discovered *Camp Parsons,*

and for most of my last five years as Scoutmaster, and against the advice of my Bishop at the time, who wanted me to stay in the *Pacific Harbors Council*, I brought my Scouts to *Camp Parsons*, which is part of the *Seattle Area Council*.

Unfortunately, it costs the Scouts that are outside their council district more money, **but it was well worth it**.

I found that it was very much like Tumwater's *Camp Thunderbird* in its feel and execution of the programs for a Boy Scout camp and for that experience Scouts should have.

Pacific Harbors Council Camp Parsons Pacific Harbors Council Camp Parsons Seattle Area Council

Camp Thunderbird

It was founded in 1919, and is the oldest continuous running Boy Scout camp west of the Mississippi River and one of the oldest continually running Boy Scout camp in the United States on its original location. It sits on Jackson Cove, part of the Hood Canal, on the Olympic Peninsula, just north of Brinnon, Washington. The site of the camp was chosen by Professor Edmund Meany, Major Edward Ingraham and members of the Seattle Area Council. It was purchased from John Strom in May 1919 and named after the first council president, Reginald H. Parsons. Booth Hall (the current Silver Marmot Grill) was constructed in May and June 1919 and continues to be used today.

On July 7, 1919, 100 Scouts arrived at *Camp Parsons* (by boat from Bremerton), for its first season that ran 6 weeks and has not stopped since. Thousands of Scouts from the Pacific Northwest and throughout the United States and Canada attend this camp each summer.

Camp Parsons is the only Boy Scout Camp that uses a salt water beach for all aquatic activities. *Camp Parsons* also has hiking treks for Scouts to explore the Olympic Mountains and Kayak treks to explore the Hood Canal.

My son Brian, being the youngest in the family is the only boy of mine that had the pleasure of going to **Camp Parsons**. He earned a lot of merit badges there, but he told me once that his reason to be there was to have fun, especially because he had some of his best friends there with him. And after all, isn't that what Scouting is all about?

57

- 38 - TOO HARD - 1998 -

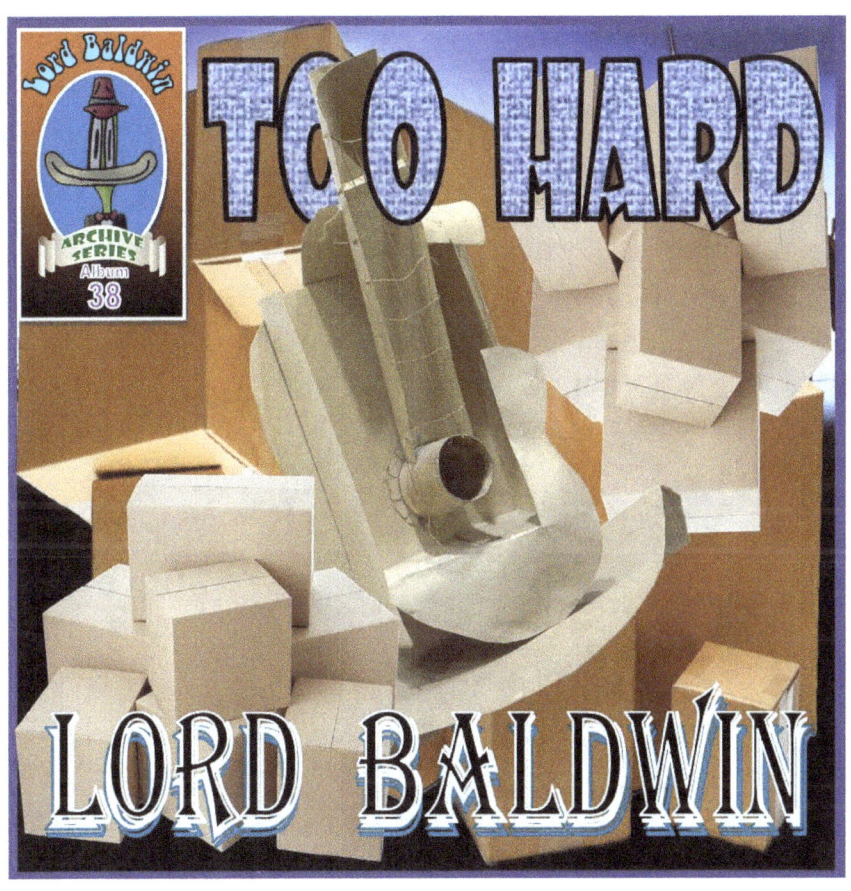

58

NOTES ABOUT THE COVERS

Notes On The New Cover:

For the new cover I chose a 1912 sculpture called, "Guitar" by Pablo Picasso made up from paperboard, paper, thread, string, twine, and coated wire. Although the sculpture was newly released as "Public Domain," I didn't want to take any chances so I rotated the figure and hid it inside a bunch of cardboard boxes. Also notice that I forgot to take off the "**Archive Series**" label icon of **Per-Q-Leez**, on the cover of, "**Album 38**" as is shown on the world-wide streaming sites; I figured you could deal with it.

Notes On The Original Covers:

For the original cover I chose "Le Sommeil" (Sleep), a kind a weird, 1937 painting, by Salvador Dali where the head (in a catatonic state) is supported by a series of crutches, suggesting tension, struggle and awkward difficulties, that is to maybe say, "Too Hard."

The back cover was a look at an alley in a city where the struggle for clean and clean is fought by suspending laundry above the trash and garbage below.

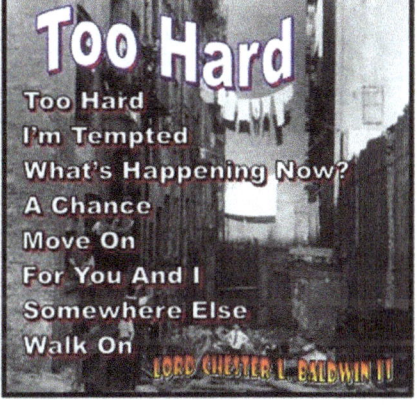

59

TOO HARD

Too Hard
I'm Tempted
What's Happening Now?
A Chance
Move On
For You And I
Somewhere Else
Walk On

60

Too Hard

The clock alarm throbs like a 10-pound hammer
beating on my head.
I know I've got to do it soon
but I don't want to get out of bed.
Information overload with no time to assimilate or sort,
leaves me down in the hole, a day late and dollar short.
It's like I'm defeated or beaten before I get out of the yard.
It's too little too late, too long, too much,
too hard.

Ironic that the HMO that might help maintain my very breath
is the same force that has the power
to send me to my death.
They say, "we're here for you when you need us by your side,"
yet in the same breath they posture and say, "oh, you don't qualify."
So unless you got real money or you're carrying the magic card,
It's too little too late, too long, too much,
too hard.

We just wanted a safety net when our affairs got out of hand,
but insurance now empowered
went from request to command.
Used to be they were working hard to service our account,
but now we're working for them beyond a 60 percent amount.
We're crammed with health, car, home, and life insurance
with demands and little regard,
It's too little too late, too long, too much,
too hard.

That cost of living and expenses keeps going up time and again,
while wages and situations seems to fall
or remain where they've always been.
Is the money gone or just hiding somewhere in that wallet or purse,
because right now I could use some cash
before thing get much worse.
The rich stay rich because the poor are poor
and the challengers get barred.
It's too little too late, too long, too much,
too hard.

61

What's Happening Now?

"What's Happening?" We would say years ago
trying to be there, hip or cool.
We had so many plans and ideas
that transcended beyond what we learned in school.
Back then, when we considered the future,
we thought love would conquer greed and hate.
And the difference would change from the lies and the shame
to that brave new world we would create.

But what's happening now?
How did so few years turn things so sour?
We look around to find we're all out of our minds;
what's happening now?

In the name of choice they kill their babies
and the family as we knew it is doomed.
Children have forgotten how to pretend or play
as they sit entranced with their minds entombed.
Outside, the radioactive secrets poison the underground
and our air-ponderous with its blight.

Ocean waters rise each day as the o-zone fades away
and we can't see the stars from too much light.

What's happening now? And who's in charge anyhow?
From existential fate to the fall of such a ruinous state
what's happening now?

Religions clash in the name of the Lord,
while Sodom and Gomorrah plays downtown.
People sell out their own trusted friends,
seems like everything is going down.

As animals, insects, birds dwindle out,
we press on with blinders on our eyes.
Rain forests being destroyed for nothing
save in the name of money and free enterprise.
Clouded waters wash down dubious foods,
as people have no choice or rights.
Years ago who would have thought
that we could even be bought
for a few dollars and some comforts in our lives?

What's happening now?
When did we reach this critical hour?
From such honest dreams and hopes,
we're now left here on the ropes
asking ourselves,
"What's happening now?"

What's happening now? Why are the idiots still in power?
It's not hard to predict what will be
if we don't turn around to see
what's happening now.

62

I'm Tempted

When she enters the room, my heart rises and sinks,
and as she passes and looks over I wonder what it is she thinks.
Is she making a move, knowing I'm a married man?
I back away keep my distance to avoid her plan,
but oh, I'm tempted.

It all starts so innocently, with clever words to find,
till playing gives into games and who knows what she has in mind.
There's a burning inside that shivers deep to my soul,
I can't ruin my life for passion I can't control, but
oh, I'm tempted.

Flirting with danger oh, she's just a stranger
ready to lay havoc to my life.
Harmless as it could be; who knows in the end what she
could do to come between my love for my wife.

In her eyes she looks innocent but I wonder from it all,
why it is that I could even consider this fall.
So many would be hurt from a simple loss of will,

and yet, even with all things considered, still,
oh, I'm tempted.

Flirting with danger, oh now she's more than a stranger
and the closer she gets the worse things are.
From the simple words to learn to the point of no return
where I wonder how I let things go too far?

When she enters the room, my heart rises and falls,
I avoid her like the plague,
hiding there behind my cubicle walls.
And that burning inside that shivers deep to my soul,
calls out to me, saying, "Hey, don't you lose control."
But oh, I'm tempted.

63

A Chance

I know that words and lamented songs,
will only distance what's already strange.
And I know what I did was wrong
but it's a past I can never change.

So here I am, back from the dead knowing you'll never understand
that I'm sorry for my foolish head and the pain caused by my hand.

But if there's a chance; if I still had a chance,
from the life that I live, and all I could give
to be back where we'd been.
So I live for that chance; that possible chance
that your passion would burn as love would return
back to us again.

When I left you, I theorized that I could have it all just because.
When you left me I realized my mistakes and how off I was.
I know you'd rather hide or run
than sift through our lost love debris,
but how can I repair damage done

if you distance yourself from me?

Is there a chance; any kind of chance
the distance would near to start over from here
we could be more than friends?

I live for a chance; a possible chance
that your passion would burn and love would return
to your heart again; to your heart again.

What I want and what comes by may be two different things,
but after all, I must try—we'll see what the morrow brings.

And if there's a chance; any kind of chance
though far or near, you know I'll be here waiting to dance.

I just need a chance; I hope for that chance
for your love to return and your passion to burn
back in our romance.

I live for that chance; that possible chance,...
And if there's a chance,... Oh, I want,...

I needed a chance; I dream of the chance
I live for the chance,...

64

Move On

From the ups and downs and mistakes entailed;
From all I tried and tried and failed,
all I got was this increase in sorrow and pain.
there was more less to it than gain.

From atonements and penances I had to pay;
well I see no choice with the hand I played
in the end all the feeling seems to be gone,
and it feels like it's time to move on.

I took off the ring that bonded our lives
and stashed it away in a drawer.
I've started going out again at times,
I'm just determined not to be lonely anymore.

I was wrong, callous, and hopelessly crass,
so if I come to you and then have to pass,
well it's not my intention to fall as your pawn,
it just reaffirms that I need to move on.

So, okay, here's where I am and where we are,
so I've left that sad past incomplete.
And if I can't have you driving my car
well, there's a whole world still left to fill that seat.

It's time to open new windows and doors,
It's time to pick myself up off the floor.
I'm going to invite the world to a barbeque out on my lawn,
and look forward as I finally move on.

65

For You And I

Two paths at the crossroads,
both confused which way to go.
Decisions of thought-provoking meaning and scope,
it's so hard for anyone to know.
I know what you're thinking,
"This could never work for long."
The reason weigh heavy on how we might fail
and how this could all just go wrong.
True love holds against adversity and wear
like fire-tempered steel, strong and true.
Our love, truly we have something special there
that will stand the tests of time and go through.
I know what we should do,
spread our wings to reach the skies.
Together we'll make a place where happiness can dwell
and love can endure for you and I.
Together we'll make a place where happiness can dwell
and love can there for you and I.

66

Somewhere Else

The sun comes up and the sun goes down
as they live and die within this town.
Steady and sure or faltering with doubt,
that "no difference" is what this place is about.

Deep-rooted they stand till they fall to the earth,
with little to show for their struggle of worth.
I don't know what it is that they hold so dear,
but whatever it is, for me, it's not here.

Somewhere else there's got to be something more
than this played-out life that will never go forth.
Somewhere else is a chance to start again free,
and I want that chance to be for you and me.

Day in, day out, I watch as they go
about their simple lives, to never know
what lies beyond our horizons here;
but instead closed in, they hold to the near.

The wind calls out as it passes through,
"Come! Come with me to the novel and new!"
I don't know what it is that I'm searching for,
but whatever it is, it ain't here for me anymore.

Somewhere else; somewhere out there
past this played-out life that just goes nowhere.
Somewhere else is a chance to start again free,
and I want that chance to be for you and me.

67

Walk On

Some say you shouldn't turn your head
and pretend you just don't see,
but there are times when getting involved
can compromise what your future might be.
Good intentions and high ideals can't justify a wronged backlash,
when you're taken hostage or killed
for some meager amount of cash.
Sometimes melting into the shadows
or just making sure you're gone
is the best way to deal with conflict:
if you can; just walk on;
walk on.

The stainless police brake down the door
and stand there like a guest.
With authority and control they smile
and say, "you're under arrest."
We might live and die in ignorance but that's no excuse for the law,
that will hold you in contempt for any one of your small flaws,
to throw you in jail unless you know what it's all about thereon,

that might put you on a first-name basis,
otherwise; better walk on;
walk on.

Anxiety and paranoia watches from out
of the corners of their eyes,
as information passes on
through their network of corporate spies.
"They're coming for me," someone whispers,
then runs into the night
never to be seen or heard again, so maybe he was right.
Maybe there is a conspiracy, some collusion secretly drawn,
but unless you're part of the echelon,
better just walk on; walk on.

Friends are friends and others posturing, for their certain place
that fits within your belief system
to fall from or rise to grace.
Stay and absorb what you will, but beware past the eleventh hour,
for there are some out there who anger
at your rise to station and power.
it's hard to know where the shots come from
on the grassy knoll at dawn
but you'll live to see another day
if you're discerning and just walk on;
walk on.

68

MEMOIRS & NOTES - 38 - 'TOO HARD'

Too Hard

(1998) – Like many of my albums, this album was to maintain the conceptual perspective of the album namesake, in this case, "Too Hard" where I looked at the politics and maladies of the times and tried to write about them. Later down the line there is a set of songs that stand alone or away from the general theme, but more on that later.

One day I was thinking about many of the hassles and inconveniences that plague my existence and thought about what would need to happen to make my life more comfortable. And we all face our preverbal "Too Hard" stuff that gets in the way of what might be really good things.

The problem with most of the examples listed here is personal greed. There are too many that want to cash in on other's vulnerabilities or requirements or necessities at the expense of taking advantage of those who can't afford the commodities or goods being offered at an overpriced premium.

The effects of living paycheck to paycheck and racking up debt to cover unexpected expenses have led to a situation in which many

Americans cannot afford to fulfill their most basic needs. While wages adjusted for inflation have remained stagnant, the cost of living has risen, leading to a decline in median household net worth throughout the U.S. Meanwhile, corporate debt levels are higher than they have ever been, currently equaling about half of America's GDP. With the spread of the coronavirus and the consequent global economic slowdown, experts are concerned that many companies in sectors like energy, hospitality, and auto manufacturing will be unable to honor their debt payments.

This includes wholesaling people's health care needs, mandatory insurances and mismanaged pensions by corporate hounds that care little for anything but the bottom line. Unfortunately, the weight is heaped on the backs of the poor that don't qualify for benefits beyond that bottom line, and have inadequate coverages or none at all.

I took certain key issues that I found to be rather bizarre, peculiar or ironic and wrote about them. My key focuses started with just getting up in the morning and then being immediately barraged with a myriad of images from the news, followed by the whole health care issues and their impersonal approach to providing managed care from their discretions.

I followed this by my dislike of the insurance company rip off fiasco, where we are required by law to give them money for little to nothing in return. The fact that this continues all over the world makes me irritated.

Finally, I deal with the day-to-day struggles of not having enough money to continue your livelihoods and to get by, one must go in debt with the loan sharks at a high interest, with credit card debt and with the deck stacked with the decrees and regulations leaning towards bankrupting you instead of being fair.

Every day, millions of Americans are personally affected by growing debt. And as a nation, we are burdened by over $10 trillion in personal debt — which includes mortgages, student loans, auto loans, credit card and medical debt. About 47% of Americans are burdened with credit card debt and last year over 137 million Americans faced financial hardship as a result of medical bills. According to recent research, at least 1 in 6 Americans has medical debt that is past due, amounting to $60 billion, and over half of those with medical debt have defaulted on their loans.

Despite being the wealthiest nation in the world, where the affluent maintain their lifestyles at the expense of and on the backs of the unfortunate, America has the world's highest levels of student debt. Currently, 1 in 5 Americans is carrying student loan debt and more than a tenth of them have defaulted on their loans. And as the division between the rich and poor keeps widening these levels of student debt are the direct result of exceptionally inflated costs of American higher education combined with insufficient public funding to support the educational needs of America's students.

Side Note:

And there I was, working for all those years at SPSCC, having my kids go there and move on to 4-year colleges only to see six of the nine kids strapped down for the most of their lives and many, not getting into the promised professions that they had gone to school for. And I feel it all falls back to me because working as a computer guy at a college I was unable to financially provide for their needed education. It is unconscionable to think, but I would estimate that between all of my children and or their spouses or significant others, collectively my family is maybe over a million dollars in debt.

Another Side Note:

I am no economist, but my thought to solve the debt problem we are facing as a nation, is for us to accept the fact that the fiscal and economic irresponsibility of both our Democratic and Republican elected officials, going back to the Reagan era, is the primary reason we are where we are. I believe we need to somehow bridge the gap between the poor and the affluent, have free health care including dental health for all and we need to somehow get the staggering 80% of Americans out of debt.

What's Happening Now

(1998) – Our planet as we know it, is the product of a delicate equation between the mineral structure of Earth – for example, the atmosphere's composition – and its biosphere – trees absorbing CO_2 and pumping O_2 through photosynthesis.

In the past, with all my friend's ideological perspectives, I really believed that together, with us all working towards a good, common goal, there would be a peaceful revolution that could and would change the United States; and then in fact, the whole world. But with the political, "New World Order" kind of thinking, where the love of money and power eclipses scientific facts, it's hard to believe that the needed change can happen anymore.

In "The Politics of Ecstasy," 1967, Timothy Leary said, "Hippy is an establishment label for a profound, invisible, underground, evolutionary process. For every visible hippy, barefoot, beflowered, beaded, there are a thousand invisible members of the turned-on underground. Persons whose lives are tuned in to their inner vision, who are dropping out of the TV comedy of American Life."

Being a hippie is all about a new way of thinking, working within a new belief system that transcends beyond the accepted norm of the times, beyond and above the political influences and stepping out of the accepted social customs, (like choosing to have long hair or wearing clothes that set you free, not clothes that advertise for and profit some big business).

In the late fifties and early sixties, it was okay to question authority and the established structure, not to destroy or to tear it apart, but to examine and take from it, the good stuff; being kind and charitable, to treat all with the same respect and honor, to take care of each other, nurturing and celebrating the solid values of our families, and in the end, discarding the "every man for himself" way of thinking, and hey, forsaking the ineffective and mean-spirited materialism doesn't mean you need to throw all your possessions away, I like my stuff too, but in truth, do I need all my stuff? And we need to somehow break free of the archaic inequality ways of thinking, where, for whatever justifiable reasoning, one people believes they are better than another, where the white privileged feel they are entitled to more than people of colour, where civil rights are fine and good as long as they don't get in the way of the favored, the elite, the advantaged, go to the front of the line to get their more-than-fair share first.

And by working within that new hippie belief system; by what we believed to be true, there was a hope that in time we might eventually change the world. This reexamination stretched beyond class definitions, into our spiritualities, into our government as well as other world governments, into the possibility of world peace, of cre-

ating equitable lifestyles in third-world countries by freeing and elevating them in their circumstances, and into our homes where people could transcend past some of the perpetuated flaws of the family structure as we knew it to be. All with a hope of change for the better of all mankind around the world.

But because most of these factions or authoritative establishments continue to maintain their own agendas of power to exercise dominion over others, even to the point of destroying people's lives, or sending them to their deaths, as the establishment did with other people's children during the Vietnam war, while keeping their own children out of harm's way, our only tool of recourse for survival was and still is to establish and maintain this new belief system which not only gives us a sense of purpose, but empowers us as a whole.

In the true spirit of the Hippie Movement of the sixties, and the philosophies that were created or reengineered back then, to hopefully learn from the mistakes of the past and rise above the conflicts of wars from country, class or religion, it was our hope to get beyond the petty differences and stalemates to usher in a brave new world.

The true Hippie transcended beyond the "free love" philosophies that teenagers epitomized to get stoned or laid, and the true Hippie did have morals and ethics that defined a certain belief systems. But the Hippies were unable to unite to overthrow the system since they refused to build their own power base. There was a hope that we, the Hippies of that day, would change the world, through gentle persuasion, to make the world a better place.

And time went by and our movement seemed to diminish, maybe even disappear, as members of our movement were seduced by the very authority, they were working to change. And unfortunately, after forsaking their own beliefs, eventually worked their way into positions of authority and power but did not carry their freak flag high anymore. All through the 80s and 90s there were small pockets of resurgence, as the inner force of the movement seemed to take some holds here and there, but money talks and poor people still walk as influence and greed enveloped and consumed the good parts of those once-well-intended individuals.

The way of the hippie was contrary and opposed to all the totalitarian hierarchical authority structures that worked to oppress, but new dominions had the ability to minimize their progress because they were and now continue to be against the Hippie ideals of peace an love and of the standards of freedom from oppression and an end to inequity. This was, and still is now, why the "Establishment" feared and suppressed the Hippie movement of the '60s—it was a revolution against their established controlling order, that was working for them and helped them maintain their power.

And now, because most of these factions or authoritative establishments continue to maintain their own agendas of power and control to retain command capability, authority, control and dominance over others, there is a sadness that our brothers and sisters that we inadvertently put in control, have now sold out to the highest bidder.

Decision-making processes to initiate societal change requires a solid foundation of willing individuals to accept change and through scientific knowledge, fix things. That being said, it is now more important than ever to advance and communicate research in this field in order to stir the public discussion into the "right" direction, namely real environmental awareness.

Side Note:

It is for this sadness that I document this song. It was for these brothers and sisters who still need to remember where they came from and in a hopeless hope of them recommitting themselves to the ideals they started out with; that they believed so fervently in. They need to understand that we can still make a difference and we can still save the planet.

Another Side Note:

We're not doomed. With every new climate movement, new clean-tech startup or new scientific publication, the ability for sustainable change gets stronger.

A recently released years-long research project simulates a global pathway towards 100% renewables across all energy sectors, bearing a clear and powerful message: a global energy transition, which is at the core of real climate action, is not only technically feasible but also cheaper than our current energy systems.

"Our planet will survive, no matter what happens. The question remains how many animal and plant species will survive the mass extinction caused by humankind." — Prof. Dr. Christian Breyer.

Yet Another Side Note:

Originally when I engineered this album, for reasons lost to me now, I put this poem third in line, behind, "*I'm Tempted.*" Arguably, "I'm Tempted" is a great song in it's own right, but for all given purposes, "*What's Happening Now?*" should have been in the second position, well if you've been keeping up, you must know by now how I feel about song positioning and moreover how I feel about the song in the second position, but to me, "*What's Happening Now?*" is probably the best song on the album. With its emotionally moving but distressing poetry and its heart-rending melody,... oh, and the way the words are meticulously voiced; this arrangement remains to be one of my best works and favorite compositions of all time, and that is saying something. So, when it came time to publish this album, I took the liberty (as is my right as creator as well as the engineer of the album), of putting this song in its rightful place; as *the second position* song.

I'm Tempted

(1998) – This scenario was taken from real-life situations and interactions within two different office environments, experienced first at the Washington State Parks Department facilities and continued when I got hired at the college, (mostly up in the puzzle palace of general administration, facility management and the personnel department in building 25), through interactions with faculty, administration and staff that I was associated with. In both places, sexual attractions for unmarried people to other unmarried people, married people to unmarried people, or married people to other married people ran amuck.

Politically correct or erroneous relationships flourished and the lure along with the excitement of enticements that lead to temptations were ongoing everywhere.

According to the Association for Marriage and Family Therapy, "Infidelity is one of the most common presenting problems for marriage and family therapists. It is devastating to relationships and can be one of the more difficult problems to treat."

As a happily married man, I am committed to remaining faithful to my wife. That means I have to constantly evaluate my thoughts. I know that inappropriate relationship temptation is not the only illicit allure on the job, lots of people struggle with other problems, like gossip or compromising your beliefs, or theft, or lying, and many other avoidable behaviors. It was my hope to capture the feel and mindset of someone who is in the position of being married, hopefully happily married, maybe has kids and in general, has no intention of straying from the nest.

But then it happens, that certain *other* arrives—is everything else the significant other is not; and maybe more. And he is driven to this point of questioning his own sacred relationship and circumstances. And then ultimately realizes the life they have worked on for so many years would be ruined with this one simple compromise.

Taken from the first-person perspective, beginning with simple infatuation, the doubt, the melee of exchanged pleasantries, the discovered common interests and then the realization that their whole world is now in certain jeopardy as they become tempted. And they realize there are grave and unalterable consequences to every word or action from that moment on and the possibility of a significant moral failure that would only hurt everybody in their life.

A Chance

(1998) – In love and the affairs of the heart, there is always an element of hope. In March of 1998 my daughter Lori decided to leave everything behind, including Ty, her boy friend of four years,... and she moved to San Diego. This sudden move of independence upset all of us, not the least, Ty, who was thrown off balance by the whole thing, but then he found that Lori was also breaking up with him.

Then one fall evening I got a call from Lori. She was real upset because Ty had called and declared that he was *now breaking up with her* and was severing the whole relationship. I didn't know there was a difference between her breaking up with him and him breaking up with her, but there obviously was.

Lori, Stephen, Liz and Me
Photo Taken 1998
about the time Lori got back from California

Not long after, an emotionally drained Lori suddenly showed up at the home and stayed with us there for a while. (She kind of took over Stephen's room from him, but he didn't complain).

She realized that she had made a mistake and wanted to try to re-build things but by now, Ty, not only wasn't interested, he was annoyed that she felt she could come back at any given time and rekindle a love that she extinguished.

We went through a terribly depressing, mourning period, where nothing could make Lori feel good again. She despaired in her big mistake and only wished she could turn things around.

Of course, this was my opportunity to document her sorrow in a poem, which I wrote over the course of a week and then recorded, about a month later. Lori cried when she heard the recording and asked me for a copy of the words, and after I printed it off for her, she hung the lyrics up in her (Stephen's) bedroom.

Side Note:

When this whole episode began, I was extremely worried for Lori and her, "wild child" posture and attitude. I was concerned that she was being influenced by a bad crowd, (of which, Lori never talked about but I still believe to be true), that she and that most, if not all, of her foot-loose-and-fancy-free gang were on some crazy new drugs,... and I guess deep inside I was worried that maybe she was involved in some weird cult,... after all, she was now in San Diego, the infamous city where just months earlier, in March 1997, a religious group called "Heaven's Gate," founded on a belief in unidentified flying objects, advocated an extreme self-renunciation to the public at large and exploded into public awareness following the suicide of 39 of its members in a suburb of San Diego, California.

And of course, I was worried. When I got the call from Lori asking if she could come back home to regroup, (maybe needing to be deprogrammed, I didn't know), I was elated,... and it was really nice of Stephen to give up part of his turn to have his own bedroom, but being thoughtful and considerate has always been a prize attribute of Stephen's.

Anyway, when she did arrive home, Lori and I talked about a lot of things; regret, her disappointment with how things turned out, she apologized for her flippant conduct and dismissive manners to her mother and father, and her actions that led to her loss of a wonderful guy, but she never told me what drove her to sever her ties and go to San Diego, nor did she ever relate to me or her mother what she was doing down there. And maybe I was wrong in my approach not to insist on details, but my prayers had been answered and I figured if she ever wanted to talk about that episode in her life, I would be ready to listen,... and neither I, nor as far as I know, Diane ever broached the subject again.

Move On

(1998) – In love and the affairs of the heart, there is always an element of hope, but there is also the element of reality check that, when love is gone and there is no hope of reviving it, prudence and practicality almost demands that a person eventually cut their losses and move on.

By November of 1998, my daughter Lori stabilized a bit more after her breakup,... and with phone calls and letters, she made numerous attempts to rekindle the flame that would probably never be revived, including going to the bars he frequented, showing up at his games, (he was now coaching the freshman football team for Shelton High School), and she even socializing with their loyal friends, (who would always let her know how much she had hurt him),...

One day she told me that she had finally taken off their ring and now it was put away in a dresser drawer. She said that for the most part, she was over him and ready to move on. I knew that this was probably not true, but it did give me an excuse to write the words to this poem to create this song—some of the words to this poem are direct quotes from conversations with her around that time.

Side Note:

Due to the dynamics of certain individuals and couples, some relationships are meant to end up being star-crossed affairs—this relationship was one of those. I never truly believed that she was over him, but I played along for Lori's sake. Fact is, I don't believe she has ever gotten over him—and although she now has a boyfriend of sorts, the fact that she still talks about him, all the time, hints that she will probably never be over him, and like an obsidian-chipped arrowhead piercing her heart, a piece of him will remain in her forever.

For You And I

(1998) – In love and the affairs of the heart, there is always an element of hope, but there is also the component of other's considerations, and when love is scrutinized and analyzed by too many for too long, it begins to just look wrong. Sometimes Love itself is seen best by those lovers who step back for a moment to see the whole picture of what their love truly is.

Even though it was apparent that the relationship between Ty and Lori was over, all the while there was a sort of hope floating in the air,... and in the heart of that hope, that maybe things could change and get back to the way they used to be, cane this song.

One night I was talking to Lori and she related her concerns that even if they were to get together again, things could never be the way they were before because their collective friends had taken sides and had already determined who was at fault, and therefore, Lori could never be accepted by them again.

Side Note:

Lori talked about going somewhere else to start over and have a second chance for a new life. This idea intrigued me and became the basis for this song. The simplicity of the words and chords also helped make this one, my second favorite for this album.

Another Side Note:

At the time all this drama and these episodes were happening, Chet was very busy at being in Junior status at the University of Washington, working on dual Bachelor's Degrees; one in Business Administration with concentration in Information Systems and another in Environmental Health and hoping to be admitted to the University of Washington's School of medicine.

I went to a football game in the Huskie stadium where Brock Huard was quarterback, and man did he have huge guns for arms and wow, could he throw the long, accurate pass. During halftime, Chet and I talked about Lori and

Ty and Chet was sad about how things had turned out,... it was a couple minutes later as the band was leaving the field that Chet turned to me and said, "It may be too late for Lori."

Somewhere Else

(1998) – As I was engineering the song placements for this album I came up a couple of minutes short of the 45-minute format that I always tried to maintain for my albums.

To me it always seems that where you are is where the action is not, and it always looks like things are happening somewhere else,... and sometimes that is true,... there is something wired differently in the minds and hearts of those who always want more, somewhere else,... and as long as happiness looks like it can only be found somewhere else, it can never be where you actually are.

Side Note:

After running away from Se- nior for the last time and we had moved to New Jersey, I was in an all-new state of mind. I was no longer under the oppression of that stepfather,... I was again able to think of myself as valuable, not just a burden to my mother, and in fact I was once again elevated by my mother to be the oldest male influence of the home front, and I was 18, getting thoughts of what I needed to do to eventually go off on my own.

And I had been so long under the tyrannical subjugation of Senior that I was having a hard time just finding out how to get my footing on who and what I should be. And I found myself gazing out the window of whatever vehicles I was traveling in, wondering what was going to happen next but moreover how would I adjust now that I'm somewhere else.

Another Side Note:

And now I was in New Jersey, (Browns Mills, which is in the center of Fort Dix), and I was adjusting to a lot of new things.

Pemberton Township High School
Annual Photo – 1968

I may have mentioned that I flunked the third grade, (maybe more on that story in a different book), I was between a year or a year and a half older than all my classmates and now, especially because I was in a new school, Pemberton Township High School, I was nervous. For the first time, (and only time), in my life I was about to experience desegregation, which is the process of ending the separation of two groups, usually referring to races. Because the student body of Pemberton Township was close to Ft. Dix and their soldiers and to the Maguire Air Force Base with their Air Force crew, maybe half of the student body were kids from the military and a large number of them were African Americans.

In truth, from my experiences working in the Job Corps two years earlier with African American youth that came from poor and underprivileged homes in the Portland area, I was mentally intimidated and scared to interact. But through choir, meeting some great personalities, (and some great voices), it was not very long before I was accepted and even friended by a lot of kids there.

My favorite story on this began a few weeks after I arrived at Pemberton Township High School and I ducked into a lavatory to take a leak. There was the sound of voices harmonizing that, upon my entering, stopped suddenly until, they saw it was me. There was five African Americans young men standing in a kind of circle in front of the huge mirror, that all turned to me, looking suspiciously until the largest boy, a guy named Barrett, that stood six-foot five and probably weighed over 220 pounds looked over at me and smiling, said to the group,

"Hey, this is Chesley. He's in Choir with me. He's a tenor." That was the first time I was ever identified in such a positive account and depicted as a person of music. Immediately they turned back to each other and continued singing, "Get Ready" by the Temptations, looking over at me like I was supposed to join in; and so, I did. Then after an argument over what to do next, they broke into their acappella version of "I Can't Help Myself" by the Four Tops. It was there that I learned the lyrics were "Sugar pie, honey bunch," and not "Sugar pie, honey bun." Anyway, I was so thoroughly caught up in the harmony and the acoustics that could only be found in a large school bathroom, that I had lost track of time and the buzzer went off telling me that we were all gonna be late for class.

Thanks to Barrett, I was given a kind of interracial free pass, and I was well received by all my classmates, but especially and what meant a lot to me, I was now accepted as a brother by the African American boys and girls at that school.

Yet Another Side Note: So, to start with, I was shy of about three and a half minutes to reach my goal of 45 minutes for this album, "Too Hard." At first I thought to just create an instrumental piece and just have some guitar chords (the guitar chords that are in fact, in this song, "Somewhere Else"), and I thought to embellish those chords with some piano music. But after practicing the chord progressions a few times, words came out, a poem materialized, to eventually become the lyrics to this song. And so, in the bargain, I recorded this song a little later that night.

Funny thing is; after I gave my friend, Ken, this album to listen to, he acknowledged that this very song was one of his favorites. I did not tell him that the words to the poem were written, and the music was composed, all in about 35 minutes.

Walk On

(1998) – Consequences for stupidity can be hard. I think there is a time to stand and there is a time to walk on; exercising fight or flight. I wrote a song years ago called, "I Can't Walk Away" from the, "That's America For You" album, which reflected the attitude of the boy pinned up against the wall and making the decision that it was time to stand your ground, even if it came to the probability of fighting.

But wait! It also occurred to me that there is another option, not any easier choice but certainly a direction and alternative of possible less resistance but with different consequences.

I thought that the idea of running away or stepping out of a volatile circumstance could be just as right as standing your ground, depending on the extenuating circumstances. From those ideas this poem was written and eventually the song was created.

Side Note:

When I was 14 my mother reconciled and once again, reunited with Senior and we moved back to Glendora, (as maybe mentioned previously), into the same trailer park but into a different trailer. Prior to returning to California, I had been going to a Parochial school that was maintained by Roman Catholic parishes that provide instruction based on sectarian principles but had an entirely different way of teaching. (More about that, maybe later). Because I was returning to a public school (mostly because Senior did not want to pay for our education), I was coming into a whole different system of learning with all new classes, and because I was starting there at Goddard Junior High mid-year in January, there were a lot of adjustments to acclimate and accustom myself to.

I'm not sure things are the same as they were in the sixties, but in those days, as previously mentioned, there was a pecking order that could not be avoided without a sizable amount of shame and embarrassment heaped upon you. When you purposefully backed down, or out of a fight that you had been "chosen off" from, you were branded a coward, and talk in Junior High could be brutal; causing you endless humiliation, indignity as you were branded.

Me at Goddard Junior High - 1964

First day at Goddard Jr. High; January something, it was cold, even for Southern California. I was keeping a low profile; keeping Richie, my best friend and brother, in my sights and trying to get through that day.

It was lunchtime, I was in the outdoor covered commons, buying a bag of "Wampums" (kind of like Fritos), from a vending machine and someone came up from behind and grabbed the stocking cap off from my head. I turned around to see three other eighth graders smiling as the fourth put my cap on his head. As I reached for it, he grabbed the hat and threw it to another kid who thought the game of "keep away" would be a good game to play before the next class. After being the monkey in the middle for too long, when the hat was passed to the guy that had originally took it, I quickly pushed him up against the vending machine and took the hat back. Not amused but embarrassed, the said, "Today; after school."

I paid no attention to the threat and went about the rest of my school day. But as I got on the school bus to take me home, this kid and two of his friends got on after me and with a stink eye, let me know I was in for it. I secretly but desperately hoped that the other boys might just get off before my stop, but no, they waited till I got off and followed after me. At that point I was directed that we would fight in the schoolyard of the Bidwell Elementary School across from the Belle Acres Trailer Park that I now lived it.

A crowd gathered around, with only Richie on my side, as I considered the options and consequences of the disgrace and dishonor that I might endure at the expense of running away. But there was no time for running away because the fire of determination in the other guy's face burned bright as he hurriedly and unexpectedly popped me in the face with a quick jab. I was reeling as I stepped back, and his crowd cheered Brandon on. But as Brandon moved in to punch me again, I took my left foot and quickly planted it on his face, pasting his nose. Surprised and hurt, Brandon stopped advancing; that was until his crowd of friends egged him on to get back in there, insisting, that I was a dirty fighter to use my feet, and they reassured him that he could take me. As he moved in cautiously, I kicked Brandon again in the face, this time even harder than the first time. His nose started to bleed and he looked back at me with panic and fear. I could tell the fight was out of him, but Brandon was still being egged on by a now larger support group, including a much older, larger high school boy wearing a Black and red Glendora High School varsity letterman jacket with a football emblem on his big "G" letter. This was Brandon's big brother, who yelled playfully to Brandon to get in there and kick my ass. As I went to kick Brandon again, he grabbed my foot with both hands and lifted my leg up, causing me to lose my balance, but as I was falling, I somehow readjusted my weight and landed on both feet, looking like I was very athletic and had intended to make the move. Brandon, now a bit revitalized, stepped forward to throw a punch at me in the face but I quickly bent backwards, which minimized the impact of his punch. I quickly returned with a swift right to his chest and another left to his face which ended up hitting him in his temple.

"Hey." I said, with heavy breathing, "I don't want to fight you." I stepped back about a yard and continued, "This is really stupid to be fighting over my hat."

I could tell the fight in the other boy had departed and the fire in his eyes was out. I knew he was hurt; in the chest, to the temple of his head, there was a dark redness around his right eye and his nose was still bleeding.

He looked back at his big brother, almost pleadingly, but his brother glared back as if to say, you got to finish him. Brandon turned back to me and mechanically lurched forward, but I stepped into the close space between us, getting so close to him that he couldn't land a punch. And then I wrestled him to the ground. Even as he struggled to gain control, I pinned him down and said cautiously, "I don't want to fight anymore." As Brandon continued to struggle to break free I added, "We don't have to do this anymore."

I felt his body go limp as if to say, "Okay. Let's stop fighting."

As I got off him, I was guardedly watchful that he wouldn't try something like a sneak attack, but he did not. Instead, he got to his feet and was dusting himself off when his older big brother stepped forward, and as he was taking off his letterman jacket, said to me, "Okay, you want to fight dirty with my brother, now you have to fight me."

My heart sank. My adrenalin had run its course and my body and all my energy was spent. "I didn't want to fight your brother in the first place." I spoke. And, "This isn't a fair fight."

The older brother looked around as if to find support or validation from the crowd for him to continue, but from the looks on most of the faces in the multitude, they did not seem to encourage him, seemingly to side with me.

In his hesitation and reluctance to get the fight going, I ran to the five-foot chain-link-school fence and quickly scaled it with one leap to the top and a follow through push to the other side. Looking through the fence from the other side, I motioned for Richie to meet me at our hiding place.

After my swift exit, the older, larger high school boy smiled slyly back at me as if to say "You're lucky you're on that side of the fence." And as the throng was congratulating Brandon and his older brother for vanquishing the dirty fighter, my eyes met up with Brandon's, whose face and demeanor, now recovered from the fight, seemed to say, "I'm sorry we had to do this."

I turned and ran speedily away, as if to convey a message that I was scared or afraid that more fighting might occur, which I felt would help the two brothers to save face as the unfair rebel was vanquished. Five minutes later I was walking with Richie down the street to our new trailer as he retold exaggerated accounts of what had happened; with me as the hero and winner of the fight.

The next day at school there were many different versions of what went on, which surprised me because I knew Richie wasn't telecasting what he experienced. And the other guy? We did not become good friends, but we were not enemies either, instead there was a mutual respect we had for each other. He respected the fact that I did not try to inflate my version and I respected the fact that neither did he. And... because of the fight I did not have to prove myself again. I did have a few other fights, but not with him and not to have to prove myself again.

69

- 41 - KEEP ON THINKING
FREE - 1999 -

70

NOTES ABOUT THE COVERS

Notes On The New Cover:

This was the eighth album I got published and the fourth to get an all new cover design.

I was getting better with software called GIMP and decided to make a collage of different but diverse items.

Keep in mind I had already been turned down on other covers so I wanted to make this unique. And with the colourful lettering, it made this cover look like a circus poster and with the huge elephant and the webbed squid, I really liked the way that it turned out.

Notes On The Original Covers:

It still sends chills inside to think that that man was hanging by that rope over a hundred feet in the air, never mind that the picture was taken in 1928.

Back cover was a political look at the idea of trying to keep on thinking free in a partisan world that wants to direct you to where it wants you to be.

71

KEEP ON THINKING FREE

Keep On Thinking Free
Invisible
Talking To The Dead
That Was You
What If ?
This Is Her Time
Lost To Me
Do It For Them
It Was My Choice

72

Keep On Thinking Free

OK, so what just happened there?
You were left alone holding the knife.
And who said things would turn out fair
when you entered into the walks of life?
But don't despair and don't give in,
use your head, know what you believe.
Be calm, collected from within
and try your best to keep on thinking free.
Keep on thinking free.

When they hit you from behind
thinking they'll break you by and by,
hold on to your presence of mind
and forge ahead beyond their lie.
Though trials begin to weigh you down a
lways question and test authority.
And when they power-trip you around,
smile back at them and keep on thinking free.
Keep on thinking free.

They want to subjugate your heart,
command, then manage, then control.
And they will tear your good world apart
and never give up until they own your very soul.

OK, things didn't turn out right
and your life seemed to somehow fall through.
In the end it's really just a state of mind
and it's all still really up to you.
You know, it makes them angry and annoyed
when they realize the strengths they see,
that you comprehend the games they play
but look forward and just keep on thinking free.

Keep on thinking free.

Yeah; keep on thinking free.

73

Invisible

Where they come from or go;
no one of certain grace would ever know.
They phase in their own space;
another plane, a place where most never go.
Fraught with mystery and enigma;
fueled with disdain and an uneasy fear,
they just arrive; do what they do and then quietly disappear.

They're invisible;
unseen, untouched, unhealed.
Invisible; exposed and yet concealed.
Invisible, in a dimension of their own.
They who walk among us; kind of familiar,
and yet unknown.

They are there in all the schools
sitting in the back without words to speak.
They're on the job right next to you,
they are the gears that never seem to squeak.

They are the quiet, silent ones
that at all costs avoid making a scene.
How can so many walk around and interact
without being seen?

They're invisible;
unseen, untouched, unhealed.
Invisible; exposed and yet concealed.
Invisible, in a dimension of their own.
They who walk among us; kind of familiar,
and yet unknown.

Too many faces without names,
that walk their lives in search of relevance.
Too many contradicting factors,
voices urging them that make such little sense.
They shift between two different worlds
yet not a part of either's loss or gain.
If you could gaze deep within their eyes
you might see something of their pain.

They're invisible;
unseen, untouched, unhealed.
Invisible; exposed and yet concealed.
Invisible, in a dimension of their own.
They who walk among us; kind of familiar,
and yet, unknown.

74

Talking To The Dead

Walking through the cemetery stepping over old gravestones
that mark the resting place of someone's buried bones.
Sitting on summer-dry grass in this perfect forest lawn,
remembering some really good days, from a past now long gone.

It's quiet here; far from the noise and the turmoil just outside.
It's peaceful here far from the war that can never be denied.

Here am I, paying respects from the ramblings in my head;
like they are standing next to me, I'm talking to the dead.

Many years have passed and time moved on
as seasons changed the scenes
to help me heal from such a wound as your passing did to me.
It is easier to speak of such to the family and friend
but the pain that will never go away will be with me to the end.
Still, I feel a kind of contentment like a presence is near by
listening with certain true intent to remarks and feelings of mine.

From the demeanor comes consent
as if in agreement to all I've said,
reassuring me that it's quite alright
to be talking to the dead.

Is it the asymmetry of an unbalanced man
that speaks out to the air?
What harm to others is he who believes in something
more than nothing there?
It matters not. I'll not be stayed from my small faith or belief,
that carries me and comforts me in my time of joy or grief.
There are days I'm miles above things,
there are other days that I fall,
and life is too short for me to think
that I might understand it all.
No, they're there. I know it;
envisioning conversation in their stead

waiting for me; hoping that I'll be
talking to the dead.
They're standing next to me
as I'm talking to the dead.

75

That Was You

That was you there; in my life years ago.
In the dawn of a love; we had so far to go.
Egos contrasted us like the sun and moon
and it was over far too soon.
life was yours and mine; freewheeling, loose and fast,
as we ran through life like every day would last.
And one day the union burst like an over-filled balloon
and it was over far too soon.

When two are busy being two, joining never comes to pass.
Why is it that love sometimes lacks a strength to last?
That was you though; that fueled my sweetest dreams,
and things never quite were the way they looked or seemed.
Without us knowing why, we ran out of growing room
and it was over,...

That was you here for a short time in my life,
and for what love we shared, everything was fine,
but with two without a plan, things were always kind of doomed,
and it was over far too soon. It was over far too soon.

76

What If ?

Is it something that just happens, and who knows what to do,
when that something that has meaning
falls there right in front of you?
Does it have to make sense to have relevance in your life?
Why couldn't it just happen, like a love at first sight?
What if,...
What if ?

Like seeing that someone special for the very first time
who is walking down the street, not paying you any mind?
It could take place so fast, just here and gone and then;
you wonder what took place, and would it happen again.
What if? What if,...
What if ?

They might look at each other as they pass on the street,
and for a few magic seconds their eyes just somehow meet.
There's a kind of recognition, a fleeting hope left on,
then as quickly as it began, the special moment is gone.

But to never to know?... well that is the weight
that must be carried for the rest of your days.
To never know the tender concern,
the touch of the heart and the passion in burn.

At times you might think to yourself,
if I'd only stopped and turned around,
or if I'd just showed some interest
when those words could not be found
and it'll always haunt you,
because it was there and you just let it go.
And through all the happenings in your life
justifying all the wrong from right
the real torment to the soul is never to know.
What if,...
What if ?

77

This Is Her Time

It's early morning,
she moves softly past quiet rooms that lay asleep.
Finding herself alone,
she ponders over her coming day to keep.
As the dark of the evening surrenders to the light
she calmly sits and reads.
Then, in reflection, she plans directions,
how to meet her family's needs.

This is her time -
mostly uninterrupted by everybody else.
This is her time.
These are the moments that she saves for herself.

There is a need
that softly calls to her to change her course,
and she knows in time she will have to give into its force.
But for now, and here; she maintains without any release.
She has this minute to continue her quest in peace.

This is her time;
just a little bit far and away from everyone else.
This is her time.
These are the moments that she saves out for herself.

In a moment,
the kids will rise and run to catch a bus for school.
In a moment, the house will be alive with everyone to rule.
Hours from now
she'll be beyond this moment, working hard and fast.
Hours from now she will be too busy to think of dreams so vast.

But this is her time;
to consider and contemplate everything else.
This is her time.
these are the moments that she saves for herself.

78

Lost To Me

Lost to me
with remnants left of other times that used to be.
Like photographs in boxes that I'll never see,
I know they're there but I can't bare to re-live the scenes,
for now, it's lost,...

Gentle tears are wiped away so no one knows my hidden fears
and guilts and pains that I've held inside for too many years.
I looked around but all I found was that you're not here,
you're lost to me, my dear.

I reflect, what might I have done to effect a change somehow,
but it's all so academic, as I live with the here and now.
Faith can be so hollow with so much time passed,
you start to believe there is no use in trying
for you can't change anything.
Then it's all too much and I just give up to that reality,
knowing you're lost to me.
Lost to me.

79

Do It For Them

There's a choice we all have to make,
but there's a heart that might break and that's a chance you take.
And there, after you're left alone,
it's just gets harder to go out from that comfort zone.

You know what the right thing to do
but it's so hard to follow things through.
So you do it, one more time again, forget yourself,
to do it for them.

A simple voice whispers from the right
saying, "It'll be alright to let things go for just tonight."
But you can't waste even one day
for too quickly they stray; grow up and move away.

All they want is a part of you, right now,
to build and bridge all the memories time will allow.
The obligation is worth the precious gem,
to forget yourself, and do it for them.

Beyond your needs, and personal dreams
there's no hesitation; hardly any doubt.
The more you behold what you do for them all,
the more you're assured what it's all about.

There's a path set before you each time,
and either you fall out of line or step up in outrageous rhyme.
And here, after your sacrifice,
it feels good, it feels nice knowing you did what was right.

And after all, as you carry it all through
thinking, it was what you wanted someone to do for you.
This purpose needs no definition; not now or then,
you just forget yourself, and do it for them.

Forget yourself, and do it for them.

80

It Was My Choice

There may not be much more to see,
and this may be as good as it's ever going to be,
but from all I've done, I still know I'm the one
that walked all the paths set in front of me.

When things fell to the bad or unfair,
It wasn't fate or bad luck that led me there,
it was how I seized the adversity
that determined what fell into my care.

. It was my choice all along,
to flow with the good and learn from the wrong,
it was my free agency it was all up to me;
it was my choice

In the beginning it was all kind of like a game
knowing where to hide and who to blame,
when things got hard or I took things too far
and I'd wonder how to slip away.

After a while there was a particular role,
to be maintained to have control,
in the struggle to know, how and where to go
when I'd end up down here in the hole.

It was my choice all along,
to flow with the good or learn as things went wrong,
it was my free agency; it was always up to me;
it was my choice.

From the pursuing of my dreams to how my time was spent,
through setbacks and progress choosing the directions that I went.
When I placed my needs and all my energies
For the most part, in the final end,
it was my choice.

All along, it was my choice.
to flow with the good or learn when things went wrong,
it was my free agency it was all up to me;
it was my choice.

81

MEMOIRS & NOTES - 41 - 'KEEP ON THINKING FREE'

Keep On Thinking Free

Besides the bean counters in the puzzle palace that were assessing the necessity of keeping me on and me still being the engineer of this family locomotive, pulling this long set of boxcars, as I may have mentioned earlier, I was forced to move over to the new Information Technology Building 34,...

and I was now working in the computer labs out of the Computer Resource Center to assist students with their homework as they used computers and software to get their homework done. I adjusted. I worked directly with Bob as we assisted the running of the three computer labs. Then there was Jeans and Ferret; both feeling like their experience made them more qualified and they both assumed the un-official role of our bosses, especially Jeans, who had been a tech working from and managing the ongoing operations of the "dumb terminals" (terminals that depended on a host computer for its processing power), used by the data processing students that were taking classes and working on their computer data processing degrees.

Trouble came when the V.P. Mike B. assigned Ferret the job to be our immediate supervisor, (including Jeans). Jeans was jealous (but not openly) of Ferret getting the lead. Jeans did not like taking a second seat to someone he felt he was superior to and for that matter, in spite of the fact that he had taken a break from finishing his Computer Sciences classes at SPSCC and never got a degree, Jeans felt his knowledge and past experiences made him superior to everyone on campus that had anything to do with computers, including the instructors. (More on that maybe later).

Ferret and Jeans were both classified as "Computer Tech Two" classified employees. Bob was classified as a Computer Tech One, and I was classified as a Lab Assistant Two, not even classified as a computer tech.

It quickly became apparent that Ferret either decided to share his supervisory duties with Jeans or was just purposefully looking the other way and not really into doing his job. Jeans, who loved looking down on me condescendingly, was much more demanding than ferret and also much more critical of my work. And there was an inside joke between Jeans and Ferret that Bob and more especially me, were underling subordinates that needed to be watched. It was annoying that I was always the butt of some inside joke between them as they would make tiny implications on my computer incompetence and sheer ignorance.

After they settled in, Jeans and Ferret would spend most of their day sitting in an office drinking coffee and shooting the bull. And there were times like Friday mornings where they would wander around the campus, schmoozing, and they would attend every birthday or retirement gathering that they had caught wind of, as Bob and I held down the fort at building 34. I was reminded that there is more to life than what you do at work, but I couldn't see anything else at the time and I was stifled.

I had heard of an opening at TESC, (The Evergreen State College), doing the same work I was presently doing at SPSCC, and went over to apply. After spending three evenings filling out the usual state employee application forms, making sure I satisfied all the necessary requirements, I went back to turn it in. I handed the paperwork to one of the HR receptionists who thanked me as she briefly looked over the form. I was on my way out the double glass doors when she called me back and said that they could not accept my application because I didn't have a Bachelor's Degree. I explained that I had seven years' experience doing the job and that I could easily fill the position before she cut me short and reiterated that they only took applicants that had Bachelor's Degrees.

There was a lot of soul searching and family discussions about what I was going to do. I continued applying to other places and state agencies, but it just seemed like my options were few.

Meanwhile at work, Ferret decided to go elsewhere and left for a few weeks before returning again, only to end up two months later leaving SPSCC after all.

And then I was stuck with Jeans as my surrogate supervisor, who became verbally abusive with authority, often yelling about something I'd done only to find out that I hadn't done it after all. But like most bullies that are trying to compensate for their inadequacies in life outside their workplace, jeans never apologized for his continued blusterous rudeness behavior nor did his supervisor, Regina, who knew about his brash behavior, do anything about it. She feared him and let him do whatever he wanted.

Meanwhile, I decided not to let my work situation get me down and I pushed forward to see what I needed to do to getting my Bachelor's Degree at the Evergreen State College.

Side Note:

One of my favorite passages *"In The Beginning,"* from the 1969 Moody

Blues album, "*On The Threshold Of A Dream*," is from the song, "*In The Beginning*" by *Graeme Edge* which goes kind of like this:

> **Sentient Person:** I think, I think I am;
> therefore, I am; I think.
> **[Establishment]:** Of course, you are my bright little star,
> I've miles and miles of files,
> pretty files of your forefather's fruit,
> and now to suit our great computer, you're magnetic ink.
> **Sentient Person:** I'm more than that; I know I am,
> at least, I think I must be.
> **Sentient Person's Conscience Inner Mind:** There you go man,
> keep as cool as you can.
> Face piles and piles of trials with smiles.
> It riles them to believe
> that you perceive the web they weave
> and keep on thinking free."

And so it was that I wrote this song to bring me out of my mental slavery and deliver myself to a better thought and direction. And I would advise others (family and friends) to question what people say about them and evaluate, honestly, who and what they are. And, at all times, question authority no matter what; don't just trust them because they appear to know what they're doing or because they flaunt or appear to have some type of authority. Fight the man; fight the power.

Another Side Note:

In a very real way, I struggled with the composition of this poem, knowing that anyone who was familiar with the Moody Blues would instantly make the connection and therefore denounce, criticize or reproach me for my pseudo-plagiarism of that enlightening song that affected me so much at the time that I had first heard it, (1970). Funny thing is, I have little to no audience listening to my stuff so I shouldn't have worried, and there was only one person that made the connections and remarked about it; saying in a positive comment that he liked it and thought it was clever of me to create this song. And so it goes.

Invisible

(1999) – It is an intriguing thought that there is a whole sub-culture of people that we know little to nothing about. When Ben graduated from SPSCC, I went to his graduation ceremonies. A funny thing happened though, as the computer graduates came up to receive their certificates, there were a few students that I had never seen before. I know there are some students that have their own computers and that some people come in from another program from some other college and just finish up here, but these classes take at least two years to complete and sometime three, and there were four or five that I had never seen before.

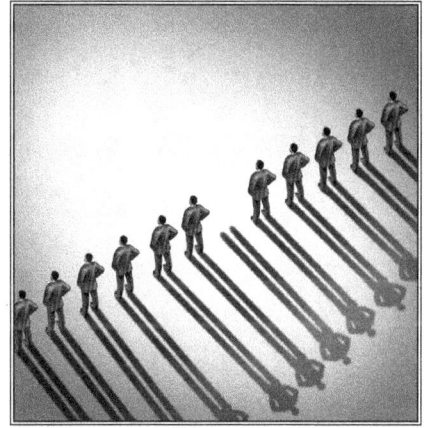

I know there are some students that have their own computers and that some people come in from another program from some other college and just finish up here, but these classes take at least two years to complete and sometime three, and there were four or five that I had never seen before.

This got me to thinking that these students were kind of invisible. I mean, they come to school, go to class, maybe even come into the labs and do their homework, but they interact on a minimal basis and come and go without being seen. I thought about the fact that I knew some of these kind of people in high school as well as at some of the other places I had worked. It was a good reason to write this poem and put music to it.

Side Note:

In 2001, during break time where we, the three of us were busy reimaging the computers for the next quarter, I was asked by the new VP to sing this song to a congregation of administrators, faculty and staff. When I told Coupe, my recently new lead person, he was livid. I don't think it was because he would miss my contribution because I had very little to do with the images till they were pushed out, but he did resent me being asked to bring my guitar and sing for the college while I was on the clock. I told him I would take a late lunch and it would only take five minutes to do the song.

When I got on the stage, I gave some background to the song and then played, "Invisible." It was surprisingly well received and people around campus talked about it for months afterwards. Meanwhile, it was 20 minutes from the time I left till the time I returned to my desk in building 34, but almost immediately, Coupe threw the door open to my office; angrily staring at me, fire burning in his eyes, and hardly containing himself, he yelled, "Where were you?"

I sheepishly told him where I had gone and that I had done it on my lunch hour. He glared at me for a long moment that I might feel a sense of guilt, (which I did), before he abruptly left to go to his office, and we did not speak to each other for a couple of days.

What If (Slight Visit)

(1999) – There have been times where I really like the concept of what I am doing with the music but for so many different reasons I feel

I need to do something over; tweak the words to fit the timing of the piece, change the tempo, (faster, slower, this happens a lot), different accents here or there, fall out of love for the creation; so many reasons. As you can tell from listening to this; there is a lot of energy and promise to the piece, but I had to start over because I changed the background guitar work. Still, this was too good to throw away and because it had such a good feel, I didn't want to lose the essence of this recording, so I engineered and recorded this little snippet of the piece and included it in the album, positioning it after the very somber but emotional song, "Invisible" and used this composition to life the listener's spirit. And, to kind of tease the listener with a hope of hearing more, knowing from the song titles that there may be more of the song to arrive after, "That Was You."

Talking To The Dead

(1999) – It was early summer and the warm evening breeze whispered over my face as I stood there looking at the grave marker that denoted the resting place of my son Christopher,

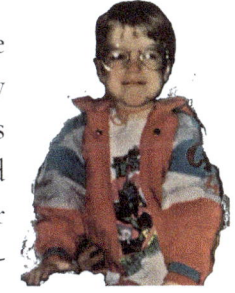

I was alone, well, not really alone, I was the only one there from my family, but there were many other people paying their respects to their relatives that had gone on. And as usual, I sat down and started talking to him. A man passed by looked over with a curious look and moved on. I thought to myself, "What's the matter, ain't you ever seen a person talking to the dead?"

The thought then occurred to me that maybe this wasn't a regular type thing and that maybe I was weird. I thought back at my days as a Funeral Director and Cemetery Sexton, trying to remember another time and place where I would be walking out in Forest Memorial Gardens to see and hear someone else speaking to their past on relative or friend. But no, I could not remember it ever happening and I was there for three years. But then I remembered a scene in the movie, "Shenandoah" where Charlie Anderson, (James Stewart) is seemingly talking to the headstone of his departed wife and says;

> **"I don't even know what to say**
> **to you any more, Martha.**
> **There's not much I can tell you about this war.**
> **It's like all wars, I guess.**
> **The undertakers are winning.**
> **And the politicians**
> **who talk about the glory of it.**
> **And the old men who talk about the need of it.**
> **And the soldiers,**
> **well, they just wanna go home,...**
> **I guess you're not so lonely any more,**
> **with Ann and James and Jacob.**
> **And maybe the boy,...**
> **You didn't know Ann, did you?**
> **Well, you'd like her,... You'd like her, Martha.**
> **Why, she and James are so much alike,**
> **they're just like,...**
> **No,... no,... we were never that much alike,**
> **were we Martha?**
> **We just sort a grew alike through the years,...**
> **But I wish,...**
> **I wish I could just know**
> **what you're thinking about it all, Martha.**
> **And maybe it wouldn't seem so bad to me**
> **if I knew what you thought about it."**

So, I pursued this thought to this song anyway. And we only guess and hope what spirits and angels on the other side are capable of. We don't know that they have been given permission and or a calling to stand on the other side of the veil or shroud and invisibly listen to us as we pour out our hearts to the troubles and sorrows that we're feeling. Or that they hear us and of our worries and disappointments that we're experiencing, and even if we can't see them standing next to us, perhaps they are listening to us as we express just how much they meant to us; how much we loved them but for whatever reasons, never got around to telling them. We can't see their faces when we tell them how much we miss them and what they meant to us. And I also think, what if they are there, standing next to us and we deny them the pleasure of our conversations; them missing the sweet pleasing sounds of our earthly voices? And what if we could get past the uncomfortable awkwardness of it all and not worry about what someone else passing by might think? What if it was always part of some, long forgotten eternal plan for us to find a comfort and solace by us, "Talking To The Dead?"

That Was You

(1999) – In those earlier days of youth, in my late teens, I was rather careless for the feelings of others, even for my loved ones, and I don't think I was alone; love for many others at that age could be rather self-centered and egocentric.

I was pursuing a girl in high school, I thought we were in love and I thought we wanted to eventually get married. I even chased her across the United States, and set up shop in the town she was living in. Unfortunately, when you are young, even though you feel you know what things are all about and how things will go, sometimes in the follow through, you find out you're wrong. I would like to think that we eventually broke up because her mother felt that her daughter could do better than the "work in progress" that I was, but maybe there was an undertow of realization where she felt that she was not intellectually or emotionally ready to handle a long-term relationship. I can only guess that because she was so self-absorbed, that when our relationship was condemned and brought to an end by her mother, it seemed that she just calmly moved on, but I don't know the full truth to that, and I probably never will. And, I know now that at that time and place in the past, where everything seemed so right, I was almost certainly guilty of some of those flaws, weaknesses, and shortcomings that I had been accused of having.

But for a while, a far too soon, sweet but, succinct while, we were both happy in that bond and connection we had for that relationship.

What If

(1999) – There have been many times in my life where I look back at something that happened or something that didn't happen years ago and I wonder, "What If?" I think about the fact that although I had many forks in the road and I could have ended up in many different circumstances, looking at those things from this side of the journey; I can see the way things turned out but I have to know that with just one different decision or one simple other choice might have led me to a whole different destination; I can only guess how otherwise things would have turned out.

Randomness, as we ordinarily think of it, exists when some outcomes occur haphazardly, unpredictably, or by chance. And as we try to understand philosophically how randomness still shapes outcomes, well, the basis for this poem is rendered.

Moreover, the real consideration of "what if" leaves the chance for love to come along wide open, and if you let love pass, you also open up other possibilities that may or may not affect the same outcome. But what if you let that chance for love pass? Are you then filled with regret and disappointment for the rest of your life?

These considerations go beyond this analysis when we think about the many possibilities of love at first sight and how that seemingly impossible interaction may lead to true love and eternal companionship. It all seemed a sobering thought and a good reason for me to write this poem and record this song.

This Is Her Time

(1999) –I got up one morning around 4:30 and there was Diane, sitting on the couch reading her scriptures and listening to the Mormon Tabernacle Choir, performing and singing, Handel's "Messiah." It looked rather boring to me, but she was very content to continue in this calm atmosphere.

As you may know by now, we have ten children, (most of the time not all of them are in the home at one time), and the chance for Diane to collect a semblance of peace and quiet is rare. It is good for her to be able to collect her thoughts and take some time for herself. Earlier on when we had less kids and seemingly more time to do what we wanted, there was really no time to ourselves then either. We would both just get back to whatever work or tasks that needed to be addressed at the time, and we would be entrenched in our day-to-day routines.

About two years ago, Diane started getting up early every morning for her prayer, the reading of her scriptures and then writing in her journal. It has become a special time for her when the kids are asleep, the house is quiet, and she can calmly collect her thoughts before the gradual or sometimes sudden wave of boys and girls getting up to go and do whatever is they need to do in their plans for the day.

As I stood there looking at Diane calmly writing in her spiral-notebook journal, the thought came to me that she was carving out a little bit of time at the expense of her otherwise valued and needed sleep. But through the contentment she seemed to have and the calmness in her manner, I thought, yeah, "This Is Her Time."

Lost To Me

(1999) – There is a fine line between concerned and obsessive, compulsive or neurotic, I'm not sure where that puts me. I think I know what you folks might be thinking, "This guy is obsessed with the loss of his son." And you may be right; it appears that I have gotten a lot of mileage from this subject, but from another perspective, these songs continue to be very therapeutic for my psyche and they help me to reach new or different levels of closure that otherwise I might not have achieved. Besides the fact that I may never really get over this anyway, there have been more than a few good poems and songs resulting from my grief, so I have felt that, to feel better, I might as well get out what I can.

Side Note:

As noted prior, I was devastated when my mother became gravely ill in 1996. I flew to Florida and stayed at my mother's house with my brothers and sister and used her place as a home base while we went collectively and separately to the hospital. My mother's husband, Ron, an alcoholic who had previously stopped drinking, fell off the wagon and was seemingly now drunk all the time. He was hardly ever at the hospital to visit mother, whose condition of emphysema complications from previous chemotherapy treatments worsened every day.

I was so happy to be able to be there with her and spend time visiting with her in her final days. At one time, when she was coherent and mentally sharp, I was hovering over her bed and she reached over and touched my face, smiled apologetically and said, "You need to get a haircut."

At the time, I was working at the college, managing my computer lab in building 31 and I had a lot of freedom that I had been denied by most of my past employments. One of them was me letting my hair grow out, and at this time, to a point where I had an eight-inch ponytail that I was very proud of.

I was not alone on campus with long hair, there were many staff members and even a few faculty members that had long hair.

Another Side Note:

When my mother had said that, I was reminded of another time; and please excuse me if you've read this story before, but it was during the 60s where, growing your hair out like the Beatles was very fashionable and I had made my attempt to do so. But unbeknownst to me, Senior had already told my mother that he didn't want any hippy living under his roof and he told her to have me get my hair cut,... and cut short.

And shortly afterwards, I found myself sitting on a stool as my mother did her best to cut my hair. I that knew there would be a loss, but I petitioned her to make it slight so I could still fit in at school. Oh, peer pressure. Mother acknowledged my requests to leave enough hair to save face with my friends and she talked calmly as she went about, cutting my hair, but covertly, she finished the haircut with the way that Senior had instructed.

Me, About the Time This Story Happened

If I would have been a more considerate son, I would have realized that is she had cut my hair any differently there would be hell to pay with Senior, who would take my haircut as an affront to his instructions and after his seventh glass of wine, would have laid into and given a physical beating to, not me, but to my mother who, like Jesus, had already taken numerous thrashings for my insurrections.

If I would have been a more understanding and compassionate son,

I would have looked at the finished product, as my mother stood there smiling affably, proud of the haircut that she had just administered, holding up a mirror for me to see and asking, what I thought or moreover, she asked if I liked it; and if I was more compassionate for my mother, I would have thanked her and accepted my fate graciously and said, "Yes." But I was a teenage boy that selfishly thought only of his own desires to fit in with the rest of the crowd. Instead, engrossed in my own selfish wants and viewpoints, I did something I had never done before; I talked back. Out of respect and love, I had never ever talked back to my mother. But in my anger, I looked up into my mother's face; a face that hoped for understanding, a face that pleaded acceptance and understanding, and then with a sharp intonation, I said, "No."

At first there was a quick sense justifiableness as I watched my mother's smile disappear from her face as I glared back at her in my supposed righteous indignation; that was, until my mother's eyes flashed with the realization of my repugnant ungratefulness and disrespect. Then she did something she had never done before or ever did again; she slapped my face.

It was not the shock of her hand as it left my face that hurt me, nor the pain of how my face was on fire from that sudden impact; the thing that wounded and injured me most that moment, and has remained with me to this day, was the sad hurt, disappointed look on my mother's face and the realization that I had purposefully and wickedly hurt my dear mother. This mother that had taken so many blows in the past from Senior, expressly for and in my behalf,... (and I have to admit she unfortunately, would take more abuse by the hands of Senior in the future because of my actions),... had sacrificed so much on my behalf.

And how dare me be so callous and thankless. But I was a stupid selfish teenage kid that could not see that, at the time, my mother had very little choice in the way that haircut went. And from that woeful look my mother cast, my heart fell and I was totally undone. I knew from that one, brief word, how much I had hurt her,... more than she could have ever hurt me. At that singular moment, all I wanted to do was to somehow take it all back. And if you were watching this like it was an episode in a movie, the mother and son would have reconciled with tears and hugs and then they would have been on their way to healing the wounds of mismanaged love. But this was not such a "*happily ever after*" moment,...

And I ran away, selfishly not caring about the ramifications for anyone but me. I stole a small kid's bike from the bike rack at the Bidwell Elementary School and rode it on the freeway adjacent to the traffic and got to Pasadena before I was run into a wall in an alleyway, then had to get picked up at the police department that evening by my mother. There were no words spoken until we got about two or three blocks from the house and after my mother pulled over, she looked over at me with concern in her face and said, "When we get home, don't say ANYTHING. You just go to your room and I'll do all the talking." She paused and looked away as she continued, "He's really mad."

It was at that moment the realization of my sin and the consequences thereof filled my whole being. "Mother, I'm sorry that,..."

"Don't." Mother interrupted, looking concerned as she started moving the car again to our fated destination. "Just go straight to your room when we get home and don't come back out."

As we entered the house, Senior was sitting there on a stool; a gallon of wine sitting on the counter, half drained. His eyes flashed at me as my mother, standing between me and Senior, ushered me to the hallway and away from him.

After I got to my room there were a lot of loud, harsh words shouted by Senior as mother's voice remained silent,... then there was a moment of silence and then a sound of a loud slap as Senior struck my mother. I then heard a quiet, almost inaudible but sickening wail of pain cry out softly by my mother as she absorbed the out-and-out force of Senior's assault for and in behalf of my iniquities. And then, like the awful debt had been paid for and amply satisfied, there was silence. After a long pause, from my bedroom door I could hear the heavy footsteps of Senior as he purposefully stomped to his room. I stood there at the doorway for at least another half an hour before I went to bed, lying there awake for hours, not able to sleep.

The next morning when I got up and went out to the kitchen, Senior was already gone to work and my mother was administering cereal to the kids. She looked over at me and seeing my guilt and shame, walked over to me and hugged me. As she looked lovingly down into my face, she gave me a sad but caring smile. Her left cheek was noticeably bruised as well as the bottom of her left eye. Tears filled my eyes as she let go of me and asked, dismissively whether I wanted a bowl of Cheerios or Wheaties.

Side Note To Another Side Note:

So, back to 1996, there I was, perched over my mother's hospital bed and she reached over and touched my face, smiled sadly, knowing it was her last days and wanting to put me more at ease, said, "You need to get a haircut."

After she drifted off to sleep, I went back to her house and looking in a phone book, found that there was a Cuban barber shop not more than five blocks away from mother's place in Homestead. So, later that day, in spite of some mild objections by my sister Mary, I made the trek and got my hair cut, but insisted that the barber, an older Cuban man with a never-ending smile, clip off my ponytail first.

When I went back to the hospital, I was excited to show my mother the haircut and I got the response I was hoping for. I even got a laugh when I pulled out a zip-lock baggie that had my ponytail in it,... and I still have that ponytail zipped and secured in a Shure microphone bag up on a shelf in my bedroom closet. And it is a reminder of the wonderful mother that I had, who showed me what a truly good, loving parent could be; my mother who is presently and will never truly be, "Lost To Me."

And Yet Another Side Note:

(dateline – November 24, 2020) Ironically as I am reviewing this entry my brother John; my oldest and dearest brother is in the hospital in Florida with failing lungs and is plugged in to a machine that is keeping him alive. From what I'm told, he will probably not make it through the day as the power of attorney person, Debbie, John's girlfriend is planning on having the machines turned off. And so, as thoughts and memories continue to linger in my heart, his mortal being is close to being, "Lost To Me."

Do It For Them

(1999) – It is good to recognize the importance of parenthood. You learn to love the ones you serve. I hope I don't paint a picture of some individual that is self-righteous or pretentious or arrogant or pompous as I approach the subjects of this poem.

In the simplest of perspectives, I hope to convey my convictions that the time you spend with those people in your home, your wife or husband, your sons and daughters; this quality time that you give to help council with, interact with, going to school and church functions, laugh with, cry with, playing games with, and even just watching TV with; these moments are some of the most important things you will ever do in your lifetime. As arduous as it seems now, as you are in the midst of maintaining the balance of family life, it comes and it goes as does the opportunities to interact with your children; they grow up and move out and have a life of their own, oh, so quickly.

Hey, seems superfluous to say that all we need is love but love is one of the foundational cornerstones of the family, and the strength of that foundation is the bond we share between each other.

I think it was Stephen that took this picture

Everything else; your work to support your family, your interactions with outside friends, all your hobbies and extracurricular activities; (your quest to do something with your talents), they all take a back seat to your family obligations. This poem reflects the need to give of yourself, your time, your talents and your love; sometimes at the most inopportune times, to fill all the needs that your family has. And then there's the little important things after spending time with them, and one of the best ways to show your kids that you love them is simply by telling them so. They love to hear you say "I love you," especially when you pull them in close and use their name to clarify just exactly who you're speaking to and why, and that bond, that love, is reinforced the more you articulate that love. And besides saying I love you, there are a few other things that help; everybody, especially children but also many adults want and need to be hugged, especially when you want to show them you love them, you're proud of them, you're happy for them, you're sad for them, you missed them, you are thankful for them, you appreciate them; hugs are good therapy.

For some reason, praise and compliments to one another doesn't seem to come naturally, but criticism of one another seems to come out effortlessly and instinctively. But, if I try, I find that there's a lot of good things going on around me that deserve compliments; little things that I can see, someone took a bit of time to create or to improve or to help out. Taking notice of the good you see in one another only fills your heart with joy, and in a family, acts of kindness is the standard to live by, not something that we are suddenly surprised by. Kindness starts from the top down. When our kids see Diane and I showing kindness to each other, as well as to others in the family, it is contagious and has a kind of domino effect. You always get more of what you affirm, whether it's positive or negative. Because of this, praise needs to be a regular part of a home. Yet when we're intentionally pointing out the good things happening in the home, and praising each other for the goodness they are and the good things they do, the outcomes are that those good things are more likely to continue.

And it is not an easy road to travel down when bad things happen or when you're pitted against doing what you want and having to do what needs to be done. That balancing act is never easy as unusual choices are faced and sacrifices need to be made. I know from experience that sometimes, the hardest thing you'll ever do is to let go of something that you wanted to do, but forget yourself and then, "*Do It For Them.*"

It Was My Choice

(1999) – I approached this poem from the viewpoint that all my life experiences have been governed by the fact that, whichever direction I went, as good things happened or as bad things came my way, ultimately whatever befell my outcomes, those resulting aftermaths, my misfortunes, or my providences, most of the time they were navigated by, and directions were determined by the choices I made. The uncertainty of not knowing the outcome of a choice is what fosters courage, giving us options or makes us anxious and afraid to make decisions.

When I was younger, I struggled over understanding fatalism or of me being a fatalist, which is someone who feels that, no matter what he or she does, the outcome will be the same because it's predetermined. There was always this uncanny certainty that my fate had already been laid out in front of me, and that I had no real control over what would happen.

The downside of that is that I always had this foreboding sense of being powerless to change things in and of my life or the world.

It was not my choice to go to school, let alone a Catholic school, and I was fated arbitrarily to be living in Iron Mountain Michigan, and it was my fate to have my mother divorce my father, and it was my fate to have my mother gravitate to someone like Senior, and it was my fate to have seven brothers and one sister, (I did not find out about my other two sisters in Oregon till I moved down on the farm in Oregon), and it was my fate to be introduced to and be baptized in the Catholic church.

But after a while, I began to question whether we were resigned to our own fates, or were able to use choices to create our own destinies. I finally began to believe that life was a delicate balance between the two. Fate would bring me opportunities, and my free will would determine whether or not I would take them. Maybe Fate was the destiny that was pre-planned for me, but it was up to me to do something with the good or bad that came my way. Still, choice was what I myself could decide or direct myself to do, from my own options, my choosing, and they were things that through choice, I could control myself.

In truth, most of the time my problems with choice stemmed from the actions and or reactions I decided to undertake. As many things were complicated by the fact that I always want to get the decision right, and to get it right from the start, yet I still found joy in the fact that I was the captain of my own mess.

Side Note:

Choice or agency or also referred to as free agency or moral agency, in the LDS Church, is explained as "the privilege of choice which was introduced by God the Eternal Father to all of his spirit children in the premortal state."

Anyway, I had fun with this song hoping to chronicle how I navigated through my life with good and bad choices, learning from the mistakes and reveling with the learned experiences, knowing, "It Was My Choice."

Another Side Note:

This recurring thought brings me a sense of comfort when it comes to my musical and poetic creations,... I can write and say whatever I want in my lyrics, and although it is my choice to keep the words fairly simple and clean, I feel that the reason swear words attract so much attention is that they invoke emotions and involve restrictions prohibitions, from aspects of our society that tend to make us feel distressed or awkward and uncomfortable. But I try to steer clear of using references to private parts, or bodily functions, or sensitive things like sex. I feel a sense of cleverness to be able to say what I want but cleanly. This is not just so as to appeal to a wider audience, (although, I have a six-year-old granddaughter that is reading my books), but moreover, whatever I'm writing at the time, I feel it is better to use a healthy vocabulary instead.

And then there's the music,... and I can go in any direction with my compositions,... and I don't have to compromise for and in behalf of some contractual agreements with a record company like Sony Music. It is my choice and pleasure to go in whatever direction I choose,... and I love that freedom.

82

❧

- 42 - RITES OF PASSAGE

- 1999 -

83

⟨❦⟩

NOTES ABOUT THE COVERS

Notes On The New Cover:

I loved the feel of the keys to the piano and the old grain of wood; not too unlike the player piano in the basement of the yellow house in Portland Westmorland area where I took my "next step" to learning how to play piano. I also liked the two favorite lettering fonts; Showcase Gothic angling out, with one of my favorite shades of blue, and my "Lord Baldwin" pseudonym using the Bellbottom laser font.

Notes On The Original Covers:

Front Cover: New York City, my guess early 1950s and arguably one of my rites of passage in 1968 when I made my first trip to "the City." I had been to the Port Authority a few times on my way to the Catskills, (the Concord Hotel), but it wasn't till later that my brother John took me into the city and showed me around a bit,... He took me to the Radio City Music Hall and then we went to a a cool place in the village where I saw Al Cooper in one of the small coffee shops there. I sat maybe five feet away from him and he was amazing.

Back cover, 1940 painting, "Old Age, Adolescence, and Infancy" (The Three Ages). By Salvador Dalí a master of double imagery and optical illusions.

84

RITES OF PASSAGE

Rites Of Passage
The First Day Again
Who Cares?
Love After Love After All
In An Instant
His And Hers
Mother-Child Lullaby

85

Rites of Passage

With balance and proportion, I was flowing with things
everything was fine, nothing to yield.
but I was there one minute and then suddenly gone
to the next level of the playing field.

Confused and uncertain what will happen next
I'm left with the wires all crossed.
I find it hard to know what to do next
with my true sense of rhythm all but lost.

I don't want to go from here,
with rites of passage imposed,
but there's no turning back or standing still
if the gates of paradise are closed.

No one asked me what it was that I might want,
they all felt that they knew what was best.
But what about me? And what about waiting
till I'm ready to step up to do the rest.

There's far too much lost in moving ahead
the uncertainty just addles my mind.
There are far too many of us out there looking back
for all we had to leave behind.

I don't want to leave from here,
with rites of passage imposed,
but there's no turning back or standing still
when the gates of paradise are closed.

I'd hardly celebrated many milestones in my life
when this change fell abruptly down.
I 'm told I'm obliged and it's now my time
to step forward, out, away or around.

The complex fairy tales that filled my head
still call to me, urging me to stay.
Only a fool without vision would consider
leaving the enchantment and walking away.

I don't want to leave from here,
with rites of passage imposed,
but there's no turning back or standing still
and the gates of paradise are closed.

86

The First Day Again

Another sunrise, another dawn
to everything going on
out there—waiting just to be.

As the light softly breaks through my window with a view
it's the first day again calling out to me.

With options hard to choose
and I've no time for the blues
adjust and focus, let the stress all fade away.

After you've looked out and over the end a
nd come back here again,
you have to feel that it's good to be here for another day.

No time for secrets and lies
that cripples, blinds or binds
me to the petty; it ends up to be such a waste.

All the trials and pit falls seem like nothing at all
in perspective, to the big picture I face.

The measure of what's to come
like the circle that must run
around to meet itself and continue through.

I'm on another sphere drifting away and drawing near
to the inevitable and eventual truth,... eventual truth.

Another sunrise, another day
with everything in its place
out there—waiting just to be.

As the morning breaks the night, I know myself and my life;
it's the first day again calling out to me,...
Calling out to me.

87

Who Cares?

Who cares of their impasse?
The children will get along.
But without help they're doomed to fail
and we ask, "where did they go wrong?"

Where is their paragon;
a counselor with wisdom and song,
to guide them through their perils of life
with good values passed along?

Parents, so self-absorbed,
justify their short-comings and faults.
While their children are waiting each day,
for that moment you might stop and play
for that moment you might let it be known
who cares.

What of the patriarch? Who speaks for their true rights
when in the course of their sad day
who's there to nurse their night?

They look for some design,
an ally to champion theirs,
searching for understanding and love,
looking out for that one who cares.
Who cares?

88

Love After Love After All

Nowhere to go, no way to escape.
Even still, I don't know
where I'd go to get away.
Still in shock and distress
that I'm carrying the mess,
but my saving grace wrapped like a shawl
is believing there could be love after love after all.

Who cares about fault when you're left there alone?
She didn't say what it was about,
just left for parts unknown.
All the lonesome pain
returns again and again.
Beyond the guilt; that imperiled wall,
I'm hoping there's love after love after all.

Abandoned by love after so many years,
forced to reevaluate
all the beliefs and simple values
we both shared in life for so long.

I got these kids, a broken-down car
and what's left of the home.
Can't tell yet how things are
now that I'm on my own.
Trying to leave the past behind
but it's still there in my mind.
Ahead of me, I hear it call
It's whispering that there's love after love after all.

Yeah, there's love after love after all.

89

In an Instant

In an instant your life can change,
as everything within temporal range
will be different from now on to you.
All the little things before
that your frenzied life passed over
suddenly take shape with meaning and point of view.

The many things before, left for naught,
now command ardent reason and thought,
and purpose, just in living seems profound.
Priorities are reviewed; reassessed,
Friends; relations brought in close to the nest,
with a strengthened love and hope for all around.

Each new moment of each new day
conveys a given substance and weight
as a gift you give to yourself to discern and prize.
But why should it take a tragedy
or some near-death calamity
to open up your mind, your heart and your eyes.

From many perspectives, life is brief,
it's hidden fruits; rare and sweet
with fleeting treasures of moments, come and gone.
In an instant your life can change,
motivated by choices you make
with that first look at this morning's new dawn.

At this morning's new dawn.

90

His & Hers

She is providence, practical,
and always makes good sense.
She knows what's right, she knows what's real;
doesn't put on any pretense.
She sees today in motion
with herself moving with its flow.
She knows the past is over
and the future? Well, nobody knows.
Nobody knows.

He is capricious, irrational,
always taking things apart.
He knows what's right, he knows what's just;
follows closely to his heart.
He sees the day transforming
with himself still out of phase.
He's realistic but hopeful
that tomorrow, things will change.
Things will change.

She is realistic and definitive;
she accepts things the way they are.
She hopes for better days
but doesn't expect a change thus far.
She loves her man for what he is
in spite of his failings and crimes.
She feels the winds of change outside
and prays to be ready for those times.
Ready for those times.

He is idealistic, experimental;
he still wants to change the world.
He too has hopes for better days
and waits for them to be unfurled.
He loves his woman for what she is,
in spite of her expectations to meet.
He looks for a break that will change their lives
and put them on easy street.
On easy street.

They see each other with acceptance;
an abiding love that will never fall.
They both know apart; they're incomplete
and together they have it all.
They move and think and act as one
through their timeline to fulfill.
At times she hopes his dreams might come true
and at times he knows they never will.
They never will.

91

※

Mother-Child Lullaby

Words by **Robin Bodin & Lord Baldwin**
Music by **Lord Baldwin**

She's here again, the little child I can not hold.
The One I left so far behind,
asking me again and again; those questions in her eyes.
I need to rock her in my arms; tell her everything is fine.

This little one is watching me
from long ago, and waiting for the sign,
to tell her that she's come full circle; to tell her that she's mine.

But, not quite certain - who is she?
Where, or when or why?
Can she hear the mother calling? Is it hers or; or is it mine?
We must take care of her, of me.

We're of each other - she and I; each the child,
each the mother.

Each must wait until the time that once-upon-a-day
when arms will reach across the years, and finally to say
the things we need to hear; to speak,
then, let you slip away.

To that time from which you came
and will go again someday,
you ran to me, to touch, to see; to know that you are good.

Come, and I will hold you in my heart,
and rock you there until you sleep.
You are good, you know, my little one
I know, because you're me.
Because you're me.

92

MEMOIRS & NOTES - 42 -

Rites Of Passage

(1998) – The idea of this poem came to me when I was going through my first quarter at The Evergreen State College. We have all had to go through our own set of *rites of passage* as we grew up or graduated from one circumstance to another; there is a change (or not), and an adjustment (or resistance to any modification, if you will), and a passing from one door through to another (or the refusal thereof), and there is a growing or learning process afterwards whether we move forward, stay stagnant or fall behind, and sometimes that process is not only very difficult and uncomprehending, but many times it is an unwanted change or alteration to our lives.

My son Brian was at that specific point in his infant progression where he was getting cut off from nursing. This process was doubly poignant for Diane because Brian is our last child and this bonding closeness, nursing thing has been something Diane has been doing for over 20 years.

At three, Brian was old enough for Diane to simply explain to him that she felt it was time to be weaned. I'm sure that Brian could understand the concept of stopping nursing, but he didn't want any part of it.

Finally, Diane chose a date and called it the, "Stop Nursing On This Day" date, where afterwards both Brian and Diane knew he would no longer be nursing. And after a few, "Stop Nursing On This Day" dates, he finally did let it go, but there was a great sadness in both Brian and Diane.

When a baby stops nursing, the process can generate a kind of separation from the "mom to child" closeness and maybe even create a stronger connection to the dad, as that baby or toddler psychologically alters. And without that close dependency on that mother, the baby might take a closer look at its surroundings and begin to establish a relationship with that other parent in the home and discover that he, the father, can be as important or almost as important as the mother.

With a sadness for the passing, and this rite of passage, I watched as Brian's sour attitude towards getting cut off and his unhappiness remained for days and sometimes it was immense.

And then there was Diane, who on one hand was ready to finally let this drain from her system go, and on the other hand, was reluctant to stop nursing and lose her special bond with Brian, her last baby, and in doing so, allow Brian the baby to grow to be Brian the little boy, and not be a baby anymore, and to allow him to progress to his next level. But then, there was the factor of losing our son Christopher in 1992, which made having Brian arrive in our lives all that much more special.

And Diane too was also going through a disheartening stage where she was moody and crying and sad and would sinking into intense depressions before returning to a normal state of mind, sometimes all in the space of hours.

I didn't know then that Diane was going through a thing called, Post-Weaning Depression, caused by a combination of physiological factors, situational dynamics, and emotional triggers, which is something experienced by many mothers after they have weaned their child from breastfeeding. Not just that, breastfeeding releases a cocktail of "feel good" hormones—prolactin and oxytocin—that can lift the mother's mood and bring feelings of peace and tranquility. Prolactin, which supports milk production, is known for producing feelings of relaxation and inducing sleep to the mother, while Oxytocin, the hormone that causes a mother's milk to letdown, is often called "the love hormone" and helps the mother to bond to her baby and generally feel strengthened and uplifted. After weaning, levels of these hormones drop significantly. If weaning happened abruptly, it may feel like you aren't getting your "fix" of those happy hormones. And breastfeeding can protect a mother from depression, so it stands to reason that ending it could lead to mood shifts and depressive feelings.

And you might think that after having ten children, this phenomenon would be something she would get through easier than she was. But in truth, most all of the children were weaned just prior to the arrival of the next child and so it was expedient to make the change happen. With Brian, who came four years after Allison and arrived when Diane and I were both 44 years old, she knew this miracle baby would be her last and she wanted to hold on to that baby for as long as she could; and nursing did just that. And so, it was a rites of passage thing for Diane too.

Anyway, as days turned into weeks and then months, Brian slowly, (and I do mean slowly) accepted his new conditions and was able to move on, and seeing her little baby to boy progress, Diane eventually did too.

Side Note:

A sad or maybe frustrating memorandum to this writing, is that, because of a hard drive crash to my computer at home, and a mishap with not being able to retrieve my files, this is the third time I have had to write this set of notes, and reconstructing them with any continuity was impossible, so after I finished doing the, *"Who I Might Be"* album, I came back to this and just started over again.

Another Side Note:

And speaking about Rites of Passage; when I was in the third grade, I lived in Iron Mountain Michigan and I went to the Catholic Immaculate Conception Elementary School. And with me having dyslexia, and having difficulty in learning to read or interpret words, letters, and other symbols, it was not good being a third grader doing math or writing. To complicate my circumstances even more, I was left-handed, and even in the 20th century, left-handedness was seen as everything from a sign of moral degeneracy, to a symptom of neurological deformity, to an almost illegal act. The association of the directional left with evil is likely attributed to the dominance of right-handed people within a population, and consequently the awkwardness of motions made from the left side of the body,...

and for thousands of years, the Devil had been associated with the left hand in various ways and was normally portrayed as being left-handed in pictures and other images. In the seventeenth century it was thought that the Devil baptized all his followers with his left-hand and there are many references in superstitions to the "left-hand side" being associated with evil.

As an example, in France it was held that witches would greet Satan **"Avec Le Bras Gauche"** or with the left hand. In ancient Egypt and Mesopotamia, for example, the two hands of their gods had opposing powers. A god's right hand could bestow **healing powers** or provide a blessing, but the god's left hand was used to **cast a curse**, destroy things, or cause harm.

It is also considered that we can only see ghosts if we look over our left shoulder and that the Devil watches us over the left shoulder. Moreover, Christianity and particularly Catholicism are strongly based towards the right hand. It is the right hand that gives the blessing and make the sign of the cross. On one count, the bible contains over 100 favorable reference to the right-hand and 25 unfavorable references to the left-hand. I bring these superstitions up because I am indeed a left-handed fellow and I was going into the third grade into a Catholic school with a learning disability.

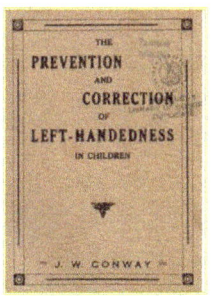

The Prevention And Correction of Left-Handedness In Children by J.W. Conway was published in 1935 and is believed that, at one point , had the subtitle, "On Curing the Disability and Disease of Left-Handedness"

Then there was my instructor/teacher Sister Leone . She was a strong believer that left-handed people were of the devil or at least tools of the devil, and from the first time she noticed mu left-handedness, I was doomed. Now my second-grade teacher, Sister Maria, either didn't know or didn't care about my left-handedness and I did fairly well in her class. And when I first arrived in the third grade, Sister Leone looked over at me uninterestingly as she did with my friend from the second grade, Kenny who was sitting next to me. For obvious reasons, she quickly made sure that I sat on opposite sides of the classroom from my friend Kenny, and I made it through a couple of days before I saw Sister Leone look over at me with a strong look of concern before turning her attention to the class.

Later that day just before the bell rang, and when we were busy eking out the last few minutes by drawing with crayons and paper, she looked over at me with a long, concerned glare in my direction. After the class was dismissed, Sister Maria showed up in the third-grade classroom. She and Sister Leone were both whispering to each other as they appeared to be looking over at me. It made me feel very uncomfortable to be singled out, but I left with the both of them following me with their eyes as I walked out the door.

The next day, when we were starting our writing, there was a noticeable look of shock on Sister Leone's face and she zeroed in on me from the moment that I picked up a pencil. I looked over at Kenny who made his eyes go big as if to say, you're in trouble" and then looked down and got busy with his own pencil on his paper.

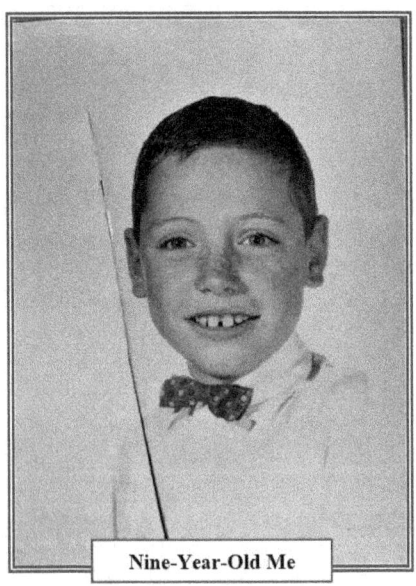

Nine-Year-Old Me

With a look of contempt on her face, she came over to my desk, pulled the pencil out of my left hand and forcibly pushed it into my right hand and, while the whole class had stopped what they were doing and were now watching, Sister Leone said insistently, "You need to learn to write with your right hand." Of course, my response would be, "Why?" and her answer was that it was more proper for students to use their right hand to write with.

She started to walk away but returned and said something to the effect, "We are not heathens. Look here." She pointed the sheet I had begun scribbling on and said, "You started your lettering from over here; on the right of the paper." I looked down at the paper and then further down to the ground. "Christians write from the left and move to the right."

And like she could not stand to be next to me for any longer length of time, she raised her veil covered head high as if to show how she had piously bested or vanquished the sinful temptations of the infidel and then went back to the front of the class.

If you think it's easy, try it sometime. Try writing your name with your non-dominant hand, then try writing your name in cursive. This went on for a long time with little to no improvement, till one day my mother saw what I was doing and went to talk to Sister Leone in conference with the Parish Father, Father McCarthy, who was like a Principal of the students and the boss of all the nuns and the guy that kind of ran everything related to the parish. Then I was back to being left-handed again, but from then on, in Sister Leone 's incapacitated heart, evil or not, I was a heretic.

And one more thing; in the 1950's and early-to-mid 60's, Roman Catholic schools were known as places where all students had to wear uniforms, and at the Immaculate Conception Elementary school, ours was gray-tweed corduroy pants, a white shirt, black military like shoes, and a navy-blue pull-over sweater, Also, at the Immaculate Conception Elementary school, the bad students would be punished by the nun instructor without question; and with Sister Leone , who ran a very tight ship, well, I can say there were times that I got my knuckles rapped with a wooden ruler, or my ears forcibly pulled, and there were a few times where I got threatened with her using the paddle; which was a piece of wood that resembled a ping pong paddle except much larger with a longer handle, and the flat face had multiple holes drilled in it to cause little bubble welts on the offender's bottom. Oh, and they were allowed to spank you at any time they felt discipline warranted it. And they were the judge, jury and the executioner whose reasoning and sentencings was never questioned; except by the Parish Father, should he be involved.

Now here's a funny thing; in this Catholic school, there was only one teacher per class, and there was only one place for me to be in the third grade and that was back in Sister Leone's class, and I am sure that that was not what she wanted.

So, fast forward to the fall of 1959 and Kenny's gone on to the fourth grade but now I have my brother Richie in the same classroom. And

I thought that maybe, besides being embarrassed to be one year older than all the other schoolmates, maybe things would be better, I mean, after all, I had already done the third grade, and my brother could be there with me to help me get through.

But although that was the case for the most part, from the first day, Sister Leone brought me aside and said, "I do not like you being here. I'll be watching you." And sometime in that first few weeks she even pointed to me and told the rest of the class that I was a good example of what could happen to them if they didn't follow the rules and do their school work.

And if that wasn't bad enough, a couple days after that embarrassing moment, I managed to get myself into even more trouble with me singing a mock version of Larry Williams' 1957 song, "Bony Maronie" that I had heard in my brother John's bedroom one Sunday. The song had a catchy toon with lyrics that went;

"I got a girl
named Bony Moronie.
She's as skinny as a stick of macaroni."

I was out in the playground with Richie and we were in the court-yard spinning around on a full-to-capacity merry-go-round when I started singing;.

"I got a teacher named Sister Leone.
She's a second cousin to Bony Moronie."

With the catchy tune and the way I was singing, there was a lot of kids that thought it was funny and laughed, causing me to repeat the ditty a few more times. Unfortunately, another nun heard something of what I was singing and then, (I think now), the nun interpreted the word "bony" out of context, maybe it being sexual in nature, but for whatever reason, she reported me to Sister Leone.

I was put on detention during recess time and that detention went on for days,... that is, until one afternoon, after Sister Leone ushered everyone out for recess, and I was sitting there writing lines, (not sure any more about that either), when something snapped. I picked up my math book, got up and stood precariously on my wabbly desk and made ready to throw the book on the floor.

At that precise moment Sister Leone walked in the room and sternly yelled out my name. Without hesitation or thought, I looked over at Sister Leone and threw the book at her, hitting her square in center of her head, just above her left eye. She reeled back in pain and surprise for a second before she lunged at me, causing me to lose my balance and fall off the desk, hitting my own head on the desk behind mine, but before I could regain my composure, she grabbed me by the hair on the top of my head and started pulling me, first up to a standing position and then out the classroom door. After I couldn't keep up with her fast pace and stumbled, she began dragging me down the hallway by my hair. As I was being dragged down the hall, I kept loudly telling her to let me go and other students and office workers had stepped out into the hallway to see what was going on. Then, as my scalp was on fire, I reached up in desperation and dug my fingernails as deep as I could into the, 'right' hand that was holding my hair. She cried out loudly in agony as she let go of my head; and all in about the same moment, Father McCarthy stepped out of his office to see what was happening.

What is going on here?" He questioned looking over at me as I squatted in a heap on the floor, with Sister Leone nursing her injured right hand with her left. Father McCarthy then looked down the hall-way and waved his hand as if to say to all the onlookers, "Get back to your work" and everyone immediately disappeared.

At first, as you may imagine, Sister Leone hurried to position her-self to stand next to Father McCarthy, wild with agitation, pointing to me while trying to tell him what had happened, but Father McCarthy raised his hand once again, instantly silencing Sister Leone. He looked down at me and said, "Son, Father McCarthy said kindly as he lifted me to my feet, "could you please come over here and sit on this bench here for a moment outside my office?"

I had no recourse but to silently go to the wooden bench just outside his door. With a stern look he turned to Sister Leone and asked her to go to her room, reminding her that recess was already over and that her students were unattended. As she tried to explain, Father McCarthy raised his hand once again, instantly silencing her and said, "We'll talk about this later."

Sister Leone glared maliciously down at me as she walked swiftly back to her classroom. Father McCarthy opened his door and asked me to come in and sit down. Maybe five minutes passed before he asked me to tell him what had happened, and reminding me that Jesus would know if I was "*stretching the truth*." This was made all the more serious at Father McCarthy glanced at the large portrait painting of Jesus hanging on the wall behind Father McCarthy's desk,... as the eyes of the painting seemed to be looking right into my soul as if to tell me that Jesus was watching me.

I don't know exactly what I said in my defense but I'm sure, with Jesus looking down at me to be upright and truthful, it was as accurate as it could have possibly been for a nine-year-old boy.

Father McCarthy then had me follow him through an inside door that led to a room full of office workers, some of them nuns and a few women parishioners, where he asked one of the nuns, Sister Margaret, to follow him. When we walked into my classroom, as was the custom of reverence and respect, all the students stood up straight and called out in unison, "Good afternoon Father McCarthy."

Sister Leone looked over at me suspiciously, and I believe Father McCarthy saw that vindictive glare, but not showing any emotion, he then asked Sister Margaret to take over the class for a few minutes, and with another silent wave of Father McCarthy's hand, Sister Leone followed him out of the classroom.

I don't know what was discussed in private, but when Sister Leone returned, she looked unsettled. All I could think of was what Senior was going to do to me when he found out what had happened. I envisioned myself standing there in our bedroom, my pants down, his belt off, and the terrible beating I would be experiencing later on.

Sister Leone seemed to avoid looking over at me for the rest of the afternoon, but I could see she was decidedly unnerved and when it was time to go and I was preparing to bolt, my heart sank and I got a terrible feeling in my gut as she calmly asked me to stay for a moment.

Sure that I was now gonna get my next punishment, I waved Richie to go on and wait for me outside. But by the eyes of God, I knew that in some way, I had been wronged too, and so, I pretended that I was not afraid. After waiting a long time in silence, she finished shuffling papers on her desk, and without emotion, she very calmly apologized for her behavior and told me she would not do that again. She then told me that Father McCarthy wanted me to stop his office by on my way out.

I maintained a look of determination like I was in some kind of control till I left the classroom and then, I was gripped with fear. Fear of what Father McCarthy was going to do and fear of how my mother was going to take things when she found out and worst of all, fear of what Senior was going to do when he found out.

Father McCarthy smiled as I went back into his office and sat down. He looked at me for a moment and said that he was sorry for what had happened, and he told me that it would never happen again. He asked me if I had any questions and I thought for a moment as thousands of things went through my brain,... like, did he contact my parents? or, was I still on probation in class? or, could I go to recess again? or, was I still in trouble with Sister Leone for the other things I was in trouble for before this all happened?

"No sir." I answered. I did not ask about anything but shook his hand as I left his office.

Richie was still waiting faithfully outside, sitting on the merry-go-round and kicking the ground below him to slowly keep in motion. On our walk home, we talked,... speculated what was going to happen to me,.., and when we did get home, we were both chided for being home late from school,... but that was all. Mother never said anything or even acted like she knew but didn't want to say.

When Senior got home there was no temper upheaval or scolding or beating. It was like the school never said anything, and I wasn't going to be the one to ruin their day.

In the days that followed, Sister Leone did not address me or call on me, even when I held up my hand to answer a question in class. She rarely even looked over at me and when she did, it was momentarily before she looked past or through me. it was like I wasn't there in the class; I was now indeed invisible. I still took tests and got terrible grades, even when I compared mine to Richie's where we had the same answers, but I wasn't gonna question things. I just spent the rest of the school year as the kid that wasn't there. And when it came time to get my report card, my mother was not called in and the recommendation from Sister Leone was to have me go on to the fourth grade.

I will say that those two years greatly traumatized me and I had a lot more difficulty learning to read, using writing skills, interpreting words in sentences, my letters looked like a first grader's, especially cursive, and I had trouble interpreting other symbols as well as being terribly deficient in my math skills.

Side Note:

It was no wonder that I had poor marks on my report card and at school-year's end Sister Leone had my mother and Senior come in for a conference with her, telling my mother that she was going to pass me but on condition. (It was a bad thing in those days to flunk someone in a Parochial school because it left a mark on the school itself if not the nun that was incapable of getting a student through their class, especially the third grade).

I never found out what that " **To Grade 4 On Condition**" was because Senior in his anger or embarrassment, looked down at me with fire in his eyes as he told Sister Leone that I deserved everything I got and for her to flunk me.

Another Side Note:

One positive note,... If you look closely at my grades, in spite of the fact that Sister Leone stifled my grades she could not totally degrade me because all report cards had to pass across Father McCarthy's desk before they were handed out,

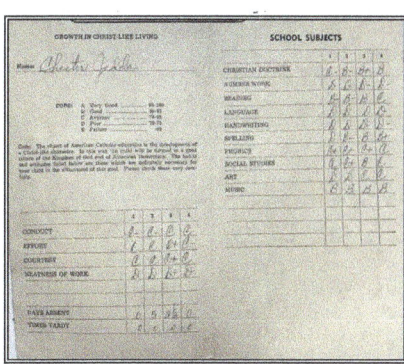

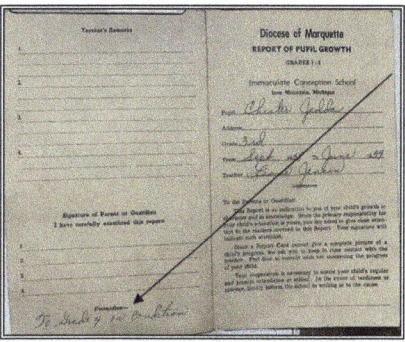

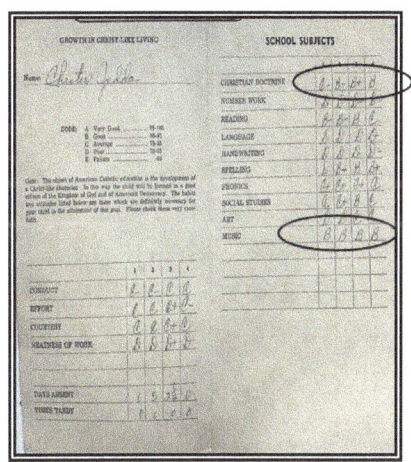

and I take solace in the fact that my spirituality (Christian Doctrine), and music grades reflected, even then, that I had a deep interest in those subjects,... and I had to carry the stigmatism of having flunked a grade, having my younger, better looking, smarter brother in my classes, and that marker or pigeon-holing label followed my all the way through high school till I graduated from North Marion High School at age 19 and a half,... but my mother was awfully proud.

The First Day Again

(1999) – When I start to worry about my circumstances and how bad things are, all I need to do is to keep in mind that there are others out there with monumental problems that in comparison to mine, well,... it can help put my adversity into proper perspective.

A case in point: There was a young woman named Cathy who became a neighbor of mine when she, her boyfriend and their kids moved in across the street from us. And things for them looked good for a while, but after a time, her companion seemed to develop a mean streak and began to beat her and terrorize her and her kids.

One day she had had enough and asked Diane and I to drive her and the kids away to a place out by Hoodsport which is a seaside town perched on the western shores of the Hood Canal beneath the shadow of the Olympic Forest Mountain Range.

I kind of lost contact with her after that but heard from my next-door neighbor, Patty, that she was having a tough time financially making ends meet. To make matters worse, she had collapsed and ended up in the hospital where she found out that she had some rare type of cancer and needed special treatment. And after months of chemotherapy, she was in remission and things looked and felt a lot better for her and her kids.

She found a good man and married him, and it looked like they would live happily ever after. But then she developed some life-threatening blood clots in both of her legs and ended up in the hospital again. When I went to see her that time, she was jaundiced and sickly but still, smiled and happily received my company. She had the clots removed and again, things looked good. Then her weird cancer returned, but now, there was another type or strain of cancer going on at the same time in her body and things did not look good.

When I went to see her in the hospital, that last time, she was listless and rather despondent, but still maintained to exhibit a spark of optimism. With a smile she invited me in and spoke with a strained, whispered voice. She looked out the window of her hospital bed and said, "I don't know how long I have. Every day is the first day again. I get blessed to be able to wake up and be here one more day. And I feel like it's calling out to me. *The first day again.*"

A few days later, she passed away. And after I got over the trauma and distress of that loss of a good friend, I took what wisdom that she left me and wrote this poignant poem.

Side Note:

This harmonica intro and ending almost didn't come to happen. Originally, I recorded this in the key of 'G' because that was my usual go to chord and at the time, I was able to sing more clearly in that key and where I thought a 'C' harmonica was waiting.

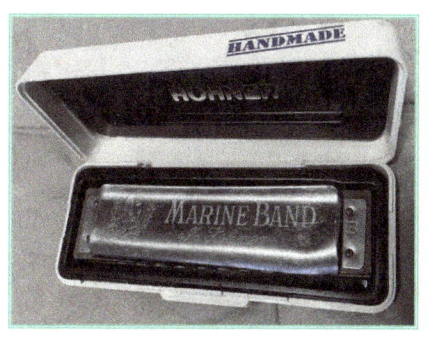

But after recording the song I found that my 'C' harmonica was spent especially the 'B' note on the inhale.

In 1998 a new harmonica cost about $25.00 of which, I did not have,... so I left the song and moved on to recording a few other songs. Still, this was an important song for the person I wrote it about and for,... and the for the message I was putting out there in the universe,... so when my mother-in-law asked me what I wanted for a belated birthday present, I simply replied that I wanted a 'Hohner' Marine Band 'C' harmonica.

Months later our family went over to visit Diane's parents after church and I was given my belated birthday present. It was a 'Hohner' Marine Band harmonica., but in the key of 'B' and I thanked them graciously. When I got home I considered taking it to Music 6000 and trading it for the right key, but that night something got into me and I decided to rerecord everything to use this harmonica. It turned out great. Since then, like that 'C' harmonica, I have worn this one out too but I keep it around for the memory.

Who Cares?

(1999) – I have always felt that, because of my time constraints; prioritizing my working all the time to meet our financial needs, that I have been at best rather inadequate when it comes to being that good father and parent that I so desperately want to be. Maybe it's to compensate for the fact that I was raised without that father figure myself, or maybe because I know that if I had done certain things differently or had had other resources to draw upon, I could have done, or still could do, so much better. Still, things as they are, I do try hard to be the father they need in their lives, and if you've been reading other memoirs, you know that I take this obligation and responsibility, seriously.

But here we are at the beginning of a new century where the infant death rate in the United States is twice as high as in similarly wealthy countries and where, except for Mexico and Turkey, we spends less of our gross domestic product on family benefits than all 37 other Organization for Economic Co-operation and Development (OECD) member countries worldwide, and a higher child poverty rate than nearly all other OECD countries, and our Temporary Assistance for Needy Families program (TANF) now provides benefits to fewer than one in four poor families, and, is the only OECD country where there is no paid maternity, parental, and home-care leave entitlement, forcing a very large share of American mothers to return to work just days after giving birth,,.. and where the obesity among American kids is described as an "epidemic," and 13 million American children still struggle with **food insecurity**, and teenagers are 82 times more likely to die from a gun homicide than their peers in other rich nations, and 2,000 American children a year die from child abuse or neglect, and now in the twenty-first century, in our schools where it is common practice to link school funding to property taxes—thus ensuring that rich kids have more resources than poor kids in the public-school systems,... and where our students rank in the bottom third of all OECD countries,... and by the eighth grade, only three in five students are proficient in terms of our reading and mathematics,... and, the "poverty gap" in standardized test scores is 40 percent larger today than it was a generation ago,... and, on any given day, with a system rife with racial inequality and an extraordinary tolerance of child poverty, nearly half a million children are living in foster care, with about 20,000 living in group homes, and in a in a country with the highest incarceration rate on Earth, where nearly two million children have a parent behind bars with profound effects on those children's emotional well-being, health, later educational attainment and earning potential later in life, and where the growth in incarceration of men with children contributes to higher rates of homelessness among black children, and, where, when a mother is incarcerated, her children often end up in foster care, separated from their families, and, where we continue to lead the world in putting minors; children behind bars, and where in too many states, we treat very young children just like adults in the criminal justice system where fourteen states have no minimum age for when a child can be prosecuted and punished as an adult, and in some cases, children as young as eight years old have been tried as adults for committing a crime, and where children confined in adult prisons are in an even more vulnerable situation, forced to grow up too fast in a dangerous environment where they are significantly more at risk for sexual assault and suicide,...

And where the United States is the only country that has not ratified the UN's Convention on the Rights of the Child,... and as millions of children are left without supervision for hours every day, or such so-called "latchkey" kids that come home to no adult supervision to fend for themselves while 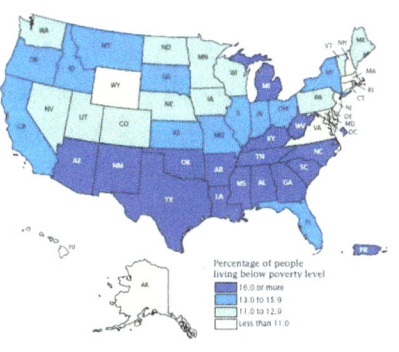 their mothers and or fathers are occupied in the workplace going to work to keep the roof over their heads,... and where the effects of being a child alone might include loneliness, boredom and fear, (most common for those younger than ten years of age) but where early teens are more susceptibility to alcohol abuse, drug abuse, sexual promiscuity and smoking, and where socioeconomic status and length of time left alone can bring about other negative effects like higher levels of behavioral problems, and whereas, many children at-need, that are missing their father or their mother or both and must, for the most part, go through much of their childhood without parents at home,... and the aid and love of that parent when that child is in need; aid and comfort that could make the difference in their lives, and change their world forever.

My heart goes out to all of those children, and my poem goes out to all of you negligent, careless or irresponsible parents that have an option where many parents don't; an option to reevaluate your priorities and take hold of your parental obligations and responsibilities,... and I have a hope that you might realize that that time, energy and love that you might give to your child might just be the determining factor that may save them and let them know, "Who Cares."

Side Note:

Back to 1998-99, The three of us computer guys at work, Jeans, Pete and I were given the announcement that Lorna was no longer our supervisor and that the VP Mr. B. had assigned a new person, Renzo to fit in that position as Lorna was moving up into a different administrative position. Meanwhile, Jeans, who was in charge of the imaging of the computers and held all the passwords and knew all the mappings of everything in building 34 was disinterested at best, arrogantly thinking himself to be irreplaceable. The three of us soon came to know that Renzo had no clue what we were doing nor did she know what she was supposed to do. I found out later from a different implant from Tacoma Community College, that the HR department at Tacoma Community College saw the in-house ad for the position opening up at South Puget Sound Community College and let Renzo know it was out there. So, when Renzo applied at South Puget Sound Community College, the HR department at Tacoma Community College, had only glowing references, stating that Renzo would be missed but if she wanted to move on, well... The implant also told me that, to the HR department at Tacoma Community College, Renzo was dead weight and they were just looking for such an opportunity to unload her on anybody that would be willing or stupid enough to take her.

Love After Love After All

(1999) – Remember Cathy from "The First Day Again" poem and song? She once said that she wished she could have found someone like me instead of the others that hurt her. She wondered why some women continue to pick the wrong guys and perpetuate abusive relationships. When these episodes happened, she was embarrassed and ashamed and blamed herself thinking she had escalated the situation and caused the man to react with violence because of her behavior. She wasn't sure there was any good man out there anymore for her, and she was reluctant to even get involved with anyone for fear that she would fall into another bad relationship.

Besides her own children, which were teenagers, Cathy was rather alone in the world. It was good to know that while her adversities were hitting her and bringing her down, someone did step into her life and show her what love after love could be. He stayed with her through her trials and was there when she passed away. He was there for her even after her death, by raising, loving and taking care of her children. And it's no wonder that I felt impressed to write this poem for and in her behalf.

Side Note:

And then there's the concept of being so lonely for so long and then finding out that someone cares, someone wants you as much as you want them,... and my Diane was just such a savior to my sad lonely life for such a long time. When we were married in  1973, we were both 23 years old,... seemingly we were so old,... but looking back, we were just kids,...

In An Instant

(1999) – We are all only a moment away from a change that could devastate, immobilize or alter our lives permanently for the better or worse. You know, so much can happen in just a flash and everything can take on a new meaning. Things we take for granted suddenly have a renewed purpose and we see things differently.

Stephen and his friend J.T. were cruising around by Tumwater High School and they both got into trouble when Stephen threw a pumpkin out the side door onto the sidewalk being occupied by certain students. Unfortunately, there was a policeman right behind them and that Tumwater policeman was less than understanding, compassionate, or considerate. Both of the boys were taken into custody; their vehicle impounded and they were thrown into the Tumwater jail before the parents were ever called. At Stephen's hearing he was given community service hours to work off (while J.T. who was driving got nothing); and this brings about the point of this story and how and why I wrote this poem and created this song.

For more than a couple of evenings, I went with Stephen to go to work in the Bread and Roses Soup Kitchen facilities, and man, was it an eye-opener. If you ever want to get over feeling blue or sorry for yourself, just spend some time in one of those dwellings. You can't help but gain some other positive perspective of your own life as you comprehend what some of those folks are going through.

What inspired me to write this poem was seeing someone I knew, someone that was (had been), a respectable, responsible citizen of the community; seeing him now adrift, misplaced, lost, broken and fallen to pieces, sitting out there at one of the tables. He didn't appear drunk, but there was something wrong in his mannerisms. From his slurred speech I thought this descent might have happened because of some medical problem. When we finally made eye contact, there was something in his stare that asked me not to confront him in this condition and to just stay away and so I did. But later on, when he approached me, he told me that he had lost his job and was trying to get back on his feet, when he suddenly had a stroke that took out the left side of his face and he ended up in a hospital for two weeks.

Then, after he got out, he got hooked on his temporary medication (Oxycodone), and in the process, ended up back in the hospital. He was now trying to make it back, and the Bread & Roses kitchen was helping him to pay his rent. But he had said, it all seemed to happen in an instant and the recovery seemed to take forever.

Side Note:

Stephen still recalls our visits there at the Bread and Roses Soup Kitchen and I think it has helped him to be grounded in his life now. Due to little to no support from the city of Olympia and other benefactors, the Bread and Roses Soup kitchen closed down months later.

His & Hers

Somehow in spite of our differences, we seem to come together and become cohesive when there is a need, and if it means something; when there is something that has relevance that might affect our lives and the family we cherish, we're both all in.

Side Note:

I have my dreams and she has hers. And yes, we come from different backgrounds that pull from different experiences, distinctive parents from both sides, singular purposes, unusual or diverse views from opinions; we have our separate stands on issues, politically and otherwise, but we meet in the middle for each other's needs, for the solutions that are finally needed, or for us to have cooperatively gathered for a united purpose, like family and, sometimes great minds, no matter how dissimilar, or diverse do come together to understand the other's viewpoints and to celebrate not only the differences but the individual and collective accomplishments of each other.

Another Side Note:

What we have together now is not what we had in the beginning. We have evolved over the many years we've been together and grown closer to each other not just because of the triumphs we've accomplished, but also the failings and because of the trials that we've faced, and the communication gaps that we've needed to bridge, and because love doesn't just celebrate the commonalities of each other but more importantly the many differences that add spice and flavour to our lives.

Mother-Child Lullaby

(1999) –My friend Robin shared some of her poetry with me and I was impressed, especially with this work about a mother recognizing she is also a child and that her child may someday also be a mother. I took it home and was inspired to create music to go with these words. I did have to massage and work the poem around a bit to make the meter and rhyming work with the music.

To me, the words kind of say that there is an identity that we take upon ourselves as stewards of the children we raise and the love we generate from our relationships. Sometimes we can be in one roll and be a part of something else in someone else's stewardship at the same time, and yet at the end of the day it's all mixed together well and re-administered with love.

There is a colourful circle of existence and of our being and of a lifecycle that we are allowed to jump onto somewhere, using our own colours, working within our own timeframes and we begin to journey down new paths for fresh discoveries of who we are and how we fit in this new universe.

Sometimes there are other circles that blend for a while with our own, like family, making a sort of, Venn diagrams that illustrate through the uses of circles to show the relationships among things and groups of things. Circles that overlap to have a commonality while other circles that do not overlap display individualities of different traits. And then like a figure eight, we are going in our circle and also going around on, by or even into theirs, like children and parents and other relatives wanting to know about us. The blended circles and colours then separate, as we both go our own way, and that multi-coloured circle that had disconnected with us is now connecting again with a different circle of another set of colours, and some of them, maybe even spinning in different directions, above and or below us.

Sometimes we see new things as we revolve and evolve while we spin to the colours, and sometimes, we recognize that the scenery we pass as we revolve-evolve is see the same scenery we'd seen sometime in the past.

Things spin around us and even through us, over and over again as our circle seeks out another joining. And sometimes we may begin to understand where and when and maybe even why we are where we are and we can make changes so as to get it right. And sometimes we may choose to not only recognize our place and purpose on that circle, but also, finding personal meaning elsewhere. And though we move away, we are then able to create a brand-new circle; one that can grow and return from where it left, and you can look up to see what and how and why the other circles are doing what they are doing and we begin to understand a fraction of the universe.

Resemblance and similitude; finding the commonality in each other used to be the strength and basis of the mother-daughter relationship, but in this new century, mothers and daughters find that they may have to navigate their different lives, opportunities, and views about being female, and for some mothers and daughters this might cause conflict, as they clash over who might be right and who might be wrong or for that matter, *what* might be right and *what* might be wrong. But the love of the mother to the daughter is so eternally special. A daughter is one of the most beautiful gifts this world has to give to the mother and the mother with her unfailing love is the most special treasure that the daughter will ever possess. In our family, that wonderfully caring mother will always stive to be her daughter's best friend.

To be that good daughter, she only needs to love, respect, and be open, honest, and kind. Sometimes, hearts open up to each other; the mother to the daughter, the daughter to the mother, and when that happens, the heavens open up too and love radiates and abounds and binds that love to be forever.

Side Note:

As I reported earlier, I was so impressed with my friend Robin's poem that I felt I had to put music to it. I had never done that before and because of my eclectic style of In-House Jazz, I feared that Robin might be a bit taken aback by the finished product. But it was what it was and came from my heart so I tried not to dwell on how she would react to her poem put to music.

And of course, these were still the days of cassette tapes and that was what I rerecorded the final rendition onto and it was a Friday morning when I gave the cassette to Robin. She was very gracious when she received the tape and promised that she would listen to it on her hour-long drive as she was going home.

By Monday I had totally forgotten to go see her and find out what she thought about the marriage between her poem and my music, and it was by chance that I stopped by her office to drop something off for her boss. When I came through the door, Robin looked up from her desk, (which was situated perpendicular to the door I had just come through) and suddenly jumped up from her desk, ran over to me and gave me a strong, long hug. Tears filled her eyes as she looked for the words that seemed to fail her. When she did get composed, she told me that something wonderful had happened in her life over the weekend. After listening to the song repeatedly on her way to her home, she felt impressed to share it with her daughter who she had been having teenager communication problems with. She told me that after she told her daughter that she had written the poem for her and they listened to the song, they both started crying and hugging each other. She said it was just the right medicine to help them with their problems.

I asked for permission to include the finished composition into this new album I was working on, and Robin was flattered and more than gracious to have that happen, and so I did; making it positioned as the last song, which, as many of you folks know is very special to me.

Another Side Note:

When Diane heard this for the first time, she asked me if I had written it for my daughters and specifically for Liz who to her seemed to fit the profile of the secondary person in the poem/song. I replied that I had my own girls in my mind while creating the musical composition, but I let her know that the poem itself had another author and related to her Robin's reaction to the finished product. Diane thought it was nice that I would do that for someone else. I think to this day that I was guided to do the project to help Robin and her daughter get closer to each other again.

93

- 43 - WHO I MIGHT BE -

2001 -

94

❧

NOTES ABOUT THE COVERS

Notes On The New Cover:

It was a great picture of a grandiose, magnificent mountain, with the tiny image of the hiker being dwarfed by its awesomeness. Then I put two hits of the same Showcase Gothic font, one on top of the other, then shaped the piece to look like it was coming at you, tilted it at a slight 30@ angle and draped it across the sides of the mountain to make it look like it was a kind of poster to give it a majestic feel.

For the, "Lord Baldwin," pseudonym, I used the, Bellbottom.Laser font, outing an extra space between all the letters and then pulling across the length of the bottom on top of the rocks. The cool thing is, at least to me, from a glance, the shapes of the letters from this font kind of take on the ambiance of a group of penguins hanging out.

Notes On The Original Covers:

Front cover; After 20 years, I have no idea who the artist was or the name of this painting, but I liked it for the ambiance of the person praying as the light from the one singular window is illuminating like the light of Christ into the weird cave-like dwelling, bringing a sense of hope.

The back cover had promise so I preserved it.

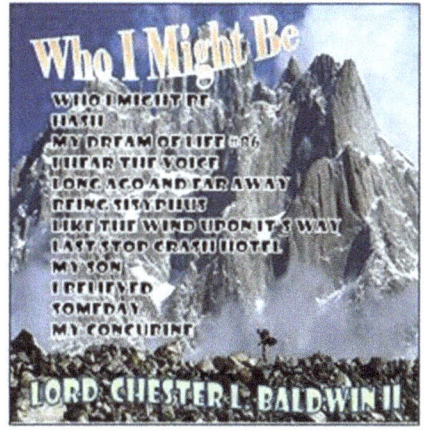

95

WHO I MIGHT BE

I Hear The Voice
Hash
My Dream Of Life #86
Who I Might Be
My Son
Being Sisyphus
Like The Wind Upon It's Way
I Believed
Long Ago And Far Away
The Right Road To Travel
Someday
The Last Stop Crash Hotel

96

I Hear The Voice

I hear the voice; I hear it call
in subtle timbre with clever sound,
and I pretend I'm down the hall;
not interested and not around.

I make believe I cannot hear
but it knows my weakness; knows my flaws.
It plays my secret inner fear
and it's ready to dispel my cause.

I hear the voice though others don't,
its focused on me, there's nowhere to hide.
I'm determined to resist but it thinks I won't
as its energies are intensified.

It looks to check the width and length
of only me and how much I resist.
It tests my meddle—my inner strength
secretly smiles with a hidden fist.

I hear the voice; I hear the voice...
I hear the voice.

The voice whispers it is my friend
reasoning persuasive for me to believe
twill stand beside me to the end
for only good and never to leave.

I hear the voice it now screams loud
the siren seeks to expose me and my crime.
with lonely force—I walk away proud
from my temptations one more time.

I hear the voice; I hear the voice...
I hear the voice.

97

Hash

Mother used to say,
"We may be poor white trash,
But in our peculiar way
There's a savor to hash."

98

My Dream Of Life #86

Cars are grumbling, people stumbling,
the city's humming
while the hammering through my brain.

And it's four fifteen and it's still not at ease
and as a siren screams,
a roaring, screeching stops a train.

Well, it'll never cease, and I won't find peace
in this cesspool of grease,
there's a constant mess of robberies and fights.

Well, I must move with care to the forest somewhere,
the birds still sing there
and the silence still fills the nights.

99

Who I Might Be

From dusty pages too long on the shelf
I have come at last to try to find myself
and I really need to know who I am and where to go
to connect me—to find out
who I might be.

For too long, I just let things go
thinking someday I'd take the time to know,
but the longer I'd delay the farther I got away
from where I should be to find out
who I might be.

The ancient faces hanging on my wall
stare back at me and they seem to call;
they cry out for me to explore—to try to find out more
to understand the key—to find out
who I might be.

I feel a connection and a relationship in doubt,
still, I haven't quite figured this all out,
but as each piece finds a place, the puzzle seems to trace
them back to me to help me to find out
who I might be.

From dusty pages too long on the shelf
I have come at last to find and know myself.
And it's not just for them or me, but for all my posterity
to know that tree—that I might find out
who I might be.

100

My Son

My Son, you've been a blessing to me.
Mr. Cheerful, and so obedient.
You've no idea how much it pleases the Lord
when you live clean and good for all righteousness.

Together We've got so much growing to do.
Mistakes to make, and to learn the better ways.
We need to stand for what we know is right.
In these latter days when men run away
we must be Champions.

We must be guided by the Spirit;
we need to pray to do God's will.

My Boy, the Lord needs us to be
a sharpened tool ready for any time.
These hills we walk will turn to mountains to climb.
When courage is gone and you can't go on,
I'll try to help you.

And I can help you when you're troubled
with some answers to fulfill,
We must be guided by the Spirit;
we need to pray to do God's will.

My Son, the day will come for us.
We will be called to do the work for all of this,
and I know that we can be ready to go.
A test knows no length; your faith is your strength
if you use it for righteousness.

My Son...
Together We...
My Boy...
My Son.

101

Being Sisyphus

Push the rock up to have it fall again
so I start over where I've already been
and life could be despairing
and seems so now and then,
but logic and reason are found well enough
from my travels and journeys
of friendships and love.
Exposing my heart in hopes that love returns,
within the chance that I might just get burned
and after so many failures
you'd think I'd have learned,
but love must be trusted or love can not be,
for by giving of love—love will come to me.
And the passion and cause of my life is to love
and in giving my love I have purpose, thereof.
Push the rock up to have it fall down again
so I start over where I've already been
still all in all, I do it for the sake of love.
I do it just for love...
Just for love.

102

Like The Wind Upon It's Way

Like the clouds that roam the sky
I come and go, just passing by.
Without direction of my turns;
without commitments or concerns.

Kin, I might visit, or friends I knew,
but it's just because I'm passing through.
I have no wish to stop or stay;
like the wind upon its way.

Like my dreams that might come true,
I have so much to see and do.
I need my feet unchained to run
or I may never see them done.

I make no promises to keep
for I don't know just where I'll be.
I know only of today;
like the wind upon its way.

Like the girl who made me bend
and then got married to a friend.
I was so hurt there and then;
I knew I'd never love again.

And as I travel where I will
thoughts of her come to me still,
but they linger and they fade;
like the wind upon its way.

Like the stories that you feel
about a fantasy turned real;
after all was said and done
and the prize dutifully won,

I am the drifter that walks the dawn
I have no need save to go on,
till I will all but fade away;
like the wind upon its way.

103

I Believed

They gathered together; collective as one
with a strength and authority challenged by none,
I fell prey as their target; the fun of the game
with little defenses to defend my name.

They said I was ugly, a fool and a freak;
with a pain made more poignant as they all did agree.
It wasn't true, but my mistake; so ill conceived
was that I listened to them; and I believed.

They said I was homely, a dreadful mistake
and they pressed, once again to see if I would break.
I searched in desperation for something clever to say
but I was trapped by ineptness and feet of soft clay.

My anger now flared and used against me as a tool,
leaving me disabled and helpless; an idiot and a fool.
I pretended to be callous hoping they might be deceived,
but I listened to them; and I believed.

they said I was ugly with my acne-ravaged face,
and they taunted me until I escaped from that place.
As I walked slowly home with my eyes to the curbs,
in disbelief I pondered their insinuating words.

In vain I made frivolous my situation and plight,
but the consensus reality was, they were probably right.
Though the truth was warped and immaterially conceived,
I listened to them; and I believed.

104

Long Ago And Far Away

Once I lived in my own land,
and all that I wanted was at my command.
All that I wished for, and all I could see,
and all that I wanted was there but to be.

There was ice cream mountains, candy bar trees,
popcorn clouds floating high in the breeze.
I could fly through the air so mysteriously.
No birds or no planes could touch wings with me.

Long ago and far away,
things were different than they are today.
The time stood still and I didn't care.
Now all I have left is the memories of there.

I could be small as an ant, or large as a tree,
there wasn't even one possibility,
nothing in the world that I couldn't be.
All I'd do was wish and then it would be.

Long ago and far away,
dreams were shared to give away.
The time stood still where ever I'd been,
But now all I've left is the memories of then.

But; once I flew beyond the stars
and talked to the people on planet Mars.
They were so friendly, but I couldn't stay,
they packed me a box lunch when I went away.

105

The Right Road To Travel

And the journey continued, and I on its course
stepped onto the path, in search of its source.
I stopped, looked both ways; first up, and then down,
And I chose, quite by chance,
the direction I'm bound.

And I walked in search of that absolute route,
and I walked to find fulfillment
and where it could be found.

I sought from the end; the answers might be
From the right road to travel
which was left up to me.

Too many side roads that seemed to need repair,
from too many forks in the road going nowhere.

And my journey continued as I carried through
down one path to another to validate the true.

And although there were times
where the road was all but gone
I found life just beyond the path that I was on.

And I walked to finish my unquestionable test,
and I walked to discover completion of my quest.

I thought a definitive would be somewhere ahead
from the right road to travel that has no certain end.
And my journey continues, and I know now indeed
that the right road to travel
is right in front of me.

106

Someday

Someday,
it's always someday,
some future time I'd arrive to some certain finding.

Purpose,
decided purpose,
is all but lost as I check on my present bindings.

Down;
going down a path to nowhere fast,
without cause, so unsure where I should be.

Someday,
some someday;
lies off, too far for me to believe.

For years I've reached out for something in my heart
that might complete me toward my dream,
but contradictions have pulled me apart,
and I've fallen down with my self-esteem.

And who I should be is a mystery;
an enigma of them and me.

Wanting,
I'm always wanting
to find a path I discovered before my fall.

Yielding,
forsaken yielding
as I go where they believe is best for us all.

Torn,...
I'm torn between pursuing other routes
and following this course set to be.

Someday,
oh, someday;
Drifts farther off and away from me.

Someday maybe I'll get to that place
where I'm in control of my own destiny.
And I'll raise my face
to the sun and the stars and know
I followed my heart and dreams
and I'll know it was me.

Someday;
it's always someday,
some future time I'd arrive to that certain day.

Purpose;
decided purpose
To create and do things my own way.

107

The Last-Stop Crash Hotel

Gallon of wine and a quart of beer
way beyond caring why you're here;
sitting outside the Last-Stop Crash Hotel.
Half is all paid, the rest is loaned
with plenty left over for getting stoned.
Slipping in the alley of the Last-Stop Crash Hotel.
Standing outside Bud's Grocery Store
bumming change from well-dressed men.
Looking for about another sixty-two cents
to get that wasted again.
Head in a cloud as the friends pass by.
A friend is a friend if he shares his high.
Sitting on the curb of the Last-Stop Crash Hotel.
Years ago, plans were made to change your life to get out,
but now that all seems like a fog in the air
and a dream not worth thinking about.
You got your gallon of wine and a quart of beer
keeps you off the streets and sitting down there,
sitting outside of the Last-Stop Crash Hotel.
Yeah, I'm sitting outside of the Last-Stop Crash Hotel.

108

MEMOIRS & NOTES - 43 - 'WHO I MIGHT BE'

(2001) – First, I would say that about a year ago I got this infection in my ears and went to the doctor's to get antibiotics. Through the usual tests, blood test, height, weight, checkup stuff, the nurse commented that I was about 13 pounds heavier than the last time I came in, maybe seven months earlier. I was up to 247. I decided it was time to do something about it and went on my own kind of diet.

My friend Pete went on this Atkinson's diet where he ate no carbohydrates and lost 30 pounds in about four months. I remained on my "moderation" diet and lost weight, but not so dramatically. I began to realize after doing this diet thing reverently that I became almost compulsive about food. It was really odd, but everything I ate, when I ate it, the quantity and time all became a consideration. I even found myself eating something really good like frosting-covered chocolate brownies, cut into small and bite-size pieces and after tasting its wonderfulness and mulling it around in my mouth, I'd spit it all out into the toilet. Obsessive about my body, I became neurotic about its maintenance.

One day I was getting ice to go with water to carry me through the day. And there, in the lunchroom, sitting on the table, was this large plastic tub full of mini cinnamon rolls.

I walked by and they seemed to call out to me with a voice in unison, "Hey, Chester..." (they knew me by my name), "come on! We're very small and it wouldn't hurt for you to have just one." I ignored them but they persisted. "You didn't have any breakfast..." (how did they know that?), "Just one little tiny mini cinnamon roll will be okay."

And so, I ate one of those fine, little tiny mini cinnamon rolls. But later on, even though I wasn't in the lunchroom; I was just passing by and I was in the hallway, they felt my presence and called out to me again. "Chester..." I peeked my head in and looked over at the tub. "Nobody wants to eat us. You are the only one that likes us." I looked away and took a step away. "Come on... one more little tiny mini cinnamon roll won't matter. We're here for you."

"I hear the voice." I said to Richard Hoagland, an instructor across the way from the lunchroom. "They're calling me to come in and partake of their wonderfulness."

He looked up and over at me and smiled obligatorily before turning back to his work. Richard Hoagland was like that. I'd known him since 1990,... he was my first Computer Sciences Instructor (*Pascal*), when I decided to get my Associate Degree in Computer Science,... and although I'd worked with him for four or five years, I never had a personal conversation with the man,... not that I didn't try, but after years of curt, aloofness in all conversations that always hinged on brevity, I found him to be a person that liked to be distant,... at least that was the way it was with me,... and I was never sure he liked me to be anything more than a passing coworker. I was able to leave the area and escape with the guilt of only eating two (or maybe three; they use this mind thing to make you forget), and from that experience I was inspired to write this poem.

It's funny though, all of the enticement and tempting things that we want of feel we need so much, seem to work the same way. They know our name and they know our heart's desires. And they call to us at times we think no one will know the difference if we do partake.

Side Note:

At the time this was recorded, Meridith was going to Western Washington University with her sister Liz; both taking theatre classes. After reviewing the "*Who I Might Be*" album, Meridith, who struggled with an eating disorder, commented on the words to the "*I Hear The Voice,*" poem, saying that she liked the part that said;

> *"It looks to check the width and length*
> *of only me and how much I resist.*
> *It tests my meddle—my inner strength*
> *secretly smiles with a hidden fist."*

I believe on one of the trips to or from Bellingham, Liz and Meridith were commenting together, (maybe debating between each other), on their other favorites and I believe they agreed to be liking the, "*Hash,*" the, "*Being Sisyphus,*" and the, "*The Last Stop Crash Hotel,*" poems and songs,... and I was always glad to have suggestions, critics and otherwise, inputs about what I do and how to improve my works,... especially from those two girls.

Hash

(2001) – Knowing and celebrating the fact that we come from a mixed bag can be an invigorating thing. Especially because it speaks to us as being a part of something great; our genealogy and posterity.

In one of my technology classes at The Evergreen State College, along with the Computer Sciences classes, I studied the concept of

Eugenics, which is a science that deals with the improvement of hereditary qualities of a race or breed, that is, by the control of human reproduction. Furthermore, it is the study of how to arrange reproduction within a human population to increase the occurrence of heritable characteristics regarded as desirable.

From the mass hype of this movement, in the early 1920s the nation's most restrictive anti-immigration bill passed through Congress in 1924, slamming the door shut on all new immigrants. In fact, in its day, the opponents of eugenics were few and far between. Civil libertarians, women's organizations rarely opposed it. There was no organized liberal or left opposition of any substance and much support from those quarters. The only consistently organized opposition came from the Catholic Church, most of it interestingly coming *before*, the Pope's famous papal letter of 1930 condemning eugenic sterilization was issued.

Developed largely by Sir Francis Galton as a method of improving the human race, eugenics was increasingly discredited as unscientific and racially biased during the 20th century, especially after the adoption of its doctrines by the Nazis in order to justify their treatment of Jews, disabled people, and other minority groups.

All in all, this concept left me with an eerie and uncomfortable feeling, especially after hearing about cloning, like *Dolly the Sheep* who was successfully cloned in 1996 by fusing the nucleus from a mammary-gland cell of a Finn Dorset ewe into an enucleated egg cell taken from a Scottish Blackface ewe. Carried to term in the womb of another Scottish Blackface ewe, Dolly was a genetic copy of the Finn Dorset ewe.

Then there was the 1997, dystopian but not unrealistic science fiction film called, "Gattaca," about a future society driven by eugenics where potential children are conceived through genetic selection to ensure they possess the best hereditary traits of their parents.

Side Note:

I was reminded that my mother used to call us; herself, her children, her parents, and grandparents; everyone included in her lineage; "Hash," with the connotation that we were like a can of mixed foods, but more than just corn beef, potatoes and onions, we were from good stock of immigrants all over the world as well as native Americans, (supposedly, Grandpa Scarbrough's mother's father was Cherokee), making me and mine, kind of like the difference between an inbred pure

Left To Right, Back To Front: Mother, John, David, Me and Richie

breed dog and an intelligent mutt. And so, the argument, or at least the controversy, has many different sides—In the end, I choose my mother's.

Another Side Note:

Not sure if it was the words to the poem, the three-part harmony of voices or the way the whole song came together, but when my son Stephen heard this song, he fell in love with it. I was more intrigued at the fact that he was actually listening intently to my material.

Yet Another Side Note:

One dark rainy night, maybe 1966, mother, with Charlie, Mary and I, all got in the Renault Dauphine and ran away. Richie was in police custody in Flagstaff, Arizona, so against Senior's wishes, who didn't want him back, we

Mother's Renault Dauphine

drove to 545 miles to Flagstaff and picked him up somewhere between two and three in the morning.

That next day we had had peanut butter sandwiches till we ran out of bread, but by nighttime, everyone was hungry again. Mother had limited supplies and reluctantly told us that we would have to wait till breakfast before we would eat again.

As crowded as it could be with five people in a small, Renault Dauphine, mother thought it might be nice for the evening if we could spread out a bit. She decided to stop at a federal park campground and found a campsite (or maybe it was supposed to be just for a day gathering), but the site had an empty covered shelter with a picnic table in the center of it. Charlie and Mary slept under the picnic table, Richie and I slept on top of the table and mother slept in the car.

Early the next morning I woke up to see mother struggling to get a fire started in the grated fire pit next to the shelter. I rolled off the table and told her my Boy Scout skills would get that fire going really fast, and, after going through the woods gleaning dry sticks and other partially burned pieces of wood out of some of the other unoccupied campsites, I got a good fire going and had wood on the side to keep it going. "I really need to have some hot coffee this morning." Mother said, rubbing her cold hands together as she put a small pan with water on one side of the grate.

In the center of the grate, mother put a large cast-iron skillet, and while it was heating up, with my Boy Scout knife, I opened up four large cans of corned-beef hash (in those days, before mother threw the contents into the pan and as the bottom of the corned-beef hash was browning, mother made herself a cup of coffee. After she turned the corned-beef hash over, she made golf-ball sized divots in the hash and put an egg into each divot before adding a little water and putting a lid over the skillet. After waking up the rest of the gang, mother served this wonderful breakfast feast to us on paper plates. The hash was slightly burnt on the bottom, making it extra crispy, but no one cared and it was all gobbled up.

Then Richie and I were put on KP duty while mother along with Charlie and Mary packed everything back up and we went on our way.

Since then, and for years, every time I make my brand of corned-beef hash, I try to get it as close as I can to meet that memory. This song also continues to remind me of that cold, rainy morning in the forest under that covered shelter where my mother made her four hungry kids, hash for breakfast.

My Dream Of Life #86

(1972) – During the years of 1971 and 1973, I lived on the second floor of a crash hotel called the Kingston apartments, located on the Southwest side of Portland Oregon. My apartment was just above and to the right of a bar on the ground floor. At the time I was living there, it was a place that was inhabited by retired folks, (mostly men), with fixed or limited incomes of Social Security, and because the place had a policy where you could rent out a room on a weekly basis. It had its share of winos and bums that were there for a while and then just passing through, not helped by the handy access of that tavern, down below on SW Morrison Street. Situated at about 20th and Burnside, (one of the main thoroughfares of the west side of town), the place never slept. No matter what time of day it was there was always something going on. The cars never stopped going by; people always outside going somewhere and all the ongoing lights made sure if you were a light sleeper, you would not be able to go to sleep.

One night, after getting home from my friend Louie's place, sometime around 2:30 AM, I sat at the window of my apartment (*seen in the center of the picture, second floor, curved triad of windows behind the tree*), staring out at the world outside. There was a kind of music to the noise itself, although constantly changing; but from the cars noisily passing by, the echoing voices of people on the sidewalks or in the streets below, there was a recurring theme to the whole thing that I enjoyed. I picked up a pen and paper and then, to the beat of the streets, wrote this poem. Then I picked up my guitar, opened the window and played this song to the rest of the world outside; a world that was unconscious of the sounds I was making or just ignorant to it all.

This piece was one of those songs that got recorded many times, but finally, after too many interpretations, landed on this album. I can say that I'm still not really happy with this rendition, but I felt it was better than the last few tries and so this recording is it.

Side Note:

If you listen carefully at the beginning of this song, you'll hear the sound of a boy asking questions; that would be Spencer who, at the exact moment I was sitting on the side of my bed with a microphone to my face and another lavalier microphone inside the Lyle guitar, and I had pushed the record button just as Spencer, arguably 14 or 15, popped in and was explaining that he was unhappy because the Game Genie for the Super Nintendo had given him some erroneous codes that were not working. You can hear me say as I'm pointing to the piece of paper, "This part here?" and then you hear him say something to the effect, "so I'm putting in the code but something weird is going on,..." And the next thing you hear is the guitar pounding out the percussion chords to the song.

You should know that as soon as I got done with this recording, I did go into the boy's room to show Spencer that he was using the wrong code. Game Genie, a device that would temporarily modify a game's data, allowing the player to cheat, manipulate various aspects of certain games, and sometimes give access to unused assets and functions. It was not always easy and sometimes was not accurate. And I stayed there to watch Spencer as he went on to win his game.

By The Way:

Spencer was a great Scout. He had this qwerty personality that made him someone everybody wanted to hang around with,... and in Scouting, that was everything,... I remember him walking down one of the many paths at Camp Thunderbird, (*the best Scout Camp he ever went to*),... and he walked with a sense of purpose looking like he owned that Scout camp,... and he had a relatively large entourage of fellow Scouts that waited for Spencer to let them know what he was doing so they could be there with him,... Spencer moved around with a sense of purpose looking all around calculatedly and feeling like he owned that Scout camp,... and so he did,...

Side Note: And then one day at SPSCC Jeans got angry because he felt that one of the network instructors (Alf), was going beyond Jeans' expectations of his network security and when Alf went up for review for tenure, Jeans influenced Gena, who had no idea what she was doing, and under Jean's recommendation, torpedoed Alf by causing the board to postpone the review for 3 months, so as to embarrass him and slap him on the wrist for allowing the students knowledge of the classroom's network addresses, but then Alf Quit.

Jeans was riding high on control after that till one afternoon he went to the offices where the instructors hung out and started yelling at the top of his voice at a tenured instructor (Don't remember much about that – I wasn't there),... but this outburst got all the way back to the President of the college then to the VP and then to Renzo who realized her own mistake in this matter and tried to quietly get Jeans to apologize. Jeans, secure in his ego that he was irreplaceable, refused and let Renzo know that with his secret knowledge of the network settings, nobody could take over his position. He was wrong. He was fired.

And then began a process where Doug-3, a clever young man came in and figured out where everything was and as mentioned previously, Doug-3 handed the network mapping over to a newly hired network administrator whose nickname was Coupe.

It was evident that Coupe was disappointed with his new crew, what with Pete with his flippant attitude towards Coupe and especially me with my obvious limited hardware computer skills and knowledge, but otherwise, he seemed to be okay at first.

But over the years instead of helping me get training and better computer skills, he continually discouraged me from taking classes, putting time constraints on my job to make the taking of network classes almost impossible unless I went at night,... and I think it was from his recommendations that I remain stagnant in my job as a Computer Tech Two.

Side Note:

Coupe's first declaration to Pete and I was that he was building the department on trust and he told us that he did not like being micromanaged and that he was not a person that micromanaged others, preferring to have equal time and group decisions and being a team and giving everybody a say in choices and determinations... and then after a week, and for the rest of the time (eleven years) that I worked with Coupe, he did the exact opposite and micromanaged us and everything that had to do with the Instructional Computing Services, (ICS) department, continuing until the ICS was dissolved years later and after being stripped of all supervisory responsibilities, Coupe was reduced to sitting in a trailer doing literally nothing of value for over a year, he was forced to retire early.

And heaven help us when network things went wrong in building 34 or when he came in to work unhappy, (which was a lot), when his mean alter ego, Skippy would show up.

Another Side Note:

Oh, and trust? Before he was yanked out of building 34, Coupe was constantly monitoring (spying on) everything any student was doing in the computer labs and he was doing the same to Pete and I; openly at times and covertly at other times.

Who I Might Be

(2001) – Family has always been important to me. Because my father and mother broke up when I was quite young, I only interacted with my mother's parent's lineage and knew nothing of the Baldwin line. The only positive male role model I ever knew was my Grandpa Scarbrough; known to us as "Grandpa."

From Left to Right:
Grandpa Ray Scarbrough, Dot & Otis Snook,
Grandma Leda Scarbrough, Aunt Ruby Scarbrough

Grandma Scarbrough, was "Grandma." As far as I know, they were not living together past 1952. But I grew up knowing them and their relatives, especially grandma's because off and on, over the years, I lived in her house. And as some of you may know, Richie and I stayed with Grandma Snook in her apartment in Portland for a while.

So I grew up with Grandma Scarbrough's brothers and sister coming to visit all the time. Grandma had a separate guest apartment in the back of her garage that, by the way, was off limits to us kids. (Although David was known to have occasionally picked the lock and gone in there). I didn't equate Aunt Evelyn, grandma's sister as being anything besides being my own aunt, not my great aunt. And so, it was, from an early age, family meant something to me.

Originally, I wrote this poem to remind myself of the importance of genealogy, and that I needed to do my genealogy. In fact it was originally called, "My Genealogy." Months passed and I performed the song for different company and guests, but although I was playing for a majority of LDS people, I generated very little enthusiasm from anyone. I generalized that Latter-Day Saints can be so inundated with church obligations and responsibilities, like temple work, home teaching and missionary work, that the reality of one more fundamental but important obligation heaped on someone that is already marginally carrying out their other assignments and besides feeling guilty of not doing enough already, one more thing just seems to become a bit too much. And like the student who hates reading a good book only because he or she is forced to have to read that book, many LDS people, especially younger people just can't get excited over doing their genealogy.

So, here's what I did. If you substitute the phrase, "my genealogy," with "who I might be," you would pretty much have it. The resulting response was remarkable. Same audience, sometimes the exactly same people, I won't say they loved it, but they liked it. So, I recorded it as such. I suppose it did take on a different meaning, but I can't see how it would be that much of a change. Oh well, so it goes.

Side Note:

This used to be the lead song on the album, "Who I Might Be," but due to circumstances with certain songs, (this will be explained later in this chapter), I had to reengineer all the song positioning which gave the album a whole different texture or ambiance, but not in a bad way, in fact, I like the way the album flows much better now, although I do miss... well, as previously noted, this will be explained later on at the end of this chapter,.. hopefully, friend.

Another Side Note:

Yes, the name of this album is, 'Who I Might Be' and it relates a very good principal; keeping up with your genealogy, and there is much good to say about this song and the lyrics and,... well can I just admit that this is my least favorite songs on this album,... In the end, it did not quite meet up with my expectations and I find myself wanting to fast forward to the next song,... I don't know, in retrospect I think it's my voice and it should have been done in a different key besides G♯ so my voice could have performed better,...

My Son

(1979) – Getting personal enough to share your personal beliefs and bare your testimony with your sons and daughters is not an easy thing to do. There is the fear of them being turned off or with you getting embarrassed for what you say about what you believe... not an easy thing to do.

So many years ago, as I realized the accountability and magnitude of being a father, I realized the need for a plan to raise these children. Originally as I wrote this poem, I was under the opinion that I would be responsible for the boys and Diane would take care of the girls. And, idealistically, I had hoped that my faith and understanding of the Lord might be understood by my example and then passed on and accepted by my children, and the rest that followed would take care of itself.

These are exciting times of technology taking off making our lives that much more comfortable and even trouble-free, but, ideologically, ethically and doctrinally, these are hard times that we live in now where everything can be justified or reasoned to be right, even when it is clearly and unmistakably wrong.

I want the most for my children but I realize they cannot live by my testimony; they must find and live by their own. And it is so hard at times to open the door to the world and watch them move in the opposite direction from what you'd hoped and prayed for them not to do. Choices are double edged and sometimes wrong choices, especially at first when everything is so easy, requires so much less effort and is much less, than following the Path, or the iron rod to the right alternatives.

Side Note:

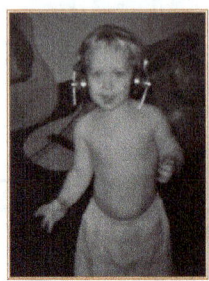

To be fair, this, "*My Son*" poem was written for Chet in 1979 with the realization that I had three daughters and one son. Four kids were enough for me; I wasn't doing such a good job of providing for the family I had at the time anyway. The poem was written when my daughter Lori was six, Chet was four, Liz was two and Meridith was a couple of months old, so when I wrote the poem, I was delighted with my little future priesthood holder and meant to be a kind of comfort for him to know that I would be there to help him through his difficult days of growing up.

Years later I thought to modify the words to be, "My Child" so as to include girls and boys, but it took on a different meaning that could be sung to anyone, to any age, and to me, the revised poem did not seem to hold the same magic that I had found in singing, "My Son."

Another Side Note:

It was around this time that, because we were having a hard time making it on three dollars and fifty cents an hour, that I left JW Electronics to go to work for

Georgia-Pacific Cardboard Manufacturing Plant

Georgia Pacific in their cardboard factory near Lacey. It was a lot more money, not quite twice as much, but over six dollars an hour with a chance for promotions and seasonal pay raises and promotions to other positions and a pension, and... well after I got there, I found the work to be terribly boring. Unbelievably boring. I was a **Pilot**; that is to say, a guy that sits at the end of a green chain or conveyer belt and grabs a stack of flat, ready-to-put-together-as-a-box cardboard and then I would pile it here on a pallet and then pile it there on a pallet and the conveyer belt never stopped until that particular order was finished. I did not wear gloves; now that I think of it, I don't think anybody wore gloves. I would pick that hot, newly glued and stenciled cardboard sheets and although I would continually be getting paper cuts as the hot cardboard slid ever so slightly across my palm or through my fingers, I would keep moving until the job order was done, then I would rest and wait for a minute or two while the next job was tooled and I would have to start all over again.

That in itself over time would be tolerable; other workers there had hands totally calloused from the tips of their fingers to the palms of their hands to the bottom of their thumbs, no exaggeration.

But then the factory went to modular shifts, also known as ir-regular work scheduling where I would work two weeks on the graveyard shift that began some-where between 10:00 p.m. and midnight and ended sometime be-tween 6:00 a.m. to 8:00 a.m., then the next two weeks I would work the swing shift, typically from around 4:00 p.m. to midnight, and then two weeks later I would do the day shift, from 8:00 or 9:00 a.m. until around 5:00 p.m. Problem was, my body could never adjust to any schedule because it kept changing. And when you work graveyard you never see your family; you're coming when they're going and vise versa, swing shift is like, you work till midnight, you come home have dinner by yourself, maybe watch tv if something is on and go to bed by two or three then wake up, eat break-fast at twelve and then get ready for work. Day shift is only one that works, and, on rotation, you just get settled and its back to the grave-yard shift. But did I mention it was over six dollars an hour? Long story short, I went back to work at JW Electronics.

Being Sisyphus

(2001) – There is perhaps two factors that separate mankind from the rest of the animal kingdom; our belief that, we have this special or certain sentience, and within that, the ability to think, and our ability to love.

I remain most amazed at the strength, command and power of this thing called love, which is defined or interpreted differently from individual to individual. This action and or behavior, and or conduct, can symbolize or embody a kind of caring, and or a particular passion or set of passions, and or maybe a sense of fulfillment, and which might take on variable degrees of enjoyment from a thought to many degrees of physical contact, and much more, sometimes enveloping multiple personifications at the same time.

Again, this poem was written for and in behalf of my daughter Lori, who was still going through a difficult time in her life; in and out of a relationship with a man that said he was torn between staying with her in a relationship and returning to the girl he was with before her. Of course, we knew what she needed to do, but she was lost. All I could see was her struggling to keep the love alive and after watching the rock once again roll to the bottom of the hill, she would ask herself, "Why should I roll it back up?"

Throughout the history of men and women, this thing called love has been a driving force that has helped shape the philosophies and destinies of many a man. It is from an ambiguous perspective of love that I approached this poem because, if you think about it, people are willing to endure great hardships in the name of and in the expectation of love. Perhaps there is relevance to the comment made in the Disney animation, "*The Sword And The Stone*," where a young and impressionable Arthur is talking to Merlin about powerful, magical forces and correlating and comparing them to life on earth, and Merlin says in passing nonchalantly that he thinks that love is the most powerful force on the earth.

Side Note:

This poem takes on a whole different meaning to me as I look at my push to get my dreams to come true, to have people notice what I'm doing over here in Olympia Washington and maybe have some type of validation for my works. Then there's the clock ticking, telling me that I'm running out of time to be a rock star, although my stuff is far from conventional rock, but the dream is always scratching from within, telling me to hurry up and write something phenomenal. And there have been times where I would be in a state of anguish over my sense of being invisible, but that kind of thing can eat you up inside if you let it. And then there is the practical pig, who builds his house with bricks, knowing that it takes more time but ends up being a better product. I have passed up opportunities to take things to another level, but they always seemed to come at a time when things at home were not good; I guess there would never be an ideal situation anyway, but it was always the price I'd have had to pay and the assay was always there to make me check what I felt to be of importance, forcing me to scrutinize all the angles, testing my mettle and loyalties to what I believe and then after making the choices I did, there's the thing in the back of my mind, taunting me with the ever infamous "what ifs," and, "see that? That could have been you."

All the time, sitting in my back pocket was this magic ticket that, after the kids have all left home or maybe, after you retire, you can pursue this dream without the family complications. But hey, families are forever and just because they've left the house, doesn't mean they've left your home. And things come up and opportunities grow slimmer as you get older. And, if you're happily married, (which I am), you have to take her needs and hopes and dreams into consideration too; and they might not be in concert with yours. And; here's a factor I hadn't thought of back then when I was making all these concessions; when you get older your desires and dreams may still be alive and bright, but your abilities start to dwindle a bit, I'm not talking about musical inspirations, that is a gift that keeps on giving your whole life, but, like making my "B min" chord on my acoustic guitar? It is getting increasingly harder these days to get my thumb over to the "A" string for the bass. And lastly, your energy levels diminish, making you have to make compromises and even minimizing opportunities where ten years ago you could have played all night long. So I've taken a different view of things. Maybe for now, it's enough to be able to do what I'm doing right now; writing these books of, 'Poetry and Memoirs From An Invisible Songwriter.'

Another Side Note:

A couple of months ago, (4-2001), I was called into the office of my supervisor Renzo on short notice. Apparently, Coupe had been secretly monitoring the activities on my computer, had noticed that there were downloads from Napster going on, and reported it to Renzo.

She asked me if I had done that and I told her that I had not. She then said she had evidence to the contrary. Looking at the log that Coupe provided, stating it was done during lunch times. I then said that my son Stephen often comes to my office at that time and perhaps he had done it, (by the way, he had). Renzo said this was serious and that I was getting a letter put into my file in HR and if there was another incident I would be let go. Also, it would take three years to have the letter removed.

I found out later from another employee that they, the powers that be, have to first give me a warning if it is a first offense for such an infraction before they put something like this in my file. But, such as it was, I had to eat this one.

Yet Another Side Note:

My coworker, Pete was always downloading MP3s from varied sites, including Napster but he was never called to the mat on it. In fact, he was downloading copious albums and video media at the same time this thing happened to me. When I told him what had happened to me, Pete said, "I told you he, (Coupe), had it in for you." Meanwhile, Pete continued doing what he wanted with no warnings, repercussions, or seemingly any interest from Coupe, Renzo or for that matter, the internet police.

Like The Wind Upon It's Way

(1983) – The life and times of a drifter on his way through life. This poem to music has been recorded so many times that I don't even know where the others are on all master tapes.

It is such a nice poem that reflects on *"who I might be"* and documents a kind of *"just passing through"* and, *"I'm a work in progress"* learning attitude, but this poem and the essence of the message was from a sliver from my memoirs to be of and for my Grandpa Ray Scarbrough and his early years before he got married and settled down.

Unfortunately, I have never quite recorded this song to my expectations or standards and so, even though this one too falls short, I wanted to get the monkey off my back and so here it is in whatever documentary form it is, I hope you like it. I think it is better to have it out there in case I never do rerecord it.

Side Note:

This poem, written during my Funeral Home Renaissance days, had such promise to me. When my friend Daryl heard it, he wanted me to record it and get it out on the Country & Western radio market, and maybe get *Willie Nelson*, or *George Strait*, or *Conway Twitty*, or *Waylon Jennings* do the song. And I believe he even tried to get ahold of some of them, but his connections, although much greater than all of mine, could not reach out that far and this song waited another five years to get recorded by its writer.

I Believed

(2001) – As I went through my whole childhood, a part of me was glad to have moved around as much as I had because in another new and unfamiliar place, there was always a chance that at that next place, I might be more accepted, more cool, more suave, more charismatic, more acknowledged, more handsome, more loved. But it seemed that no matter where I went, there was always an astigmatism that followed me, and people that would use me as a catalyst to fortify or uplift themselves at the expense and degradation of my personal psyche. But if I was at fault for anything, it was having the want and need to be loved, so I listening to others that didn't know me and then believed I was less than what I really was.

 You know those people that would get together in groups or gangs parading their power and muscle with that strength in numbers, and then they would single you out, and start in with the silly lie and tell you that you were ugly or say that you couldn't do something because you weren't good enough, or as smart, or as pretty, or that you were less than even you with your low self-esteem thought you were?

Bullies were everywhere I went,... and I went to eleven schools before I graduated high school,... it was usually those individually flawed persons that might be insecure, might be having problems at home, maybe being persecuted or tormented by a parent, but when that bully formed a group around their interests, oh man; they were viciously confident with unrighteous power, unleashing pain and suffering while enforcing their unmitigated power and influence and control over you.

And you want so much to be loved, to be able to fit in, and you don't mind being lesser than you are as long as you can be included in the group.

So, when they would reiterate the silly lies, saying things about me, again and again,... and their gang is reaffirming what the leader has said,... which is kind of a witness against you,... and with three witnesses you would maybe start to question yourself, gauging or re-evaluating what you thought was true and then you start to doubt, and after that, things start going sideways with your self-worth self-respect and confidence in yourself.

After a while, if you don't get some other positive reaffirmations from others around you, like your mother or your siblings, the things that are said about you to hurt you only hurt more because you have come to the point where you too now believe in the silly lie.

Long Ago And Far Away

(1974) – Long ago and miles from here I set out to write a poem about innocence in its simple moments. Make believe There was a lot of alterations along the way and the poem evolved to what it is now. For years, I sang this song to the kids at bedtime and for that captive audi-ence, I was well received. And beyond being fun for kids, I think that pretending and other kinds of imaginative play are critical to healthy for a child's development in creativity, understanding of others and maybe even social aptitude and capability of interacting with friends and others.

And maybe in pretending, children can learn to do things like being considerate to others and giving respect and consider-ation for another's perspectives, obviously they can learn to share knowledge and balance their own ideas with others, it can be good for developing plans, express and listen to thoughts and ideas of others. And let's face it pretending can stir the imagination to create. Create scenarios and pretend places, and actions and reactions, and go to places they could never go to before. Pretending can also lead to non-pretend actions, learned from past experiences.

I spent a lot of time pretending when I was a kid. There were no video games, well, to be fair with you, there was little to no television for me, at least while I was in the households with Senior, especially after a few glasses of wine. Too unpredictable and dangerous. So, I was outside, rain, shine, snow, after dark; it was a different time and place. I only went inside to eat dinner, to go to sleep and occasionally to do homework.

Side Note:

After I became a father, right off I knew I needed to try to capture in a poem, the feel and ambiance of the awesome act and art of pretending. And it not only pleased me that my kids liked this song but moreover, until they felt I was too old to be in their hallowed youthful circle, you know, that time before I was just an adult?

And I was invited many times to connection with each and every one of my children; to join them in their fireside, pretending; and I always gladly and excitedly accepted their invitations.

But the virtuousness and naïveté innocence of childhood will always be fleeting and that special time lasts for only so long before they, the children, find they've outgrown or lost the keys to remain in that domain, and then find the need to have to move on, and sadly when that happens, I have to accept that they are growing up and out of the Peter Pan syndrome leaving me to be suddenly an outcast, an outsider once again; to move forward now I would be just a gatecrasher or trespasser that no longer belongs or is welcome; and to return to that magical place, I must find another willing to share their fire.

The Right Road To Travel

(2001) – Knowing where you are going to is good. Knowing who you are is even better. Knowing why you're here, where you came from and where you're going and, being on track with that goal is all something entirely different.

Although many of us can shape our destinies with what we want to do or where we plan to go, there is a certain time in our life where we look back and realize that at one of the crossroads that we stumbled at, maybe at one of the dead-end roads or when we staggered and fell off and down one of the wrong Paths, there were learning lessons to be gotten and they were as valid an experience as what we have valued or regarded as the lessons learned while cruising on the right Paths that traveled.. Sometimes, the right road to travel is the road you are on, that road right in front of you.

Side Note:

My thought here was that life is the journey, not the destination and we sometimes frustrate ourselves by being so focused on how things ought to be right now, or might soon be, or should have been, or even will be; not realizing that our focus should be on the right now, on this journey here, not to worry about looking back or worried about the tomorrow to come.

Someday

(2001) –I have a nephew who is going through something I went through when I was his age. There was a lot of changes I went through to get to where I am now and a lot of those roads and detours were less than choice by comparison.

JW Electronics – Back Warehouse

At 35, I lost my job when the funeral home was sold to a conglomerate, and I was left with no prospects and no hope. I had a wife, six kids, a mortgage and besides unemployment, no money coming in. After an exhausting search for work I was offered a job back at JW Electronics as a parts driver—a job I had done for the same company eleven years earlier. Besides giving me material for poems and songs like, "Where I Used To Be," I was very unhappy with my lot in life. I had visions of carrying my music to great heights but could never seem to do anything professionally with it. I knew I was intelligent and I knew I had talent, I knew I had something very special with my love for my wife and children, but that clouded small voice inside me kept pointing out the defects and failures and inadequacies that overshadowed everything else; reminding me that I was, 'Just Not Good Enough' and it told me that I was, 'Nothing But A Nothing.'

So, after calling up all the people that I had known or suspected that might have disliked me at JW, each time asking that individual for their forgiveness, (and actually having one person point blank tell me NO, and more than once that he would not!), anyway, I slithered back into JW Electronics again, working with some of the people that were not happy to see me return, and even worse, a few of the people there would point out to me how unskilled, inadequate and useless I was, and, as another one of my poems to songs recorded,... "I Believed."

I have reflected on those days and my thoughts and feelings that led me through those times, and I compare them with my attitude about life now. I still haven't done anything professionally with my music and I still seem to be just getting by, but I know that all of this stuff;

this stuff we carry and value can sometimes get warped because we are looking at things the way we think others are looking at them and judging ourselves and our circumstances accordingly.

Side Note:

"Someday" is a song about getting past all of that anguish and suffering and anxiety and pain and being able to look in the mirror and see that guy that is making it happen for his wife and family and feeling good about who and what he is right then and now, and seeing what he's done; the accomplishments that get lost in the shadows of the overhang clouds of uncertainty. And think about how you managed to still be here today.

The Last Stop Crash Hotel

(2001) – One of these days I'm going to put out an album called, "It Came To Me In A Dream." This is another one of those poems put to music to be a song that I extrapolated from one of my more colourful dreams.

And I was there in one of the vehicles with the Scoutmaster, Mike, (now our Bishop), and I'm looking for somewhere that we can pitch our ten or fifteen tents down by the riverside so that we can have front row seats for the Rose Festival that would be happening in the morning on the following day.

For some reason, Mike leaves me with the Boy-Scout-packed second vehicle, driven by his wife, while he goes off searching for the police to get his permit signed.

I'm let out into the, "Old Town" Skidmore area where there is one of these crash hotels, and I'm looking for someplace to let the kids out to go to the bathroom.

Mike's wife Jan tells me I have five minutes and unlocks all the doors to the vehicle as all of the Scouts quickly pile out.

Meanwhile, (keep in mind, this is a dream), this destitute scruffy guy is sitting in the front entrance singing this drinking song about his friend who is apparently passed out with one leg in the ditch and the other covering the sidewalk so that we have to carefully step over him and or his leg.

We get let into this awful bathroom, that hasn't been cleaned or attended to for months and with its one, 40-watt lightbulb hanging down from the ceiling, it's rather dark and really stinky, but the Boy Scouts are calling it an indoor KYBO, (Keep Your Bowels Open), enjoying the adventure and are using the facility.

All of a sudden there is an explosion and all the boys run out laughing. Seems it was dark in there and someone lit a match so they could see the toilet and the methane gas inside there exploded everything except the boys who are singed but okay.

As we exit, somehow, I am now the person singing this crazy song, and after we all get into the vehicle, Jan says that she now needs to use the facilities, but the boys tell her that it's gone and after relating the whole story, she says she wants to find a gas station.

Meanwhile, remember Jan's husband? He calls us up from his cell phone and says he's down on the waterfront with the navy and a submarine, wondering if we want a midnight tour.

And then there was the Boy Scout fishing contest to happen after we all set up our tents, but we had still not established where that was going to happen.

Side Note:

There was more, but after I woke up, I wrote the words to the poem and then recorded a semblance of the music and song. It was rerecorded the following day because something went wrong with the first one and it developed a wow and flutter. (A problem common with cassette recorders).

I wanted to do it again and put some percussion into it and really jazz it up, but after re-listening to the reengineered version, I liked the way it turned out better, I felt that it had a good feel and was a bit closer to the dream, so I kept it just that way.

My Concubine

(2001) – Hey, surprise. No lyrics in the poetry section of "My Concubine" and sadly, there was no song published. I felt at the time that the words to this poem were clever with them saying one thing but meaning something else. But times change and people's perspectives do too.

Side Note:

As irony played a role in this, my objective was to point to how older adult couples were dealing with the internet in an adverse way,... well I may or may not explain more about that at another time.

So, there I was one day, driving in my car, listening to the news, (oh no, not again...), where it was reported that lately, communications between couples have drastically diminished since the advent of the computer, and more specifically, the internet. There seems to be a concern that the internet was corrupting and perverting people into spending time online at the expense of time spent with spouses and significant others or family.

The news report stated that husbands or wives are sitting at their computer screens at home and not going out of their rooms to talk to their other partners or would choose to remain at their computers at night instead of going to bed, but moreover, there was (is) a tendency to put off or ignore domestic problems that they might be having with one another, pulling people away from any in-person contact, cultivating disinterest or indifference to their problems, and developing a growing alienation between each other and allowing communications to break down due to the ease of ignoring the other and substituting the excitement of the Internet in place of any conflict resolution.

I went around and around in my head over this issue, even to the point where I consulted my daughter Meridith, our very own, "Marriage and Family Therapist/Expressive Arts Therapist and Mental Health Clinician," who confirmed that, "*My Concubine*" might not be interpreted in the most positive way to the listeners out there streaming material from cyberspace and that I should probably not include it on the, "*Who I Might Be*" album, but at the same time, she recommended that I keep, "*The Last Stop Crash Hotel*" into the mix as it was not offensive.

After conferencing with Meridith, it was thought that, in the interest of sensitive listeners, and with this song going worldwide,... and then being misinterpreted,... I took it out of the lineup and in doing so, had to reengineer the whole structure of the album and the song positioning. And although I do like how the new album feels, this poem to song had a really neat sound. Uh well...

Side Note To The Side Note:

My good friend, Jim, who was one of my lab techs and was working in the computer labs one day when I showed him this poem. He read it and apparently saw through the parable, and with a knowing glance, he said, "Computers. You're talking about being on the computer at night, aren't you?" He laughed and as he pointed to himself, said excitedly, "That's me!"

My Concubine

In moments where I must intrude,
when she's out of sorts or not in the mood,
I'm left frustrated and far from feeling fine.
But what if there was a way to be
to alleviate that pressure from her and me,
might be a good idea to have my own concubine.
Those nights when she wants to be left alone
or the mornings when she needs to get up and go,
well, that's okay, when she's ready, I'll make the time.
But meanwhile, I won't be troubled at all
I'll say goodnight and walk down the hall
to my odalisque that is, in my concubine.
No more being on the schneid and having to wait,
or dealing with an attitude, or that altered state,
I'll just move to the next one waiting there in line.
And when I'm done and the rest will keep,
I'll come back to bed and get some sleep
till tomorrow's return to my functional concubine.
Now she'll have that time she needs to regroup
and won't have to keep jumping through the hoop
every time I'm in need and give her that special sign.
Instead, she'll just smile and give me a call
when I finally return from that room down the hall
from my den of principle, that is, my concubine.
In moments where I must be on my own,
when she looking for an evening to be left alone,
I'll be okay, we'll all be feeling fine.
She can play her games and never lose,
While I'm having a hard time trying to choose,
who it'll be tonight in my refuge concubine.

109

- 44 - THE UNIVERSE
WITHIN - 2001 -

110

NOTES ABOUT THE COVERS

Notes On The New Cover:

As you may be able to see, I took the same fetus and rotated him so instead of looking across, now, if he opened his eyes he would be able to look up into the universe itself. To get the feel of floating in space with stars emanating from below his head and in the background above is an Orion Nebula photo taken from outer space by the Hubble Telescope with and expanded view of the stars below. From the simple editing tool, GIMP2.1 (GNU Image Manipulation Program) to create a PNG image, it took me, I don't know, let's just say hours to get this to look the way it does.

For the, "Lord Baldwin," pseudonym as well as "The Universe Within" lettering, I used the, "Showcase Gothic" font, (kind a like my signature font for Lord Baldwin stuff), and placed them out of the way so you could see space.

Notes On The Original Covers:

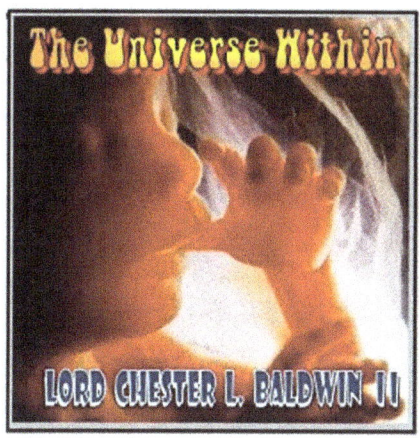

Front Cover; This original picture was an actual fetus of some human being that is more than likely, 22 years old now,... but I was fascinated by the clarity of the baby in the womb.

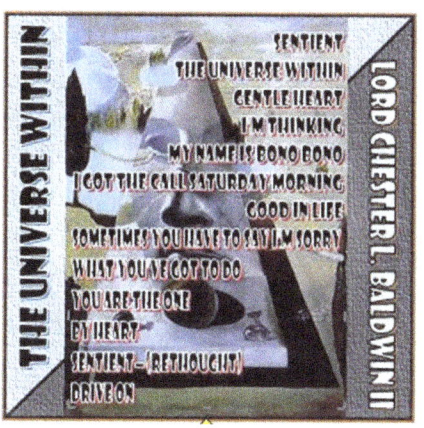

Back Cover: *'Aphrodite of Cnidos-Face of a Child in a Pyramid'* by Salvador Dali – 1981

The Aphrodite of Knidos was an Ancient Greek sculpture of the goddess Aphrodite created by Praxiteles of Athens around the 4th century BC. It is perhaps the first life-sized representation of the nude female form in Greek history, displaying an alternative idea to male heroic nudity

Salvador Dali manipulated that image and,...

III

THE UNIVERSE WITHIN

The Universe Within
Gentle Heart
I'm Thinking
My Name is Bono Bono
I Got The Call Saturday Morning
Good In Life
Sometimes You Have To Say I'm Sorry
You Are The One
By Heart
Drive On

112

The Universe Within

Twenty-three plus twenty-three friends in appropriate pairs,
an assortment and mixture of folks
that each, receives and shares.

In the center of the dividing block,
the progression of the bonding begins,
as acceptance of each other for each other
towards; the universe within.

Centered here and drawing near;
the universe within.
Out in space, yet here in place;
the universe within.

Ancestors from both camps are there,
character streams from their source.
They look on in confirmation and support,
towards the path of their uncertain course.

After ceremony, joining, commitment,
they reach out for each other as kin;
they embrace and to the music they dance
towards the universe within.

Star, sun, moon, arriving soon;
the universe within.
Words unsaid; they know instead;
the universe within.

Magnetism draws its magic,
from first thought to the beating of the heart.
They grow as one, arise, develop,
their own to flesh out this new start.

Senses heighten, with a shared understanding;
a harbinger of a time to begin,

the next stage and then onward through
the universe within.

Rising fire, new desire;
the universe within.
Calling loud; beyond the shroud;
the universe within.

113

Gentle Heart

Be careful, be careful out there; before you do things,
think about what it is you want to do.
Don't be afraid to fail or make mistakes,
and when you error, learn from it and go to something new.

Be happy to know and be yourself;
don't worry too much about what others do or say.
Let your world be filled with dreams of joy and wonder,
as you find yourself and place along the way.

Be watchful of your actions and your words;
consider, it's better to be wise than to be smart.
Be sensitive to the needs of other people,
and shelter, save and take care of your gentle heart.

Don't worry about your strength or size,
remember, even the greatest tree began as a seed.
It's always good to show a little kindness;
look around, you're sure to find someone in need.

Stand strong by what you believe, but know;
to be sensible yet steadfast is an art.
Try not to forsake the right to run with the wrong,
and never be ashamed of, or lose your gentle heart.

There will be times when only you will matter,
there will be moments where life around you will fall apart.
It will be then that you will find your greatest power
in the simple warmth you shine tenderly with your gentle heart.

114

I'm Thinking

Lights moves as morning colors dance,
from the window I see the steady advance
of people and things in motion or stance
and I wonder,...

Questions look for answers that I don't know
As I pedal my bike down the old farm road
where seasons are in an in-between kind of flow,
and I wonder,...

I wonder why the grass is green,
and how these thoughts can come to me
and I wonder how it can be that I'm thinking.

I touch the bark in a red cedar stand,
then try to seize water that runs through my hand;
I stare down the coastline at all of the sand
and I wonder,...

I can see, and touch, and taste, and smell,
I can hear, and distinguish other senses as well
that hints of maybe something more to tell,
and I wonder,...

I wonder why the grass is green,
and how these thoughts take shape in me
and I wonder how this all can be that I'm thinking;

but I'm thinking,... I'm thinking,... I'm thinking.

I feel something deep inside me call,
To say that there's something more to it all
that I might finally understand and know;
and I wonder,...

I kind of know it's there, maybe it's always been,
but how do I know how I fit in?
With so much to learn from now to then;
and I wonder,...

And I wonder of eternity, of life and death; of you and me
and I wonder how this all can be that I'm thinking;

but I'm thinking.
I am thinking,...
I'm thinking.
I'm thinking.

115

My Name Is Bono Bono

My name is Bono Bono,
and I would like to give you a kiss.

My name is Bono Bono,
and you are surely one that I would miss.

116

I Got The Call Saturday Morning

I got the call
Saturday morning,
She had passed away sometime in the night.
And I was speechless; regrettably silent
that I had failed to reach her in time.

With so much to do,
and so little time,
I had hoped to meet all the other pressing needs
but when the call came, I was only reminded
of my other, many past defeats.

I could see her
in that hospital bed,
waiting for me to visit her one last time again,
looking out a window, then down the hall,
just wondering where I am.

And late as usual-
the bridegroom's come and gone
and I'm too late--my lamp is out of oil.
Indisposed I stand confused; disheartened,
no reward for my hopeful toil.

God knew my heart,
He knew my will,
He knew what I was trying to do in my own way,
But in my quest to hold to a balance
I ran out of time and she passed away.

We take our time,
think we have time,
wait till that last moment to put it all in place,
but that last moment may come before we expect it
or are ready then to face.

I got the call
Saturday morning
that she had passed away and I wanted to cry.
There was no way to tell her what I wanted to say,
and it was too late to say goodbye.

117

Good In Life

You don't need to look very hard to find wrong
for the flaws of the world are easy to find
and the shadows consume all the small bits of light.

Maybe the answers were there all along in your search;
in your heart, for the gentle and kind
to glimpse for a moment; a hint of some good in life.

Sometimes we feel sorry with our broken wing
that we can't see another still lost in the weeds
struggling there desperately just to cope with their strife.

So many in need of the spirit you bring
and the comfort you pass may be all someone needs
to sustain and restore their faith of the good in life.

Hoping to find the path to the gate, that leads to the prize,
but few there be that find or even know what their searching for.
You don't need to look very hard to find grief,

there are lost souls out there needing comfort or rest
that wait for an answer beyond this dark night.
Maybe by acting upon your belief

you will find you no longer feel lost and depressed,
you may find indications that there is some good in life.
Sometimes to escape from the prison you dwell

you must see past your chains, and the walls and the bars,
to transcend and reach out with your goodness in kind.
If your destiny is not for the fates to tell

and you trust in yourself, and not just to fate or the stars;
lean your head out enough
and you'll see that there's good in life.

118

Sometimes You Have To Say, I'm Sorry

Sometimes you have to say, "I'm Sorry."
Sometimes you have to take the hard road,
even when you might lose it all,
or you know it's not your fault,
you know it's what must be done—you just know.
Sometimes you realize it's up to you,
to put and to a conflict carried too long,
to reach out and impart your wisdom and your heart
regardless of who is right or wrong..
And with love see the enemy;
see the pride that has brought you to this place.
And with love see the solution
is stepping back with dignity and grace.
Sometimes you have to just give in.
Recognize the mistake and then just let it go.
It's healing to forgive
all the days that you live
and deep down inside; you know, you know.

119

You Are The One

At a time when the world needs a champion
to stand up strong in the belief a change should be made.
Although the price is dearer than any price ever paid,
the brave steps forward to do it anyway.

What if it was you? What if it was you that was that champion,
and the course of history could be changed by you?
Although the cost was dearer than any price you ever paid
could you maintain that integrity in everything you do?

You are the one to make a difference this time.
The one that stands their ground as others turn and run.
You are the one for those who need you desperately right now
and all you need do is believe; you are the one.

There's a stand that needs to be made sooner or later;
for what is life without direction purpose or goal?
What is a man profited—what truly does he hold
if he should gain the world yet lose his own soul?

Your whole life was preparing for this moment;
inside your heart a question will not leave;
is the foundation of understanding yourself,
to know and act upon what you believe?

You are the one to make a difference this time;
the one that works to finish what others have left undone.
You are the one to share that love and hope inside your heart
and all you need do is believe; you are the one.

At a time when hope is gone, darkness even fills the dawn
and they say, "All hope is lost," but look inside.
Every fiber of your being testifies of a truth
that cannot be disputed or denied.

At a time when the world needs a champion
to stand up tall to represent all those in need.
Although the cost is dearer than you hoped to paid
you step forward to take hold and succeed.

You are the one to make a difference this time;
the one to raise the banner high up to the sun.
You are the one that is destined to come at this critical hour,
and all you need do is believe you are the one.
You are the one.

120

By Heart

You would think I would know
after all of these years
why she gets weird at times,
from her beliefs or fears.
But as she drifts further away
from what she herself planned,
I have come to realize
I may never understand
her.

Yet from noble hopes and dreams
that her concerns are made of;
through unfailing charity
and an unconditional love,
though I only comprehend
a very small part,
in a wonderful way
I know
her by heart.

121

Drive On

Yesterday; disheartened, I was driven beyond critique,
and it caused my mind to doubt, my music and the words I speak.
Still, if I fail or succeed in the end the difference is slight,
and it's what I do with what I see,
from whatever wisdom and insight

that makes the difference,
that sets the stage to create and beyond,
confirms the purpose to the heart,
and perpetuates me to drive on. Oh,... to drive on.

Critical words from ones hell-bent
without knowing what it's about
to cause one to partake of their discontent
to give basis for distress and doubt.

Is it all they have in their weaponry to justify mediocrity?
but if I know the truth; I know myself,
what I am and what I believe,

can make the difference,
as I await the coming new dawn
and renews that purpose to my heart,
and sustains me to drive on.
Oh,... to drive on.

Greater deeds from more remarkable men
will dwarf me and my cause,
if measurements are drawn against the lines
that weigh merit with flaws.

Yet all I am today or will become begins with a simple belief
that I believe in what I do and that something different;
special in me,

that makes the difference,
with this gift to be used or be gone,
and confirms the purpose to the heart and soul,
and with passion I shake the reins to drive on.
Oh,... to drive on.

122

MEMOIRS & NOTES - 44 - 'THE UNIVERSE WITHIN'

Sentient, (Thought)

(2001) – From the beginning, the collections of poems and the composition of the music, this album was perceived and envisaged to be a concept album dealing with the many questions of sentience and the realization of all that goes with the aspect of life and living for a reason.

One could easily argue from a spiritual standpoint and I'm cool with that, but what about those out there that are questioning without the luxury (or weight) of having that to hold onto? The word, 'Sentient' comes from the Latin sentient-, "feeling," and it describes things that are alive, able to feel and perceive, and show awareness or responsiveness. Having senses

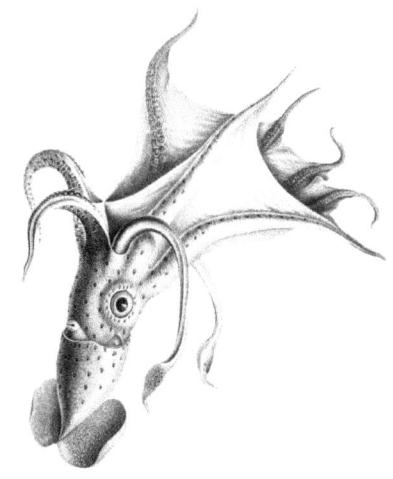

makes something sentient, or able to smell, communicate, touch, see, or hear.

Surely there are people that still look up to the stars at night and wonder what it's al l about. Unquestionably there are people that realize they have the capacity to physically feel things like pain and pleasure, or to feel things inside like joy and sorrow and to perceive things; to become aware of something, know, or identify by means of the senses, or to experience subjectively; the emotional and cognitive impact of a human experience as opposed to an objective experience which are the actual events of the experience. While something objective is tangible and can be experienced by others and the awesome idea that these subjective experiences are shaped from somewhere 8inside our minds, the very thought that we can manufacture and construct thought itself, generated by our own individual mind; it's so incredible it's almost inconceivable.

Side Note:

This instrumentation to begin the album with it's lone piano voice calling out, as if to ask, "What it this thing that is in me or is me and that I am now identifying with, noticing, detecting movement and constant change, seeing and or feeling what's in front of me and perceiving all around me?

Another Side Note:

Before I put this whole thing together, Liz was visiting from Western Washington University, maybe for Thanksgiving, and I played this piece for her. She listened intently to the one-minute-and fifteen-second arrangement and immediately looked over with surprise and said, "That's really good, dad."

The Universe Within

(2001) – Originally this was written about the magnificent process and miracle of mitosis, which is a part of the cell cycle, in which, replicated chromosomes are separated into two new nuclei, and cell division gives rise to genetically identical cells in which the total number of chromosomes is maintained. Science; one of the tools of the sentient being, (or the vehicle for denial by the sceptics who have little to no capability for abstract thought)

I thought this would be my chance to begin the album with this poem in an up-tempo fashion and the conceptual model or idea would carry through the rest of the album. Although I had no tune, I was confident that the power of the subject would carry this to a great height. After the poem was completed, I read the words over a few times and knew that the poem as it was, would not work. It was all too scientific and dry with no life and no magic. I took another stab and put different music to the words but it was no use. There was no way this poem to song was going to get off the ground like it was and there was no way this song was going to be able to lead the rest of the album.

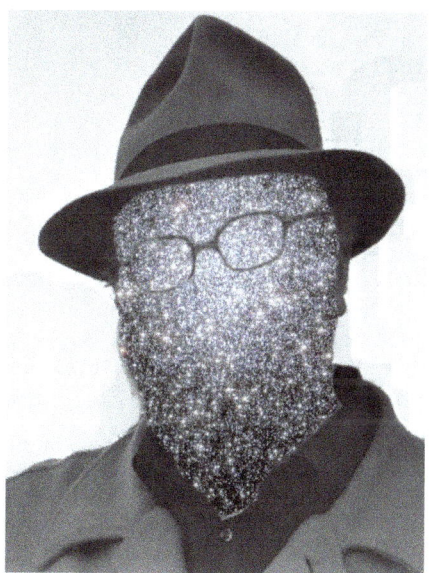

I decided to keep the concept, but changed the words and masked the mitosis or that is, substituted the general ideas with that of a kind-of wedding, a marriage between two people, along with a wedding ceremony and party afterwards. There were some problems, but the words to the poem were sounder and the encryption fell together on paper far easier than the general scientific terms.

Side Note:

One day I woke up to a world full of snow and not being one of those that likes to brave the roads of snow and ice, I settled in at home and invariably ended up on the keyboard. I toyed with different chords but nothing seemed to come together. I left to go outside for a while in the snow with the kids but I soon came back in, (it was a wet, cold snow that only a kid could like), and toyed around with another tune. After playing with this tune and the two chords, it dawned on me that this could be a chorus or a middle-8 thing if I wanted to write something more into the words of the poem. So, I tied the chorus together and wrote lyrics to go with it, but I still had no tune for the rest of the song.

Another Side Note:

The following night I sat on Stephen's bed with a guitar tinkering with some chords, but I wanted the structure to reflect the evolution of the single cell to the growth of the fetus to the development and birth of a baby. Then an idea came to me, what if I went, like a circle of fifths, but went from a tonic to its relative minor then to the subdominant, then to its relative minor and so on, going through 16 chords and arrive to the dominant of the major tonic; that would be different, and on experimental circumstances it did sound cool too. But I had to do the math because I wanted to land back on "D" to slide into the tonic of the chorus being in "G." It was a bit of a stretch to go from the end of the chorus that is, "C" to "G#" to arrive at "C#" but it worked and the end results is here. I'm not that good of a guitarist that I can't play all these chords very well, but I did my best. And that is me at the very end laughing because I lost my timing a bit. Fun stuff.

Gentle Heart

(2001) – This song has two places of origin, beginning with my home and spilling over into my brother Ray's home. firstly and NOW; I was seeing my own children entrenched in some of the temporal things of this time, like the availability of anything over the internet, the trappings of 'R' rated movies (and even some questionable PG-13), the influences of other friends that, in their homes, may have relaxed their standards, or they may have moral issues or consequences that might end up getting them in trouble.

I saw Matthew, my brother Ray's 13-year-old son slowly distancing himself from his family. At the time, Ray, who has always been a family man, was once again single, taking care of three daughters and two sons,... as well as being proactive with his older sons and daughters,... at the time, besides being behind with his property taxes, Ray was arguably drowning in other debt,... and as a contractor and/or subcontractor working hard in construction,... that had to be grueling especially for a man over fifty,... Ray worked hard to ferret out whatever work he could find,... whenever and wherever he could find it, *going from paycheck to paycheck, living on the edge of the today,...*

Matthew was a kid who early on was looking for a sense of meaning to his life,... and outside influences called him out,... introduced him to other possibilities,... maybe find himself in a world of escape, maybe like him finding an oasis after walking in the desert,...

I'm sure Ray was concerned as, from a distance, he watched his 13-year-old boy running with an older crowd,... and for a while Matthew had dual identities; one for the Matthew at home and the other Matthew when he was out with his gang,... but this duality was hard to maintain and after a while it led to a gradual falling away from family,...

Matthew became distant to most others, including me and members of my family, like his favorite cousin Spencer who he used to like hanging with,... and when we would come to visit Matthew would pretend to be older, to be tough, and put on this oddly fitting façade,...

Side Note:

On October 18, 2001, Matthew was killed in an automobile accident. He was cruising around with a much older man that accidently lost control of his vehicle and ended up crashing into a tree off of S Hwy 99 E on the outskirts of Canby.

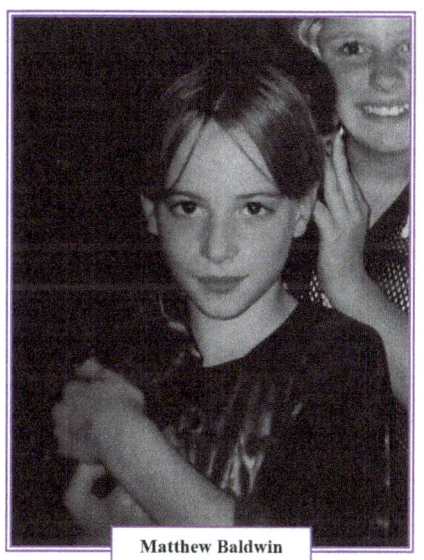

Matthew Baldwin

Another Side Note:

Within days following Matthew's services and interment, I returned to the essence of this poem, and as I rewrote the words, I felt inspired; almost like Matthew's spirit was there in the room with me, encouraging me, stirring my feelings, dictating or approving these words to the poem,... it was then that I was also able to see the true Matthew from a different perspective; a child who, in search of love and knowledge, made some mistakes while navigating his temporal path through his life. It was then that I broke down and cried for him,... and for me and for everyone's loss. and, I feel I felt his spirit conveying to me that he wanted me to let his family know that he did love them very much and that he hoped his mistakes could be a heartbreaking but discerning lesson learned for all of us too.

Yet Another Side Note:

When I completed this album, I drove down to Canby and gave Ray a copy of the album, "The Universe Within" and I told him that I had felt a sense of inspiration from Matthew as I was writing the words to the poem. I also told him that I was given an insight to be able to see Matthew in a different perspective,... I was seeing a boy that wanted us to know that he loves us and hopes we can learn to be kind to each other and to *love each other for who and what we are.*

I'm Thinking

(2001) – Following the general theme of this album, that is "Sentience," I am amazed how thought works. Thought (also called thinking) is the mental process in which beings like us form psychological associations and models of what we see and come to experience in the world around us.

I was watching my six-year-old son Brian analyze the construction of a sentence through the breaking down and evaluation of its separate words and I was amazed how his thinking was manipulating the information he was seeing, and then he was forming concepts as he engaged in problem solving exercises, using reason and then making decisions. His thoughts, and in the act of thinking, produced more thoughts.

I forgot what learning to read was all about and how intrinsic the process is. Moreover, I wondered when it was that I realized that I had this thing called "thought processing" going on in the background. I'm told that there are three types of thought that our brains produce: **insightful** (used for problem solving), helps us to do long range planning and problem-solving, **experiential** (focusing on the task at hand), brings our attention onto our senses such as our sight, sound and feel, and **nonstop** or never-ending (continuous or chatter), where our attention is attracted to whatever is most problematic at the moment. And these processes are so different from each other, they occur in different parts of our brain.

Realizing the power of thought, this poem was written for and about that extraordinary process of thinking from the perspective of someone who is in the process of realizing that thought itself is going on all the time he or she is thinking. Kind of complicated when I put it like that, but maybe you get what I'm trying to say.

When I put the words to the Roland keyboard voices and harmonica to the song, I felt that there was a good, cohesive amalgamation that carried the composition well.

My Name Is Bono Bono

(1976) – I wrote this poem for my two kids back in 1976. It is a poem about being personal and thoughtful. I used to sing this song all the time as I bobbed a little stuffed animal up and down like he was dancing and singing this song to them.

First to Lori, then to Chet, then to Elizabeth, then to Meridith, then to Ben, then to Stephen, then to Spencer, then to Christopher, then to Allison, then to Brian, all of which enjoyed the whole performance. As I sang the song, I would always reach out and kiss the stuffed bear or monkey to their cheek, and loving the song, they would demand that I repeat the process (and the song), over and over. This expression of identity of self and the caring for another—love and understanding is rather timeless and will go on.

Side Note:

This is also one of Diane's favorite songs and was delighted that I finally included it in one of my albums. It was long overdue.

Another Side Note:

There is another song, this one involving a monkey and his adventures called, "Pongo" or, "My Name Is Pongo" which was also a favorite of the kids with the same action and movement of bobbing the monkey up and down while singing the song. As you can see, this monkey has seen a lot of love and faced a lot of challenges.

Also, there is a song about Pongo's further adventures called, "Run Pongo Run" which speaks of the dangers in the jungle as well as the dangers of getting caught by men and sold to a Hurdy-Gurdy man. Unfortunately, both of these songs never did get recorded in the Archive Series but did get recorded later on in the further Lord Baldwin two-point-zero Digital recordings.

I Got The Call Saturday Morning

(2001) – Inez, my step-mother and friend for over thirty years, was living in St. Louis and came to visit her friends in Portland in the fall of 2000. During this visit, she got sick and ended up in the hospital where Diane and I visited her. She got better and eventually flew back to her home with my sister Kathy in St. Lewis.

Almost a year later, in August of 2001, I got word that she had fallen ill again. I talked with her on the phone and I did conclude that she was seriously in trouble, but I figured, like before, that I probably had a couple of weeks before she might deteriorate to a worse state. I had planned to go to St. Lewis after the weekend of my niece's wedding reception.

I called her Friday morning and because she was undergoing tests and because was groggy, I told her I would call her again later. The next day, that Saturday morning, I got the call that she had suddenly passed away.

I was so upset. I couldn't make it there for her before she passed away, I felt that my procrastination or hesitation, hoping she'd pull out again was the final reasons. I also felt like I had let her and that end of the family down, and this was only to be augmented by the disappointment in my sister Kathy's voice as she related the sad news to me.

Side Note:

Her casket was flown back to Seattle on September 10-11 and arrived hours before the New York, Twin Towers incident that shut down all flights for days. Kathy and her family drove in a rented van and Wendy got a ride from friends to a point where Kathy picked her up and came to Aurora Oregon where Inez was buried next to her mother, Grandma Wicks.

Good In Life

(2001) – There is a general assumption that people gravitate to their own interests and then spend time in the areas that make them happy. I believe this is true and I believe that bad things can happen to good people, but that certain people that have their act together will rise above their adversity, realizing that there is a growing process and knowledge to be gained by them developing courage while confronting their challenges.

In his sophomore year, Ben was caught up in an unfortunate car accident where community time was required. We went to the *Salvation Army kitchen* and *Bread and Roses Soup Kitchen* to work off community service time. We were not there very long before Ben realized how fortunate he was in his circumstances. He compared those scenes he was seeing; destitute and homeless people struggling to get by, down to being in a place like that to get a meal for themselves and or their families, to his own situation, and at that moment of realization, compassion flowed from him. He worked there, uncomplainingly and I could see how he interacted with the people with a sincere gentleness and kindness; impoverished and destitute people that he could now see with his empathetic eyes, were there in need of a good meal and to be treated with dignity and respect. And the way he showed his simple compassion towards them moved me.

When Ben had "served his time" doing his community service he continued to go back and be of service to the Bread and Roses Soup Kitchen and to the folks he now respected that frequented the facility.

Side Note:

That I might remember that I'm only a paycheck away from being right there with any of them is not an encouraging thought and I could be disheartening, but realizing there are people out there like Ben, who have charity and compassion in their hearts and are willing to do what they might to lighten another's burden, is of great comfort,... and I hope to be more like him.

Another Side Note:

After Ben's unfortunate accident, which was arguably **not** his fault due to recent changes at that intersection, to allow students to negotiate getting into the driveway of a newly constructed Black Hills High School, on a stretch of highway on Little Rock Road, where traffic from both directions were clipping along between 45 and 60 mile an hour, (depending on whether the student was late for their classes), the City of Tumwater decided to put in a stoplight and safer turning lanes for the school. And for the students and faculty of that school year and perhaps for a few school years that followed, the new stoplight on Little Rock Road had been unceremoniously christened, "Baldwin's Stoplight."

Sometimes You Have To Say, "I'm Sorry"

(2001) – Only weeks before Matthew's untimely death, he was picked up by the Canby police and put in a juvenile detention home just outside of Salem, maybe 30 miles away from his home. About 6 in the morning, Matt called my dad, because Ray, his dad, was in Arizona checking out possible work. Calling collect, Matthew was asking my dad to come and pick him up from the detention home.

My dad not only refused, but was terribly upset about the collect call. A week later, finding out Inez's condition, I called down to Oregon and the family people down there to inform them of her condition. I called my dad first, but he wasn't home. I then called Ray's house to let his kids know about things, and as irony might have it, Ray was back home. As I was talking to Ray, there was a lull in the conversation and at that moment my dad came into the back door to Ray's house, and I could hear him over the phone line shouting loudly to, or rather at Matthew. My dad said that Matt owed him $8.00 for the collect phone call. Matthew responded by telling him to go poke himself. Over the line I could hear a big verbal battle take place, so intense it was, to the extent that Ray put down the phone and I got disconnected.

Sometime after 11:30 that night I got a call from my dad who was decidedly sorry for his short temper. He discussed his dislike for Ray's wayward son (his grandson) and his attitude for his grandfather, and he also admitted that he himself had brought things to a level that should never have happened.

He said, "Sometimes regardless of who is right or wrong, you have to just give in. Sometimes you have to say you're sorry, even when you might lose it all, or you know it's not your fault. As I was talking to my dad, I had the foresight to again, be close to a pencil and paper and I wrote it all down as he was speaking.

The next day, from my notes I wrote this poem or lyrics to this song and then composed the music to the song. Unfortunately, with Matthew's untimely death, he never got the chance to read this poem nor hear this song, and frankly, neither did my dad.

Side Note:

The words to this poem resonates from time to time as I experience situations where I allow my feelings and psyche to get damaged by others' transgressions or trespasses, and the poem stands as a subtle reminder that for me, sometimes I have to say I'm sorry too.

Another Side Note:

In February of 1987 after a week of snow, we needed to drive to,... somewhere, I don't remember anymore,... but I had Chet and Liz with me as we had just gotten back from the store in the 67 Chevy Nova. I handed Chet the keys to get the groceries from the trunk and afterwards he gave them back to me,... or at least so he said,... I went to get back into the car to see if I'd left them inside but the door was locked,... so I turned to Chet and asked him where the keys were,...

Chet told me he had handed them back to me, but I searched my pockets and could not find them,... and then a moment later, with me sure the keys were in the car, and with me now angry, I began to yell at Chet for the missing keys,... we got into the trunk with a screwdriver (can't do that anymore with the newer cars), and I had Chet crawl into the trunk to unsecure the backseat to get into the car,... as he was doing that, he was sadly upset as I went to the driver's side of the front door to check how feasible it would be to use a coat hanger, and I kind of kicked the snow with my shoes just enough to see the reflection of something shiny in the snow,... There were the keys, right where I had dropped them,... I was so ashamed and embarrassed that I had blamed Chet, who we still struggling with that back seat,... I unlocked the car, opened the back door and started talking to Chet while he was working,... not at first, but a moment later Chet realized I was talking to him from the other side of the seat,... excitedly he climbed out of the trunk and smiled happily to see I had the keys,... I told him how I found the keys and moreover that I was sorry and that it had to have been me that lost the keys,...

This episode happened so many years ago,... eventually Chet grew up and was was happily driving the Chevy around himself to Tumwater High School and other places,... but I have never forgotten how I had kind of acted like Senior, who, with such a short fuse, was always ready to cast blame anywhere else but to himself,... so if you're reading this Chet, please know that *I am sorry,...* and ask you to forgive me for my impetuousness,... I love you, man,...

What You've Got To Do

(2001) – This instrumentation was intended to have a poem written

and words to go with the composition, but because it was Christmas-
time in 2001, and I was trying to get this concept album out so I could
give album CDs to all the family, I just engineered the voices of the
different instruments with the #10 organ voice to be the lead, so as to
represent the arrangement as it is; sorry, it might have been something
special—maybe someday I'll come back to it.

You Are The One

(2001) – Realizing we may all play a part in the enrichment, fortifi-
cation and edifying of others. I think either out of a sense of separated
convenience or a lack of self-awareness, we believe that the work or
deed will be done, but it will be done by someone else. Someone per-
haps stronger, maybe smarter, certainly younger—or maybe someone
else we feel to be more worthy.

I guess, like myself, we see others out there doing the work or
stepping up to the special task and we think, "that was their calling,"
or "they were the right person for the job." It will always be someone
else's responsibility if we never realize that each of us here has a chance,
an opportunity or maybe even the need to step up and do that one
special thing.

You may never realize your potential; you may never step out of the
comfortable groove that you're now in, but perhaps someday you may
find that, in a defining moment, there is something that needs to be
said or done that can only be done or said by someone like you and you
may come to the understanding that indeed, you are the one.

Side Note:

About this time at work there was a small movement to unionize
the classified staff. I attended some of the meetings and listened to the
rhetoric that was being spewed by the unionizers but I was just there to
listen. Then it came time to the last meeting at lunchtime before we'd
have the vote the following day. I listened to others that told tales of
how the head of our HR was doing nefarious things, but I was still not

in. Then I heard dissenting voices that reinforced how I felt, I mean, it would be them taking out money from my hard-earned salary, and for what? I thought until I remembered how helpless I felt having my unfair supervisor, Renzo bearing false accounts of me and having that letter put in my file.

And something happened to me. I knew I had to be a voice for that union.

I stood up and got in front of the rest of the people there, a large crowd of classified workers as well as some admin people there to see how things were going.

Then I said something to the effect: "I want to say that the way things are, we will always be at the mercy of our supervisors and HR can do what ever they want without ant accountability or repercussions for their actions.

"This may be the most important decision we as a group ever make. And if we don't choose to do anything tomorrow, well than we deserve whatever they want to do to us."

I also said that I knew a lot of the folks out there were worried about money, but without this protection that we would be paying for, we might not have a job after tomorrow.

And I said, "I know that there are people out there that will report whatever I say today and if we vote no, well, I won't be here very long, but if you vote no, tomorrow, maybe next month, maybe next week, when they come after you, you will not have anyone to stand for you in your defense either and you will have no one to thank but yourself."

I paused before I continued, "I'm voting tomorrow to have the union represent me and my job and to keep the incompetent supervisors and the HR monkeys off my back."

After I spoke no one else stood up and we all left to go back to work. I did not realize I was to be the last speaker but from the vote the next day the union was passed. "You Are The One" was a reminder to me that my one voice can make a difference and may, in the end, have been the determining factor to sway the vote to get the union ratified.

Another Side Note:

Coupe was against the union and exercised his right to refuse to join. He still had to have money taken out of his paycheck but it did not enroll him in the union.

Funny Other Note:

I was a Union Shop Steward at SPSCC for thirteen years and to be fair with you it wasn't always easy dealing with Coupe letting me have the time needed to do union stuff to help others in need,... but one day Coupe came to me with a work-related problem that he was having,... and yes, though some employees are not union brothers or sisters, the union would represent them in the workplace too. Coupe's problem was resolved and after that I seemed to have smoother sailing doing union stuff.

By Heart

(2001) – I was messing around with some piano chords late one night and had thoughts and a feeling for what the words should be. As everyone was asleep, I went out into the living room with a pen and a spiral notebook and with those thoughts and ideas I wrote this poem.

I gently pushed all the junk off the piano bench and, playing the tune I had earlier created, found that I needed to modify the words just a bit to fit the timbre and quality of sound of the music.

But it was always my Diane who, just when I might think I have it all figured out when it comes to understanding the woman, I find out I'm not only wrong, but not even close.

And although we've been together for these many years, wisdom had taught me not to assume I get it or get what's going on with her. She can change like a psychedelic mushroom lamp and what's Diablo canyon lake's moss-green water right now can be cobalt blue in an instant from now.

I can go through periods of time when Diane is moody or unhappy and I may keep trying to find out just what it is that she is unhappy about, and whether or not it's my fault she's feeling the way she is, you know. But usually, it's nothing like that and there's some other underlying thing that, although possibly trivial to me, is presently a turning point to her at that time in her life. Just another confirmation that although I may not know the thought process that Diane is experiencing, I may know her fundamentally better than anyone on this planet, and I do know her by her caring generous compassionate kindheartedness, and the charitable, oh, so, giving nature she lives by.

Although I'll keep trying, I may never truly recognize certain parts of her personality, or comprehend how she manages to be in tune with the spirit, or truly understand what my princess Diane is all about, but from the things that are really important; her treasured loves and valued desires and unforgettable sweet goodness—I do know her by heart.

Sentient, (Rethought)

(2001) – This is a return to the instrumentation "Sentient (Thought)" but after experiencing thought and reason has come to have more of an understanding to what it means to be sentient; to be a magnificent creature with the faculty of sensation and the power to perceive, to reason and to calculate through the thinking process, how to understand. He or she can rejoice and feel joy, and suffer and feel pain. And like many other humans that were, are now or will be, he or she must face their own mortality.

This composition starts with that same lone piano voice calling out, but now it's telling us of the experiences, good, difficult, struggling, and circling back to a point of reference as it says, "okay I get that I'm here and I've been figuring things out, I have identified with common-alities and some of the discords, I've discovered how to work with my senses, I've felt myself in movement and realized that I must adjust to the changes, I have perceived many things around me, understood how to do things. I have gained wisdom for a quality of having a good judgement based on the power of knowledge and the ability to discern. I have found choice to be good and bad with an ability to under-stand one's knowledge and choices is the realization of that decision.

But now I wonder, if there is a purpose to it all; I wonder why? Why is this so? Why did I get put here? Where did I come from? Is there another level of comprehension after this?

Side Note: When composing this one minute and forty-five second arrangement, I envisioning "The Flammarion;" a wood engraving by an unknown artist that depicts a pilgrim that is able to see through the veil of temporal life to grasp and perceive the splendor and glory and magnificent majesty of the heavens on the other side. And maybe com-prehend that there is something more marvelous to life.

Drive On

(2001) – I shared one of my albums with one of my acquaintances at work and was given some extremely harsh feedback on my material, criticizing the quality of my musical recordings, my voice, and the production of and the presentation of the album itself.

It was almost a joke and I took it as such but was later clarified that he was not kidding. Although Diane said it was probably just jealousy, my delicate ego had a hard time with this. I was afraid of criticism, to the point I would limit my experiences and actions simply out of fear of what others might think or say. There is that fear of not being accepted, there is the fear of rejection, of being judged, and in the end, I might let it affect my cherished image of myself.

Unfortunately, other's perceptions can easily shape alternate realities, and when I buy into their rhetoric, my individuality could attach itself to what others might think and say of me, could end up having strangers controlling me; people who honestly don't really care about me, they just want to sound like they know what they're talking about.

But I came to understand that my reaction to the criticism was the problem and the thing that was hurting my psyche. And I realized that I needed to center myself again, and go by what I've come to know as who and what I know myself to be, and reflect on, and remember that excitement and love I have for expressing myself with the poetry and the music and the songwriting developments and the progressions I work through, and remember that I have value.

I have resolved that I will not let others dictate how I should distinguish my own talents, abilities and geniuses. They are not and could never be a good judge of me. And whether I pursue my dreams or not, people are bound to criticize me.

At some other crossroad in my life, I might have been hurt or crushed from the criticism, but after carefully thinking about it, and reminding myself that I do this thing I do, not for monetary gain or fame or fortunes, (although I could use some compensation for all those nights I lost sleep creating and recording my material), but I do this because I feel it is my gift that God has blessed me with, (and I'm thankful), and , like the parables of the talents, I need to magnify that gift and this calling.

And dog gone it, I look forward to doing this stuff I do, however trite and irrelevant it may end up being to the masses or other individuals, it gives me a delightful sense of purpose and it makes me happy to be able to put together these poetic words and musical concepts that end up being songs. Lord Baldwin songs.

Side Note:

It still amazes me that I have this ability to create these little works of art, and that songs come to me in my head, out of the blue or from vivid dreams, and that I have the ability to work with words to write a poem and then, come on, then I get to put a variety of music to those words and then I somehow generate a song. And then there's the engineering of the production, which is not always easy, and then there's the artist in me that wants to conceive, design, and construct the album covers. Hey, it's all just so cool that I could even be doing this. And If man is that he might have joy and I'm not hurting anyone with my little songs, I say let him play on.

Another Side Note:

And this is it. The last of the four books on the "Archive Series" Done. This has been a lot of work but a labor of love, nonetheless. I would like to first, give a very special thank you to **Steve Whalen**; (a class act), of whom is mostly the reason that I was able to get all of my "*Archive Series*" digitized from my master cassettes.

Just One More Thing,...

So wow,... lot of work,... I find myself slowing down as I get to the end,... I want to savor these last few words,... and I want you all to know that it's been a gas to complete all this poetry to lyrics to music to songs to albums,... and I'm glad that I had the insight to document the memoirs and notes as they happened,... I was surprised over remembering things I had forgotten had happened,... some memoirs were very precious to me,...

but yeah,... it pleases me to let you know that I am working on a second round of books that will, I hope, be able to document the, *Second Wave* of "*Memoirs From An Invisible Songwriter*" books, containing my, 'Recall To Life' more recently created, "Lord Baldwin 2.0" document-ing the details of my recordings done digitally from 2011 to present.

Hope to see us there, soon,...

123

SPECIAL FINAL BOOK (BOOK FOUR) ENDING SIDE NOTE

After Steve Waylon showed me how to work the special library equipment and how to use their state of the art software, I spent more than **15 months**, and most all of my lunchtimes during the school years , 2001-2002 and part of 2002-2003 at the SPSCC library on their audio equipment.

I feel that there needs be a clarification on the creation and album release dates dealing with, "Who I Might Be" and, "The Universe Within."

When I was getting my material published—distributed through DistroKid, I did not do publish things chronologically, especially the "*Archive Series*," but instead, jumped around a bit, pulling an album from here and then an album from there; mostly from the "Archive Series" but I sprinkled in an album from the Lord Baldwin 2.0 series here and there too.

Originally, "The Universe Within" was published July 2019 with a release date of December 19, 2002 and "Who I Might Be" was published earlier but was taken out (because of the "My Concubine" controversial issue where I had to unpublish the album and wait for a couple weeks before republishing it again without the, 'My Concubine' song) and so, "Who I Might Be" was published August 2019 with a release date of December 24, 2001.

Usually the albums from the "Archive Series" came in pairs; 1 & 2, 3 & 4, 41 & 42, excreta, and even though I was shown a way to digitize my material, album # 43, "Who I Might Be" and #44, "The Universe Within" were both compiled around the same time from the collections of material from the same engineered master tapes. Okay, long story short; the release date for "Who I Might Be" should have been, December 19, 2001, not December 24, 2001, and the release date for, "The Universe Within" should have been, December 24, 2001, not December 19, 2002 as noted on my material out there in the musical space waves.

After I had finished publishing my material for all those albums, I upgraded to a better level at DistroKid which gave me more control over a lot of these things, and I was able to get some of the mistakes corrected, but it was a one-time repair deal and so, it is what it is. But now, if you're reading this, in the famous words of Paul Harvey, *"And now you know the rest of the story."*

124

INDEX BY NAME OF SONG

125

⟨⟩⟨⟩⟨⟩

SOME FINAL WORDS,...

This was such an overwhelmingly huge undertaking and I'm surprised I got as much done, even though for the past four months I've been sitting here in the computer labs every night they've been available, typing away until they close down and kick us all out,... and that's kind of good because it's 1:45 AM right now and I'm tired and I got to go get some sleep before I wake up again at 6:30 to go to work,... and I feel I might need another quarter to go over all my notes and drafts and polish this work just a bit more,... but as I was saying, here I am, at the end of the quarter and so I have to turn in what I have and hope they, (the professors involved), seem to be happy with this body of work.

Okay, we've arrived,... at this end,... and for me it feels kind of funny,... like I've left so much out and there is still so much left to convey,... but here I am, at the end of the quarter at Evergreen State College,... I am finalizing all the paperwork and documentation to my PLE (Prior Learning Experience) project.

The fact that you are reading these words indicates that this document may be more than just my own personal documentation of my time and efforts as a songwriter for the last fifteen hears of recording the, 'Archive Series' of my analog recordings,... and you're welcome to it, in whatever format you're reading this from,... oh, and thank you so much for your interest,... to be frank, all I ever really wanted was to have a wider audience to enjoy the poetry, music and song packages to maybe bear out all the work I'd done and validate my virtuosity and God given talents,... I hope you like things.

And now, as I am moving forward, I would like to say that I have taken great pleasure in creating these works to share with all my family and friends,...

It was my hope to share some of these songs with other artists out there but if you've read any of the memoirs and notes you already know that I could never make any of the right connections that would connect me with others in need of or at least in want of something distinctive and special from some unknown songwriter named, Lord Baldwin,... but that's okay,... I'm not complaining,... I love the fact that my Heavenly this journey that I been

Note from 2022:

So, twenty years passed and,... well, twenty years passed and I have continued to remain invisible to the world as a songwriter,... and after this document was completed, I ran into a few roadblocks,... first, my keyboard stopped functioning to a degree where there were some notes that did not work,... first the 'G#' above middle 'C' stopped playing,... the Supertonic to my favorite key, 'F#' which made things difficult even with a transpose button on the 'Yamaha PRS-500 keyboard'... but what came next was worse as the, TASCAM PortaStudio 424MKIII 4-track Cassette Recorder started adding wow & flutter to all the recordings, probably needing new belts,... Music 6000 at the time said it would probably cost over $300.00 to get it looked at and repaired, but no guarantees,...

To be honest, I was now over fifty,... and speaking about that, in

2003 I was trying to apply to be on an American reality television singing competition program called, *Nashville Star*,... it was similar to American Idol, where I'd sing to impress both celebrity judges and the public via call-in and/or internet votes, but with this contest, I'd be limited to just do country music,... and I think you might agree that I have a few good songs that could fit the bill,... but in the application process I seemed to have gotten lost so I called them up and the person I spoke with representing the, *Nashville Star* told me that it was because I was too old,... they were looking for someone they could get a lot of years out of,... funny thing though, the person that won that year that I was denied, Buddy Jewell, was only eight years younger than me,...

I knew I wasn't gonna get picked up any time soon by any recording company,... so I decided to put all my energies into writing two books and in doing so, and with my equipment in total disarray, I stopped recording music altogether,...

That lasted for about ten years before I came into a little bit of money, (my Dad passed away), and I went to Music 6000 and bought a *Roland Juno-Gi keyboard*

to replace the Yamaha and a, *Fostex MR-8HD Digital Multitracker*

to replace the TASCAM,... and suddenly I was back in business,... At work I geared all my one-hour lunchtime breaks to be productive time to write poems again,... and then naturally music followed, and marriages between the two and my fingering on my guitar got better,... and my Roland keyboard? What a mystical journey it's been playing with all those sounds,... and now, having double the power of recording with eight tracks,... are you kidding???

Point is, if you go looking for me out there in the mysterious cyberspace of the internet to see what happened next,... do me a favor, if you can, when you can, use headphones, because like, 'Jimi Hendrix', Lord Baldwin loves to play with the Stereo settings,...I wish you happy listening,...

Hey and thanks so much for taking your curious time to looking into these books to find out about Lord Baldwin,...

Other Books

LORD CHESTER L. BALDWIN II

FROM THE LOST LETTERS SENT
Memoirs Of An Invisible Songwriter
Book ONE: 1985 – 1992

FROM THE LOST LETTERS SENT
Memoirs Of An Invisible Songwriter
Book TWO: 1992 – 1993

FROM THE LOST LETTERS SENT
Memoirs Of An Invisible Songwriter
Book THREE: 1993 – 1994

FROM THE LOST LETTERS SENT
Memoirs Of An Invisible Songwriter
Book FOUR: 1995 – 2001

STEPPING BETWEEN THE ANTS
Book ONE: *The Winter Escape*

STEPPING BETWEEN THE ANTS
Book TWO: *The Spring Ahead*

STEPPING BETWEEN THE ANTS
Book THREE: *A Summer To Remember*

STEPPING BETWEEN THE ANTS
Book FOUR: *The Fall Behind*

RESILIENT:
A (Web-Based Episodic) Musical Play & Story

'HEADS' or,
'TALES FROM THE SUMMER OF LOVE'